# In Good Faith?

Governing Indigenous Australia through God,
Charity and Empire,
1825-1855

# In Good Faith?

Governing Indigenous Australia through God,
Charity and Empire,
1825-1855

**Jessie Mitchell**

E PRESS

Published by ANU E Press and Aboriginal History Incorporated
Aboriginal History Monograph 23

This title is also available online at: http://epress.anu.edu.au/good_faith_citation.html

---

National Library of Australia Cataloguing-in-Publication entry

Author:     Mitchell, Jessie.

Title:      In good faith? : governing Indigenous Australia through god, charity and empire, 1825-1855 / Jessie Mitchell.

ISBN:       9781921862106 (pbk.) 9781921862113 (eBook)

Series:     Aboriginal history monograph ; 23

Notes:      Includes bibliographical references.

Subjects:   Indigenous peoples--Government relations.
            Philanthropinism.
            Aboriginal Australians--Politics and government.
            Aboriginal Australians--Social conditions--19th century.
            Colonization--Australia.

Dewey Number: 305.89915

---

### Aboriginal History Incorporated

*Aboriginal History* is administered by an Editorial Board which is responsible for all unsigned material. Views and opinions expressed by the author are not necessarily shared by Board members.

### The Committee of Management and the Editorial Board

Kaye Price (Chair), Peter Read (Monographs Editor), Maria Nugent and Shino Konishi (Journal Editors), Robert Paton (Treasurer and Public Officer), Anne McGrath (Deputy Chair), Isabel McBryde, Niel Gunson, Luise Hercus, Harold Koch, Christine Hansen, Tikka Wilson, Geoff Gray, Jay Arthur, Dave Johnson, Ingereth Macfarlane, Brian Egloff, Lorena Kanellopoulos, Richard Baker, Peter Radoll.

### Contacting Aboriginal History

All correspondence should be addressed to Aboriginal History, Box 2837 GPO Canberra, 2601, Australia. Sales and orders for journals and monographs, and journal subscriptions: Thelma Sims, email: Thelma.Sims@anu.edu.au, tel or fax: +61 2 6125 3269, www.aboriginalhistory.org

Aboriginal History Inc. is a part of the Australian Centre for Indigenous Studies, Research School of Social Sciences, The Australian National University and gratefully acknowledges the support of the History Program, RSSS and the National Centre for Indigenous Studies, The Australian National University.

**WARNING: Readers are notified that this publication may contain names or images of deceased persons.**

**ANU E Press:** All correspondence should be addressed to:
ANU E Press, The Australian National University, Canberra ACT 0200, Australia
Email: anuepress@anu.edu.au, http://epress.anu.edu.au

Cover image: *Missionary Register*, September 1834, L & G Seeley, London. National Library of Australia, N266.3CHU.

Cover design and layout by ANU E Press

---

Apart from any fair dealing for the purpose of private study, research, criticism or review, as permitted under the Copyright Act, no part of this publication may be reproduced by any process whatsoever without the written permission of the publisher.

This edition © 2011 ANU E Press and Aboriginal History Inc

# Contents

| | |
|---|---|
| Illustrations | vii |
| Acknowledgements | ix |
| Introduction | 1 |
| 'This land of Barbarians': missions and protectorates begin | 13 |
| 'Godless political experiments': philanthropy and governance | 39 |
| 'All white masters belong to your King': race, identity and empire | 65 |
| 'Our country all gone': rights, charity and the loss of land | 87 |
| Deserving poverty? Rationing and philanthropy | 109 |
| Keeping body and soul together: creating material 'civilisation' | 129 |
| 'Can these dry bones live?' Religious life and afterlife | 151 |
| 'This bitter reproach': destruction, guilt and the colonial future | 173 |
| Conclusion | 195 |
| Bibliography | 199 |

# Illustrations

Figure 1. Map showing the locations of Indigenous communities and missions in Australia. Prepared by Karina Pelling, Cartographic and GIS Services, Australian National University.

Figure 2. During the 1830s, the Church Missionary Society published tales of bush life, cultural clashes and missionary work at Wellington Valley. As the picture indicates, many aspects of traditional Wiradjuri life were continuing, to the fascination and concern of the missionaries. *Missionary Register*, September 1834, L & G Seeley, London. National Library of Australia, N266.3CHU.

Figure 3. British missionary publications were even more dismissive of pre-colonial life than were their Australian counterparts, as this juxtaposition of Indigenous people and native animals suggests. 'An Australian Group', Wesleyan Methodist Missionary Society, *Wesleyan Juvenile Offering*, February 1853, Wesleyan Mission House, London. Mitchell Library, State Library of New South Wales, 266.705/W.

Figure 4. By the 1840s, philanthropists' reports were becoming pessimistic. As this choice of illustration in a missionary journal shows, Indigenous Australians were increasingly portrayed as hopeless and doomed. 'Burial of one of the natives of Australia', Wesleyan Missionary Society, *Papers Relative to the Wesleyan Missions, and to the State of Heathen Countries*, no CXI, March 1848, London. National Library of Australia, Petherick NK5726.

# Acknowledgements

This work began life as a doctoral thesis in history at the Australian National University, and became a book during my time as a staff member with the Australian National University and the University of Sydney, working as part of a Discovery grant funded by the Australian Research Council. I also was assisted greatly by a creative fellowship with the State Library of Victoria.

Particular thanks must go to Ann Curthoys for her keen, thoughtful and generous supervision of this project, and to Peter Read and Jay Arthur of the Aboriginal History monograph series, for their encouragement and support. I am also grateful to the Australian Historical Association, who helped to promote this work through the 2006 Serle prize.

Thanks must go to the manuscripts staff at the State Library of Victoria, the Mitchell Library of New South Wales, the National Library of Australia and the Public Records Office of Victoria for their assistance and permission to use images, to Geoff Hunt for his editorial work, and to Karina Pelling of the ANU's Cartographic and GIS services for putting together such a useful map. I am grateful, too, to Lynette Russell for making me welcome during a brief stay at the Centre for Australian Indigenous Studies at Monash University, and to Jane Lydon, Tom Griffiths and Verity Archer for their insights and enthusiasm. Thanks, finally, to my family, for all their love and encouragement.

# Introduction

Contemporary Australia has been shaped powerfully by legacies of colonialism. Disputes over national responsibility, guilt, denial and shame for Aboriginal dispossession have become especially notable in public life since the late 20th century. This has proven most striking in debates about the forced removal of Aboriginal children from their families (a process which can be traced back to the philanthropic projects described in this work), and while questions of national responsibility for historical wrongs have taken on slightly different forms of late – with the federal government's 2008 apology to the stolen generations, and ongoing debates over government 'intervention' into troubled Aboriginal communities – their continued relevance is clear. In this climate, tracing histories of dispossession, Indigenous rights and the mixed meanings of paternalism and state authority is a challenging and important task.

Ideas about rights, in particular, have become both notable and disputed in recent Australian political life. Questions of Indigenous people's entitlements – as colonised peoples, as Australian citizens and as human beings – continue to provoke debate. Such controversies have emerged from efforts to situate Indigenous grievances in human rights frameworks, as well as in debates over whether 'civil' and 'Aboriginal' rights are compatible, and in attacks on a rights-based discourse by those who view it as irrelevant or dangerous. Related disputes are also occurring in a wider context, where the very concept of human rights has become both highly articulate (employed by activists and governments) and under attack from different quarters. My own belief in the importance of pursuing these issues has been influenced not only by my academic research, but also by a period of time spent working in the community sector. Here, tensions between rights and charity and questions about the supposed (in)gratitude of vulnerable people towards state and benevolent agencies continue to have strong relevance. This work was prompted partly, therefore, by a belief that more attention must be paid to the evolving and problematic nature of philanthropic support for Indigenous people's entitlements, and its shifting connections to empire, charity, religion and the state.

Furthering my interest in this topic is the fact that, by the beginning of the 21st century, the historical plight of Indigenous Australians has become seen (often contentiously) as central to broader national identity. This belief is no doubt relevant to the desire which has emerged over the past couple of decades to trace histories of Australian humanitarianism, including that of certain 19th century missionaries and protectors of Aborigines. While I appreciate and support such a project, I would add nonetheless that it can be equally important to examine the complexities, paradoxes and deep cracks within these humanitarian movements; the fault lines in colonial philanthropy have, themselves, left rich and troubling legacies. The place of philanthropy within empire is a subject that warrants particular consideration. Since the late decades of the 20th century, Australia's past and future ties to Great Britain have become controversial, and at the time of writing this, both the monarchy and the republican movement appear to have dwindled in popular relevance. These areas of debate gain greater depth and significance, however, when widened to encompass issues of Indigenous policy and subjecthood. 19th century philanthropic movements provide an important window into this, revealing a complex interplay of ideas, actions and identities at colonial, imperial and local levels.

## Messages in bottles: exploring a philanthropic past

In 1840, Chief Protector of Aborigines George Augustus Robinson and his assistant James Dredge travelled through the northern districts of Port Phillip, making notes on the circumstances of the Indigenous people they met. In their diaries, amidst ethnographic observations and quarrels between the two men (both of them temperamental, discontented individuals), one unusual event stood out. When the protectors and their local host, Joseph Docker, reached the Murray River, they carved into a gum tree their initials, a cross and the word 'DIG', then wrote the following message on a slip of paper, which they pushed into a bottle and buried beneath the tree.

Reverend Joseph Docker

G.A. Robinson, Esq., C.P. of Aborigines<br>
James Dredge, A.P. of do.<br>
'AMICI HUMANI GENERIS'

Murray River, 2 miles below the Junction of the Ovens with the Murray. On this occasion the health of Her Most Gracious Majesty Queen Victoria was drunk, and the Royal Initials inscribed on a Gum Tree.

April 30th, 1840

<u>VIVAT REGINA!</u>

'Tres (in) Uno'.

WO-RA-JE-RE

This message is intriguing, alive with multiple meanings. Carving imperial signs into a tree in 'unsettled' country was, of course, typical for explorers, imposing meanings on new lands and, in doing so, implying a previous emptiness to the countryside. Elsewhere in the district, these travellers had behaved similarly, giving the names Docker, Robinson and Dredge to several places they visited.

This was complicated, however, by the purpose of the protectors' journey: not to claim empty land but rather to monitor the culture and dispossession of the people still living there. Robinson's diaries, in particular, recorded numerous details of Indigenous residence: huts, ovens, spears and signs of hunting and firestick farming. Such observations, and the protectorate project they served, were by turns sympathetic and chauvinistic, as the Latin slogan — 'friends of mankind' — suggests. This message also yields other meanings. The ordering of the men's names hints at the fine distinctions of class and status which caused tensions in the protectorate and within missionary projects in general. Furthermore, the loyalty pledged to Queen Victoria, situated so precisely within the Australian landscape, and the inclusion of 'Wo-ra-je-re' (presumably Wiradjuri, a large Aboriginal nation whose country lay to the north), marked both the land and the protectorate with a significant combination of the imperial and the Indigenous. It is, moreover, hard for the historian to resist the image of the message in a bottle, the connections to Aborigines, Queen and country both immortalised and buried.[1]

While a singular incident, this story points nonetheless to many central issues within Evangelical philanthropy, as it related to the governance of Indigenous Australia during the first half of the 19th century. The colonisation of Australia was a diverse process, but this era has been seen as particularly important, especially in the south-east. During this time, introduced diseases and species spread rapidly — often preceding British colonists themselves — and land was seized for urban development and pastoralism. In many of the districts examined in this work, the occupation of land increased exponentially within a decade or less, often accompanied by violence, alcohol and a rapidly growing population of settlers, sheep and cattle. The effects on Indigenous societies were devastating, with many suffering a rapid population decline. In central Victoria, for instance, many Aboriginal nations had shrunk numerically from hundreds of people, to mere tens, by the middle of the century.[2] This development of settler-colonies with an institutional penal heritage, where the original people were to be replaced by newcomers, differentiated settlements like those of Australia from other regions like Polynesia, where missionaries arrived early and were a major colonising force, and India, where trading interests were paramount and the British population remained comparatively small.

---

1  James Dredge, 30 April 1840, in James Dredge, Diaries, Notebook and Letterbooks, ?1817–1845 [hereafter JDD], MS11625, MSM534, State Library of Victoria (SLV); Clark 2001 vol 1: 248–256.
2  In the country around Bathurst in New South Wales for example (where the Wellington Valley mission would later be established), land occupied by colonists increased from 2520 acres with 33,733 sheep and cattle in 1821, to 91,636 acres and 113,973 stock animals in 1825. Later, in the Port Phillip settlement to the south, the settler population first arrived in the late 1830s, but by 1851 had increased to 77,345, with almost 7 million head of stock. Meanwhile, in South Australia, the land sold to colonists increased from 3711 acres to 170,841 between 1837–1839 alone, while the white population reached 17,366 in 1844 and 85,821 by 1855. See Barwick, 1998: 16; Brock 1995: 213; Goodall 1996: 30; Main 1986: 15.

However, this same era also saw the first attempts to introduce philanthropic governance and 'protection' of Indigenous Australians. Evangelical Protestants, whose influence in British social and political life had been growing since the late 18th century, had campaigned successfully for the abolition of slavery in the empire during previous decades, and between the 1820s and 1840s they turned their attentions to abuses of native peoples throughout the colonies. The missionaries they sent into the field were characterised by lower-middle class or artisan backgrounds, passionate religious faith and a strong belief in hard work, individualist aspirations and the value of the respectable bourgeois home. Their impact on early Aboriginal policy would be significant and mixed, and it is these 'civilising' projects which form the main theme of this book. *In Good Faith?* looks at missions and protectorate stations across the Australian colonies, focusing on the period from 1825 – when LE Threlkeld started work for the London Missionary Society at Lake Macquarie in New South Wales – to 1855, when John Smithies' Methodist mission in Western Australia finally closed. During this era, protectors and missionaries set up in Port Phillip (present-day Victoria), South Australia and Western Australia, and mission stations opened in rural New South Wales and Moreton Bay on the southern Queensland coast. The terrain ranged from urban institutions (notably in Adelaide and Perth) to the coastal fishing country and swamplands around Lake Macquarie; from the expansive grasslands and river country of the Wiradjuri people of inland New South Wales, to the former Aboriginal fishing villages around Moreton Bay, and the small tracts of rich bush and lakes fed by the Barwon River in western Victoria. Missions and protectorates opened at different times, but these points tended to be roughly in line with the early colonisation of the districts concerned.

Along these shifting and turbulent frontiers, complex relationships and conversations developed between philanthropists and Indigenous people. During this time, missionaries and protectors often lacked strong material and official power, and Aboriginal people, while suffering depopulation, dispossession and social breakdown, were nonetheless comparatively mobile, maintained a certain physical and cultural autonomy, and often continued to live in their traditional country. The local dynamics that emerged from this made the early 19th century an interesting period, rather different to the late 19th and early 20th centuries, when government bodies, protection boards and missionaries gained much greater power over people's working, cultural and family lives. While the first philanthropists were keen to exert (allegedly) benevolent control, their more compromised circumstances led to some intriguingly different outcomes.

Several historical works have considered early efforts to 'civilise' Aboriginal people through Christian philanthropy. These studies have included accounts of local conflict and resistance by scholars like Peter Read and Michael Christie, and examinations of religious encounters between Indigenous people and missionaries, by Hilary Carey, Niel Gunson and Jean Woolmington. Also important are attempts by Henry Reynolds – and, from a more explicitly Christian perspective, John Harris – to trace a lineage of white humanitarianism in Australia.[3] However, *In Good Faith?* approaches these projects from some new angles. My work has been guided by key themes of governance, subjecthood and rights, and the need to understand these ideas as developing through complex exchanges between imperial centres and mission outposts. While tracing philanthropists' efforts to support the wellbeing and entitlements of Indigenous people, I also emphasise the need to examine these agendas closely and to consider how they were shaped by charity, religious beliefs, personal relationships and commitments to empire. As such, I would also stress the need to re-evaluate the place of British imperialism in Australian history, especially in histories of Indigenous governance. While the historiography of Aboriginal Australia produced during the late 20th century tended to take a national or regional focus, questions of 'humanitarian' imperialism and Indigenous people's status as subjects of empire warrant further attention. This project has been facilitated by a wider research endeavour, headed by Ann Curthoys, into the relationship between Aboriginal policy making and the growth of self-government in colonial Australia, a connection previously neglected by many historians.

## Making subjects: political and personal approaches

The uneven exchange of ideas between Britain and the colonies affected a range of issues, notably the initial establishment of missions and protectorates in Australian districts, as discussed in chapter one. Here, British philanthropic publications tended to discuss Australian prospects in apprehensive, even pessimistic terms. These depictions contrasted with – but also influenced and were influenced by – the mixed accounts of paternalism, anxiety and exchange emerging from the missionary and protectorate projects themselves. The idea that Indigenous Australians were unusually 'savage' and difficult to redeem, for instance, appeared in both local and metropolitan sources, but its meanings could differ significantly, from British missionary societies concerned about their funding and public displays of success, to local missionaries wishing to stress the special hardship and value of their work.

Much of my research focuses on the type of authority which philanthropists wished to create in the colonies. While their records focused explicitly on their efforts to 'civilise' Indigenous people, their implicit concerns revolved

---

3   For example, Carey 2000: 45–61; Carey and Roberts 2002: 821–869; Christie 1979; Gunson 1974; Harris 1990; Read 1988; Reynolds 1998; Woolmington 1986: 90–98, 1985: 283–293, 1983: 24–32, 1988: 77–92.

strongly around what it meant to be British, imperial and white, questions which assumed particular meanings in a colonial Australian context. This is highlighted in chapters two and three, which examine how the relationships between philanthropy, subjecthood and government were imagined in relation to Aboriginal affairs, and how national identity and race figured in this. Here, philanthropists' mixed imperial loyalties, their dependence on the state, and their wish to incorporate Indigenous Australians as British subjects sat uneasily beside their distress at the harm caused by dispossession, their mistrust of white colonists, and their disputes with Indigenous people over questions of authority.

Important works have been produced recently considering Indigenous peoples' legal and political status as imperial subjects (for example, in studies by Julie Evans), or tracing Aboriginal rights movements during later decades (notably in works by Bain Attwood and Ann Curthoys).[4] However, the realm of subjecthood encompasses a wider range of issues that have still to be addressed. Chapters four and five of this book pay particular attention to the difficult relationship between philanthropy and Indigenous rights with regard to two key topics: land and rationing. These chapters address the strong statements philanthropists made about Indigenous dispossession and entitlements, including their recounting of Indigenous people's feelings on these subjects. At the same time, however, notions of absolute, universal 'rights' (even to the basic requirements of life) were not necessarily present. Evident instead was an interplay of ideas about paternalism, imperial obligations, and deserving poverty, as well as Indigenous people's own beliefs about entitlement, exchange and personal connections to philanthropists. This brings the lineage of white support for Aboriginal rights under closer scrutiny. In this respect, I have also endeavoured to move beyond the assumed tension between 'civil' and 'Aboriginal' rights that shapes a number of contemporary works, which have tended to focus on the problematic place of minority rights within supposedly equal democratic nation-states.[5] While acknowledging that such debates are important, I would call for a greater historicising of changing ideas about what subjects and citizens are entitled to, and how this relates to government and charitable authorities. Issues of land and labour within early philanthropic sources also provide insights into alternative (largely unrealised) visions of Australian colonialism, where Indigenous access to land, the Crown's power to control how land was used, and the superiority of agriculture over pastoralism, were prioritised in ways which rarely eventuated in practice.

Understanding philanthropic efforts to 'make' Aboriginal subjects also requires moving inward, to examine their projects of physical and spiritual transformation, as addressed in chapters six and seven. The regimes of daily

---

4   For example, Attwood 2003; Curthoys, 2002; Evans 2004: 69–82; Evans 2002: 165–185; Evans 2003.
5   For example, Peterson and Sanders 1998: 1–4, 27–28. Attwood 2003 also addresses this theme.

mission life and their place within imperial politics have excited interest in recent years, due in large part to the works of Jean and John Comaroff on Tswana missions in southern Africa. The idea of 'civilisation' as a lived process – physical and spatial, concerned with intimate understandings of the self – has been explored in colonial settings by historians such as Jane Lydon, Anna Cole, Michael Harkin and Kathryn Rountree.[6] My work is indebted to their approaches, whilst also revealing some compelling issues arising in early 19th century Australia. Attempts to recreate Indigenous Australians as Christian individuals – self-aware, introspective, demonstrating their 'civilisation' in outward, visual ways – involved some creative paradoxes. I wish to consider further the links between missionary beliefs in individualist self-improvement and the institutional conformity which they were also trying to create. Worth examining, too, are philanthropists' own contradictory roles. Clearly, they wished to establish themselves as authoritative observers and exemplars of Christian enlightenment and bourgeois individualism. However, this developed in necessary dialogue and tension with the need to make their lives and homes open to Indigenous people, and to understand their own spiritual journeys partly through their mission work. In this setting, ideas about public and private life and Christian faith emerge not as absolute ideals, but as shifting, contested and personal dynamics.

This work challenges the frequent assessment of the first protectors and missionaries as failures. It does so partly by drawing attention to the rich and complex nature of their relationships with Indigenous people, including several accounts of Christian baptisms which have received surprisingly little historical attention. However, I have also tried to interrogate ideas about 'failure' itself. This is relevant to the discussion of conversion, religious standards and 'good death' in chapter seven. It is also important to chapter eight's account of the closure of the first missions and protectorates. By the middle of the 19th century, all of the first protectorates and Protestant missions had closed. This usually happened against a backdrop of further Indigenous dispossession and scathing comments from settlers and politicians about philanthropists' shortcomings and Aboriginal people's supposed 'savagery'. Here, while acknowledging the real failure of philanthropists to stem the harms inflicted on Indigenous people, I have also considered humanitarian 'failure' as an idea, emerging from disputes over colonial authority and connected to the growing popular belief that Aboriginal destruction was necessary and inevitable. This last notion provoked mixed responses from philanthropists. It might seem a foregone conclusion that their Christianity and commitment to missionary work must have led them

---

6   Cole 2005: 153–171; Harkin 2005: 205–225; Lydon 2005: 211–234; Rountree 2000: 49–66.

to oppose such claims. However, it is also worth considering how these very factors could also limit humanitarian advocacy and their ability to imagine an Indigenous future.

## Sources, approaches and limitations

The main sources for this project have been those produced by philanthropists, both locally (mission diaries and correspondence, protectorate records, and publications arising from these) and at an international level (for example, publications by missionary societies, the Aborigines Protection Society, and the 1835–37 House of Commons Select Committee on Aborigines). It is an ongoing challenge to examine the differences between these sources, in terms of focus, material and audience, and the dialogue occurring between them. Missionaries' personal journals, for example, were written with the encouragement of their societies, provided the material for annual reports and publications, and engaged in various ways with conventions of Evangelical writing. However, at the same time, their daily and individual nature allowed for greater discussion of emotional and spiritual experiences and Indigenous people's opinions. In this context, exploring Indigenous agency and viewpoints is both important and problematic. Linguistic and cultural differences, and the partial and sometimes propagandistic nature of philanthropic sources, limit our capacity to understand Aboriginal experiences through these records. It is partly as a result of this that Indigenous viewpoints are not the primary focus of this work. Nonetheless, philanthropists' concern for Aboriginal wellbeing, and their often conversational approach – vital to the evangelising process – mean that their records include some of the most illuminating material from this early colonial period; for all their shortcomings, they cannot be disregarded. Here, I note Gareth Griffiths' discussion of African missionary texts; he argues that colonised people's voices could not be completely suppressed, however problematic the source material, due in part to missionaries' own need to report religious encounters and establish authenticity. While their narratives worked to contain native voices, these voices were also (partially) inscribed, and can be read against the grain to some degree, their silences and gaps interrogated.[7] Themes of discussion and exchange in philanthropic sources are, therefore, important to this work.

Colonial mission sources contrasted in many ways with British publications, which often took a more straightforward propagandist role, 'correcting' and editing missionary stories for public display, driven by the need to raise popular and political support. This could involve a general emphasis on Christian progress and imperial loyalty, and a downplaying of missionary obstacles and

---

7   Griffiths 2005: 155–156.

colonised peoples' views. However, as I will demonstrate, British sources also gave varying descriptions of different colonies, with Australian Indigenous issues receiving often minor or pessimistic treatment.[8]

Philanthropists' writings were characterised by self-awareness and interiority, but they were also marked by calls for action. As Isabel Hofmeyr has noted, missionary tracts were explicit in their aim of spurring their readers to moral activism, and this approach had a strong political relevance. Elizabeth Elbourne, too, has examined the importance of narrative in the work of the Select Committee on Aborigines (British settlements), as they tried to strengthen advocacy for colonised peoples by engaging the feelings and imagination of their readers.[9] Furthermore, as Catherine Hall has noted with regard to Baptist missionaries in Jamaica, the task of speaking publicly about native policy and promoting the protection and 'civilising' of colonised peoples could be important to how middle-class Evangelical male activists saw their own authority and social position. This was implicit in their remarks about the 'pleasure' of speaking on behalf of the oppressed and the dispossessed. Here, I do not wish to label missionaries as sanctimonious liars, or to defend their integrity and legacy uncritically. Rather, I wish to further understanding of how their often difficult experiences in the colonies were shaped (in practice and in representation) by broader ideas about empire, identity and advocacy. As Hall puts it, 'Being a friend to the mission was one way of being in the world and mediating one's relation to others.'[10]

As the above topics suggest, a major focus of this project has been to understand philanthropists themselves and their place in empire and colony. As Isabel Hofmeyr and Helen Bethea Gardner have observed, missionary history has undergone broad changes since the mid-20th century. Scholars have moved from praising missionaries uncritically as agents of civilisation, to attacking them as imperialist oppressors, to portraying missions as local projects, involving considerable agency from native peoples, and/or as transnational efforts, which shaped their 'home' societies as much as the colonised ones. Some historians like Peggy Brock have also begun to place particular emphasis on indigenous people's own roles as evangelists, with very different agendas and world views to their European clergymen.[11] I have attempted to place this study within a broader understanding of British imperialism, acknowledging the vital work done by historians such as Susan Thorne and Anna Johnston on missionary influences within the British world. Johnston, for instance, examines how Britons came to 'know' the world partly through missionary literary cultures,

---

8   For more in this area, see for example Gardner 2006: 16–18; Griffiths 2005: 153; Johnston 2003: 32, 34, 80–83.
9   Elbourne 2002: 284; Elbourne 2003; Hofmeyr 2005: 21–26, 34.
10  Hall 2002: 294. Also, Hall 1992: 212–213.
11  Brock 2005: 132–152; Gardner 2006: 13; Hofmeyr 2005: 19–20.

while Thorne considers how missionary work shaped class and religion in British life. She asserts 'Missionaries were considerably more successful in securing imperialism's hegemony in Britain than in their foreign fields of operation.'[12] My own focus, however, returns more to the so-called colonial periphery; while viewing imperial history as crucial, I continue to be most intrigued by its ramifications for Australia. As Johnston notes, missionaries remain intriguing figures here — both humanitarian and authoritarian — and studying their work helps disrupt any simple view of empire, as well as reminding us of a tradition of debate over the morality of colonialism.[13]

Several other explanatory points are needed here. Of the institutions that operated during this period, two are not studied in great detail. One is the Parramatta native institution and the associated Black Town settlement, which ran on and off in Sydney from 1814–1829, supported by Governor Macquarie and various Anglican and Methodist preachers. This institution targeted children, including some removed forcibly from foreign districts in punitive raids, and has been identified by several historians as representing the nucleus of policies of separating Indigenous families and institutionalising the children, which in the late 20th century would become identified under the heading of the 'stolen generations'. While accepting the significance of this institution, I have not found it necessary to examine it at length. This is partly because several historians have done so in detail already, notably J Brook and JL Kohen, Peter Read and Jane Lydon.[14] Furthermore, its character differed in several notable ways from the institutions of the 1830s and 1840s: its very small pupil numbers, its focus on students who were far from their own country and unable to travel and negotiate their living habits, its partial focus on Maori children, and its avowedly 'experimental' nature, in contrast to the more generalised Indigenous governance that many later institutions hoped to initiate. Similarly, the exile of Indigenous people from the Tasmanian mainland to institutions at Wybalenna (Flinders Island) in 1833 and Oyster Cove in 1847, following their notorious experiences of violence with colonists and the military, is relevant to this study, but again, I have not made it a major focus. The absence of a strong missionary or religious influence there, and the more prison-like setting, where the people were prevented from returning to their traditional country, led again to different dynamics. Moreover, in-depth studies of this institutional life, notably by Lyndall Ryan and Anna Haebich, reduce the need for extensive reiteration.[15] Nonetheless, these early efforts at Aboriginal 'civilisation', although quickly labelled failures by some observers, would cast long shadows over subsequent projects.

---

12   Thorne 1999: 10. See also, Johnston 2003.
13   Johnston 2003: 104–105.
14   Brook and Kohen 1991; Lydon 2005: 201–224; Read 2006: 32–47.
15   Haebich 2000: 75–130; Ryan 1981.

As stated, I have chosen to focus on Protestant efforts, due to their strong and conflicted connections to empire, government and ideas about British civilisation. Some Catholic missionaries did operate in the Australian colonies during this time: the Passionist priests at Stradbroke Island between 1843–1846, the Sisters of Mercy in Perth from 1846, and the Benedictines at New Norcia in inland Western Australia from 1846. Given that their work rarely overlapped with that of their Protestant counterparts, and given their comparatively weak connections to the state (and sometimes to Indigenous people) during this era, I have omitted them from my study. Their stories have been discussed, however, by several historians, including John T McMahon, George Russo, Geraldine Byrne and Anne McLay.[16]

Finally, a couple of observations are needed about the use of language in this work. When referring to native peoples, I have tried to name their regional identities, but due to the sometimes vague source material, or the need to make some broader statements, this is not always possible. Otherwise, I have tended to use the term 'Indigenous' more than 'Aboriginal'. This is due to a certain unease with the notion of 'Aboriginal history' as a single, unified narrative, especially for this early colonial period when traditional identities remained strong and little sense of a generalised Aboriginal affinity was apparent. Nonetheless, this work does engage with Aboriginal history as a genre, and I recognise that these issues are controversial ones, subject to continued debate.

When referring to missionaries, protectors, and writers and advocates who raised Indigenous issues, I have tried where possible to name them according to their specific roles. However, the question of how to group them together – and to what extent we should – is problematic. There was considerable overlap between the voices raised in concern for Indigenous people. Missionaries, for example, were alive to the problems of material poverty, while state-funded protectors preached the Gospel, and British philanthropic bodies like the Aborigines Protection Society were interested in both evangelising and practical 'civilisation'. Zoë Laidlaw has drawn attention to a distinction between missionary organisations and the Aborigines Protection Society, which, while religiously motivated, was more open to civilisation-first approaches.[17] I have tried to be sensitive to the various agendas and personalities involved, while also seeing them as part of a wider movement in favour of relatively humane and Christian colonisation. Terminology is difficult here. While the term 'humanitarian' has a range of meanings in different imperial settings, Ann Curthoys has noted that its use in histories of Australian colonialism became popular largely through the scholarship of Henry Reynolds. Reynolds' work used the word as a valuable umbrella term, encompassing activists both religious and secular,

---

16   See, for example, Byrne 1981; McMahon 1943; McLay 1992; Russo 1980.
17   Laidlaw 2007: 133–161.

spanning two centuries, thus drawing the reader's attention to a long lineage of European concern for Indigenous dignity and humanity. Some scholars like Claire McLisky, though, are cautious of the term 'humanitarian' for precisely this reason, warning that it may work to obscure historical specificities, and pointing out that 19th century activists themselves did not necessarily identify with this word.[18]

Alternative terms, however, can also prove awkward. 'Evangelical', while important theologically, does not seem to me quite sufficient to encompass the colonising, protective and advocacy roles these men took on. The more popular 19th century word 'philanthropy' is perhaps the most appropriate, although it too has limitations. Used more commonly by historians of poor relief in Victorian Britain (although linked to missionary movements by historians like Johnston and Thorne), 'philanthropy' carried a range of meanings – used variously as a boast, an insult, a reference to religious proselytising, or to campaigns for social and legal reform. As a movement, philanthropy was linked to a decline in older systems of local aristocratic paternalism towards the needy, as well as the rise of the bourgeoisie and the non-conformist churches, and the growing British wish to regulate and discipline the poor. While philanthropy was intertwined with Evangelicalism, some historians like Robert H Bremner have associated it with a rather more secular benevolence that focused on abolishing slavery and on systemic reform of prisons, hospitals and other institutions for the vulnerable.[19] Complicating the issue further in this case is philanthropy's traditional emphasis on voluntarism. While this powered the efforts of some advocates for Aboriginal rights, it may have had a more tenuous meaning for professional missionaries and protectors, who took this work on partly for wages and social advancement. Ultimately, I have still tended to use the term 'philanthropy', feeling that despite its shortcomings it has considerable benefits. It forces us to keep in mind issues of benevolence, gratitude and control, relationships between giver and receiver, and the awkward but vital connections between religion and political change, which resonated for these colonial projects. Given this study's comparatively narrow focus, it also seemed appropriate to use a term more evocative of the 19th century. Nonetheless, questions of language, and the wider issue of how to categorise white settlers who attempted to speak for Indigenous people, remain contentious.

---

18   Ann Curthoys, 'The Humanitarians versus Colonial Self-Government: the Australian Colonies in the mid nineteenth century', conference paper delivered at *Race, Nation, History: A Conference in Honour of Henry Reynolds*, 29–30 August 2008, National Library of Australia, Canberra; McLisky 2005: 57–58.
19   Bremner 1994: xii, 121. See also Roberts 2002: 1–11, 143–153, 229–246.

# 'This land of Barbarians': missions and protectorates begin

Records from the Wellington Valley mission began with a death. In the spring of 1832, missionary William Watson wrote of his journey from Sydney to the Church Missionary Society station about 100 kilometres north-west of Bathurst. Watson, an energetic and cranky Yorkshireman, had worked as a shopkeeper and schoolteacher before moving to the colonies; for him, as for many of his contemporaries, missionary work meant an elevation through the ranks of the lower middle classes. He was accompanied in his journey by a ten-year-old Indigenous boy called Billy Black, who had been taken from the Wiradjuri country of Bathurst to Sydney by a Major McPherson. McPherson passed him on to the Watson household, where he became close to William and Ann Watson, learned to pray, and showed symptoms of the respiratory illness that would eventually kill him. According to Watson, Billy tolerated cruel treatment from white neighbours, who took his sickness for laziness and 'repeatedly said that a horsewhip was the best medicine for him.' He died quietly one night during the journey, and the missionaries wrapped him in a sheet of bark and buried him beside the bank of the Fish River. Watson wrote with mingled satisfaction and grief:

> When his happy spirit had left the cumbrous clod behind though I felt assured of his felicity I could not forbear weeping and sorrowing exceedingly, for I loved him as a Brother or as a Son and it was with the greatest difficult[y] imaginable that I got through the funeral service over him. The ways of God are mysterious but I am persuaded always in wisdom and mercy. O that Billy Black may be the forerunner of very many of the Aborigines of New Holland to the realms of light.[1]

This early tragedy might seem symbolic or prophetic, given the collapse of Wellington Valley a decade later and subsequent assessments of it as a dismal failure. What should also be considered, however, are the ways in which it was thought symbolic and prophetic at the time. Watson's earliest writings show the presence of death, loss and grief, as well as the reinterpretation of some such scenarios in terms of Christian ideals of 'good death' and the triumph of the spirit. Watson, a man whose records were characterised by passionate, energetic use of narrative, had been warned in advance of the great obstacles he would face amongst Indigenous Australians. Through such accounts of his labours,

---

1   William Watson, journal, 3 October 1832, also, 19 September 1832, in Carey and Roberts (eds) 2002, *The Wellington Valley Project: Letters and Journals Relating to the Church Missionary Society Mission to Wellington Valley, NSW, 1830–42, A Critical Electronic Edition* [hereafter WVP]: <http://www.newcastle.edu.au>. Also, Bridges 1978: 30, 251.

he could convey to his Evangelical readers a sense of both hardship and hope, and construct himself as a significant up-and-coming missionary. Certainly, the publicity value of Billy's death was not ignored by the Church Missionary Society itself. In 1834, the Church Missionary Society's *Missionary Register* and *Church Missionary Paper* published lengthy excerpts from this story as part of their descriptions of the new station, adding their confident hope that Watson had witnessed a genuine conversion.[2] This convergence of optimism and death (unnerving to the contemporary reader) was not coincidental. Such tales fit broadly into worldwide missionary discourse; the *Missionary Register*, for example, published frequent articles about the pious deaths of native children from different countries. Australian Aboriginal demise, however, was already assuming a special significance.

This chapter uses the early records of the Australian colonies' first missions and protectorate stations to provide an overview of the origins of philanthropic involvement in Aboriginal policy. With the exception of John Harris, few historians have attempted a general examination of missionary beginnings across all the colonies, and yet this task is valuable, showing important contrasts and commonalities. There was a near-universal equation between Indigenous survival and Christian Evangelical success, and, at the same time, serious doubts expressed from the start about the prospects for such success. Despite most philanthropists describing their early meetings with Indigenous people as friendly, missionary publications also included derogatory descriptions of Indigenous Australians from as early as the 1820s, with Australia assuming a minor and often pessimistic place in imperial philanthropic discourse. However, the spectre of Aboriginal destruction took on a variety of local meanings. Particularly notable was the tendency, apparent in Watson's story of the loss of Billy Black, to read hardship and tragedy in terms of Christian inspiration, and to claim a certain fulfilment and hope in the midst of destruction.

## 'The vexations, the sluggishness, the ignorant prejudices': early attempts at missionary work

Missionary movements can be traced back to the Evangelical fervour growing in Britain since the late 18th century. The London Missionary Society (LMS) was founded in 1795, the Church Missionary Society (CMS) in 1799 and the Wesleyan Methodist Missionary Society (WMMS) in 1813. By the 1820s, this movement had assumed strong social importance. Two generations of the so-called Clapham sect had campaigned against slavery; these activists were politically influential, many from mercantile and intellectual backgrounds – notables included MP

---

2   Church Missionary Society (CMS), *Church Missionary Paper: for the use of weekly and monthly contributions*, no LXXV, Michaelmas Day 1834; CMS, *Missionary Register*, March 1834: 133.

for Yorkshire William Wilberforce and Cambridge graduate and Lancashire landowner Thomas Babington. Meanwhile, missionaries were moving into the Pacific, the Cape colony and India, where they were already objecting to many of the impacts of settler-colonialism. Unlike their superiors in Britain, most of the agents sent out were from lower middle class or 'mechanic' backgrounds and were part of the general rise of a 'respectable' class during this era. (Many experienced class tensions with society authorities back home.) Missionary work was also assuming domestic importance, as Evangelical Christianity was mobilised in struggles between new and old elites and powerful and marginalised social classes, and membership of these new churches grew rapidly.[3]

Prior to 1825, however, little of this enthusiasm had reached Indigenous Australia. Anna Johnston attributes this slow start partly to the hard-headed politics of this penal colony, and partly because the strongest surge of missionary energy did not occur till some decades into Australian colonisation.[4] A native school operated at Parramatta between 1814–20, and at Blacktown between 1823–29, supported by several Anglican, Methodist and Congregationalist missionaries and Governor Macquarie, who had alternately ordered punitive punishments of Indigenous people and hoped for their Christian 'redemption'. Its primary aim was to train young Indigenous people as farmers and labourers, living apart from harmful European influences. (Older people were generally ignored, believed to be indifferent to European life.) Initially the school wanted no more than 12 students; in practice, numbers ranged from four to 15. Some children were recruited at the annual native feasts, but others were brought in from punitive expeditions and many ran away.[5] Often referred to as an experiment, the institution aimed to prove that Indigenous people could become civilised, if only in theory or on a small scale. While many of its techniques – not the least the forced removal of children – set the tone for later efforts, widespread or regional governance of Indigenous people does not seem to have been the aim. Nor was this project characterised by tremendous optimism. The Committee of the Native Institution noted in their minutes of 1821 that prior to establishing the institution, Governor Macquarie had asked the opinion of powerful Church of England chaplain and missionary advocate Samuel Marsden, who supported the scheme in theory but was himself more interested in the Maori and warned that Indigenous Australians lacked 'the finer feelings of affection and attachment which are the bonds of social life'.[6]

---

3  Elbourne 2002: 15, 21; Gunson 1978: 31–32; Johnston 2003a: 16–17; Lester 2005: 65–71; Mann 2004: 7.
4  Johnston 2003a: 169.
5  Brook and Kohen 1991: 30–35, 54–55, 61, 65–74, 87, 129–131, 146, 173, 212; Robert Cartwright to Governor Macquarie, 6 December 1829 and 18 January 1820, *British Parliamentary Papers (BPP): Papers Relating to Australia, 1830–36: Colonies: Australia*, vol 4, 1970: 156–159; Lydon 2005a: 202, 204.
6  Extracts from the Minutes of the Committee of the Native Institution, 12 December 1821, Church Missionary Society, Records [hereafter *CMS*], reel 46, AJCP M218, State Library of Victoria (SLV).

If the Church of England's interest in Indigenous evangelising was minor and equivocal during the 1820s, the Methodists were not very confident either. Throughout the 1820s and early 1830s, the Wesleyan Auxiliary Missionary Society for New South Wales often expressed regret that they had not done more for Indigenous people, but this did not lead to much action, or even much dialogue.[7] Methodist preacher Rev Walter Lawry, for instance, wrote to the Methodist Missionary Society in 1820 calling for a mission school and a farming settlement for Indigenous people, but warned that they had virtually no notion of God; 'of all the heathen tribes they are the lowest'.[8] The Methodist Missionary Society sent William Walker to Parramatta in 1823, concluding that there was little point in establishing a larger, independent mission; Indigenous people were, they claimed, nomadic and indifferent to material bribes.[9] Public discussions were no more optimistic. In 1822, the Wesleyan Methodist Missionary Society's *Papers Relative to the Wesleyan Missions and to the State of the Heathen Countries* published a rare article on Indigenous Australians, describing them as 'perhaps the lowest and most miserable of the scattered family of man', not yet inclined to respond to Christian teaching. Total destruction loomed, the journal claimed, due to the disappearance of their original staple diet and their refusal to become farmers. Only Christ's redeeming power could save them, and thus missionary work was imperative, not the least because only a missionary could bear to 'reside among them, and to struggle with the vexations, the sluggishness, the ignorant prejudices of such a race'.[10] In 1823, the Wesleyan Methodist Missionary Society's *Missionary Notices* aired similar concerns, via a brief letter from Mr Walker at Parramatta, recording with sorrow the deaths of two of his most promising students, as well as an article describing Tasmanian Indigenous people as the 'most destitute and wretched portion of the human family', and calling for mission work to elevate them and protect them from 'extinction'.[11]

By the mid-1820s, Methodist energy was growing somewhat, as amateur preacher John Harper explored the region around Wellington Valley and found the Wiradjuri people there to be healthy and friendly. The tone in *Missionary Notices* for 1824–25 indicated a certain optimism for people in such districts not

---

7  For example, 'Design of the Wesleyan Missionary Society; with the plans and rules of the Auxiliary Missionary Society for New South Wales, 1821', 'First Report of the Wesleyan Auxiliary Missionary Society for NSW, 1821', 'Eighth Report of the Wesleyan Auxiliary Missionary Society for NSW, 1828', 'Twelfth Report of the Wesleyan Auxiliary Methodist Missionary Society of NSW, 1833', in Wesleyan Methodist Missionary Society (WMMS), *Reports of the Wesleyan Methodist Missionary Society*, 1840–1851.
8  Rev Walter Lawry to Rev Joseph Taylor, 26 February 1820, WMMS, Records, 1819–1874, mfmG3726 (Record ID: 1040441), National Library of Australia (NLA).
9  Minutes of a Meeting of the Committee, 8 October 1823: 83–93, Methodist Missionary Society, Records [hereafter *MMS*], reel 2, AJCP M119, SLV.
10  WMMS, *Papers Relative to the Wesleyan Missions and to the State of the Heathen Countries*, no IX, September 1822.
11  WMMS, Missionary Notices: relating principally to the Foreign Missions, vol IV, no 95, November 1823: 163–164; WMMS, Missionary Notices, vol IV, no 96, December 1823: 180–182.

yet intensively 'settled'.[12] Hopes for a mission there were quashed, however, by attacks in the press on Harper's motives and expertise, and controversies over misuse of society funds. When the WMMS tried in 1826 to secure another site in Bateman's Bay, they were blocked by Governor Darling, who said it would endanger settlers' interests. The society continued to comment that Indigenous wellbeing was a painful, awkward subject, adding (curiously, in the light of years of inaction) that numerous attempts had failed.[13] Claims that missionary work was hard and that 'heathens' were depraved did not, in themselves, indicate unusual pessimism; these were standard remarks in missionary discourse. However, descriptions of Indigenous Australians appearing in missionary journals were exceptionally derogatory, and the fact that these societies were already expressing doubts about any Australian success at all – at a time when very little had been attempted – suggests that hopes for this region were low from the start.

While there were cultural and political reasons behind this neglect, there were also some geographical factors. Ironically, concern for the plight of Indigenous Australia may have been lessened (perhaps subliminally) by the strategic importance of this region to Pacific missionary work. The nearby islands had attracted strong missionary interest from early days, from the London Missionary Society in Tahiti, the Marquesas, the Cook Islands and Samoa, the Wesleyan Methodist Missionary Society in Fiji and Tonga, and the Anglicans in New Zealand and Melanesia. These societies disagreed on some issues, but voiced similar denunciations of European beachcombers and Catholics. Their intensive work in the islands had ramifications for Australia, which was a vital Pacific base and transit point for missionaries travelling to the islands. They formed floating communities of sorts linking back to Sydney, where their activities were monitored, supported or hindered by Rev Samuel Marsden in particular.[14] As early as 1820, Rev Walter Lawry was praising the growth of New South Wales to the WMMS, on the grounds that it would prove 'the refuge, and nursery & asylum of this Hemisphere for missionaries.'[15] These views were still evident in 1848, when the Church Missionary Society's *Colonial Church Chronicle and Missionary Journal* stressed that British expansion in Australia was positive because it would enable missionaries to spread throughout the

---

12  WMMS, *Missionary Notices*, vol IV, no 107, November 1824: 363; WMMS, *Missionary Notices*, vol IV, no 116, August 1825: 498–499.
13  Ralph Mansfield, Report of the New South Wales Aboriginal Mission for the year ending 31 December 1825, *MMS*, reel 4, AJCP M121, SLV; Minutes of the Seventh NSW District Meeting, 2 January 1827, *MMS*, reel 4, AJCP M121, SLV; Roberts and Carey 2009 (online through Project Muse).
14  Johnston 2003a: 173; Samson 1998: 9.
15  Rev Walter Lawry to MMS Committee, 26 August 1820, Wesleyan Methodist Missionary Society, Records, 1819–1874, mfmG3726 (Record ID: 1040441), NLA.

Pacific – 'If we could plant another England at the Antipodes, the task would be incalculably easier.'[16] Indigenous Australians were not mentioned here; in this context, this might have proven a disruptive and unwelcome topic.

## 'Sitting among them': evangelising begins at Lake Macquarie

By the mid 1820s, though, hopes were beginning to stir for a new London Missionary Society station, headed by LE Threlkeld. Threlkeld's mission focused on the Awabakal people of Lake Macquarie; he set up first by the lakeside peninsula of Reid's Mistake, then later moved across the lake to a site called Ebenezer, following his split with the LMS. The Awabakal were a fishing people, living off the sea, the coastal rock platforms and the nearby swamps. They had already experienced two decades of relatively minor colonialism, since an isolated penal camp was established in Newcastle in 1804. In these early days, Awabakal had done casual farming jobs, taken crops for themselves, recaptured escaped convicts for the military, and generally retained a certain autonomy. More intensive colonialism and free settlement arrived in 1823, though, shortly before the missionary did. By the 1830s, an increasingly dispossessed Awabakal become involved in violent clashes with colonists, soldiers and other Indigenous groups, and their destruction as a people became a real threat. Threlkeld's mission, finally abandoned in 1841, would stand witness to these changes.[17]

Threlkeld's early reports showed a guarded optimism. He was told in 1825, before he commenced his work, that Awabakal people had heard of him and were inquiring keenly when the missionary would arrive. They were probably influenced by the local clergyman GA Middleton, who had lobbied local government on their behalf and encouraged them to visit Threlkeld's station. Awabakal people sang and danced to mark Threlkeld's arrival, and camped outside his cottage, smoking and talking. They agreed to teach him language and promised to work on the farm he was planning in their country. Having inspected the site, he reported that the 20 people already living there 'appeared pleased with the idea of my sitting among them.' Threlkeld immediately began gathering information about Awabakal language, totems and clans, by talking to people while they hunted, fished and ate their meals.[18]

---

16  Church Missionary Society (CMS) 1849, *The Colonial Church Chronicle and Missionary Journal*, vol II, July 1848.
17  Clouten 1967: 70–75; David A Roberts, 'Aborigines, Commandants and Convicts: The Newcastle Penal Settlement', in Roberts, Carey and Grieves (ed) 2002, *Awaba: A Database of Historical Materials Relating to the Aborigines of the Newcastle-Lake Macquarie Region*, University of Newcastle, <http://www.newcastle.edu.au/group/amrhd/awaba/>; LE Threlkeld to London Missionary Society, May 1827, in Gunson (ed) 1974 vol 2: 227; Turner and Blyton 1995: 13–14, 28–29, 36–37.
18  Henwood 1978: 34; LE Threlkeld, Mission to the Aborigines, New South Wales, 7 March 1825, 14 March 1825 entries, London Missionary Society, Records [hereafter *LMS*], AJCP M11, SLV; LE Threlkeld to

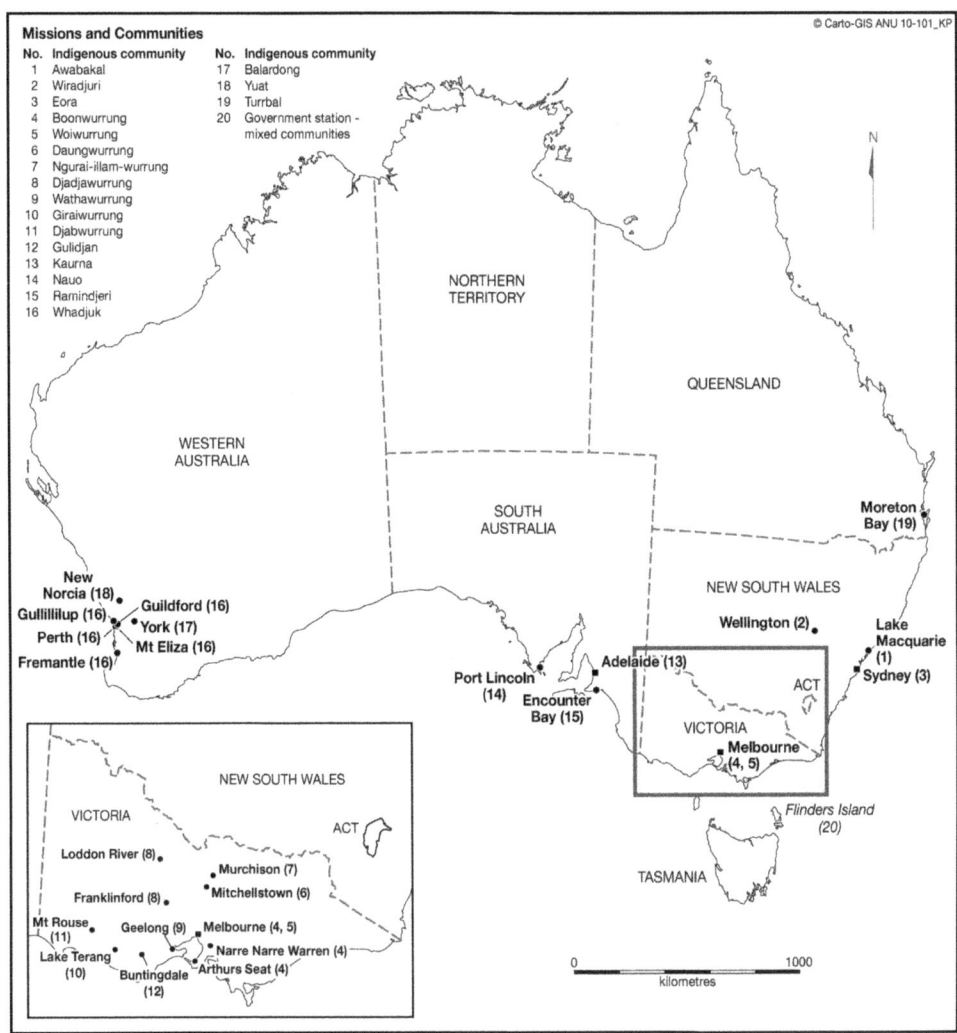

Fig 1. Map showing the locations of Indigenous communities and missions in Australia.

Prepared by Karina Pelling, Cartographic and GIS Services, Australian National University.

Threlkeld's work was unusual in several ways – notably his strong linguistic focus, his relatively subdued evangelising and his eventual political notoriety. Nonetheless, his early accounts demonstrate a number of elements common to many Australian missions and protectorate stations in the early 19th century. The first is the initial friendliness shown by Indigenous people. This was interpreted by missionaries as a promising sign of eventual conversion, but

---

George Burder, 25 April 1825, in Gunson (ed) 1974 vol 2: 182; LE Threlkeld, Second Half Yearly Report of the Aboriginal Mission, 21 June 1826, *LMS*, AJCP M73, SLV; Turner and Blyton 1995: 30; Windross and Ralston 1897: 11, 30.

it carried other local meanings. Much of missionaries' behaviour – giving gifts, exchanging names, trying to speak language, holding ceremonies and discussing with Indigenous people where they should locate their stations – may have seemed more or less appropriate for visitors in Indigenous country. Gwenda Baker, describing early 20th century Arnhem Land missions, observes that invitation, permission and negotiated passage were essential to Aboriginal people's use of space, and notes that later story-telling (although possibly rose-tinted) often stressed that missionaries were given approval to live in certain areas of land. Similarly, Fiona Magowan, focusing on the same era, argues that although missionaries' beliefs were radically different to Yolngu ones, some of their behaviour could still be assimilated into Indigenous relationships of reciprocity, caring for others and sharing skills.[19] Close comparisons with the early 19th century are, of course, problematic, and deep cracks would soon appear in these philanthropic arrangements. Nonetheless, it seems possible that Indigenous people held early hopes for beneficial relationships with missionaries.

Another aspect of early philanthropic work intriguing to the contemporary reader – and especially notable in Threlkeld's records – was the commitment to learning Indigenous languages. Threlkeld published his first, partial effort at an Awabakal grammar in 1827, continuing to produce spelling and phrase books throughout the 1830s and working on translations of the Gospels of Mark and Luke.[20] This contrasts sharply with efforts by later institutions to ban local languages. However, it should not be equated with respect for Indigenous cultures, but rather with a particular Protestant view on the relationship between language and religion. Brian Stanley, for instance, notes that from the 1820s there was an Evangelical belief that translating the Bible into a multitude of languages was essential for worldwide conversions.[21]

Denominational loyalties presented different questions. Mistrust between missionaries of different backgrounds may have had a broad impact in lessening Evangelical commitment to the Aboriginal cause; Anna Johnston, David A Roberts and Hilary Carey, for instance, argue that tensions between Anglican and Methodist figures contributed to the failure of the first Wellington Valley project in the 1820s.[22] However, there was little sign of different bodies competing directly for Indigenous converts. In 1826, for instance, Threlkeld discussed his mission with Archdeacon Scott, reminding him that the LMS did not require its missionaries to be Anglican and that he could not pledge to teach the Church of England liturgy. Scott responded 'he cared not by whom the Aborigines were

---

19    Baker 2005: 20–26; Magowan 2005: 162–164.
20    Hilary M Carey, 'Missionaries, Dictionaries and Australian Aborigines, 1820–1850', in Roberts, Carey and Grieves (ed) 2002, *Awaba*.
21    Stanley 2001: 193.
22    Johnston 2003a: 169; Roberts and Carey 2009.

civilised so long as it was done.'²³ Meanwhile, Threlkeld was virulently anti-Catholic — he had worked in the South Seas and deplored the French Catholic presence there — and concerns about Catholic influences on the white population were raised by other missionaries working in the Indigenous field.²⁴ However, Catholics in eastern Australia were rarely engaged in Indigenous issues at this time and do not seem to have worried their Protestant counterparts in this respect.

However, Threlkeld's early papers also show signs of the greater tensions that philanthropists — especially in the south-east — would develop with their white neighbours. By 1826, Threlkeld was writing to the LMS in deep concern over frontier violence and dispossession, protesting that Indigenous people faced total destruction, in 'this vile, hypocritical country'. In this context, he had to consider whether missions could ever succeed, noting that most colonists had judged his project 'utopian' from the start, based on a 'forlorn hope'.²⁵ His own earlier experiences in Tahiti led to mixed feelings about Awabakal prospects. He told the LMS that he found his new work dull after the joy of preaching to large crowds of converts in Raiatea, remarking that the Awabakal, while friendly, presented a depressing heathen contrast to 'their sable brethren in the South Seas'. However, he added, his very experience of Pacific success also gave him hope for New South Wales.²⁶ Threlkeld's early work suggests that the idea of Australia as an uniquely problematic field, while discouraging, could also create a space where Australian work could take on a particular potential value. In 1825, he told the LMS 'I glory in this work because it [is] so much despised, so much considered as utterly impossible.'²⁷

## 'To make them like ourselves': Wellington Valley and Flinders Island

In the late 1820s, the Church of England in New South Wales remained fairly unenthused about Indigenous prospects. In 1827, Archdeacon Scott told Governor Darling that he saw little hope of Indigenous improvement. He did not relish the idea of funding Aboriginal projects when there were so many

---

23   LE Threlkeld to George Burder and William Hankey, 20 January 1826, *LMS*, AJCP M11, SLV.
24   For example, Niel Gunson, 'Introduction', in Gunson (ed) 1974 vol 1: 28; James Günther, journal, 28 July 1840, *WVP*; JCS Handt to William Jowett, 27 November 1841, *WVP*; John Smithies to General Secretaries, 25 October 1843, Wesleyan Methodist Missionary Society, Archive: Australasia 1812–1889 [hereafter *WMMS*], reel 2, Mp2107 (Record ID: 133095), NLA; LE Threlkeld to His Most Christian Majesty Louis Phillip, King of the French, 8 December 1838, *LMS*, AJCP M11, SLV; Tyrell 1993: 2.
25   LE Threlkeld, Mission to the Aborigines, New South Wales, 13 March 1825 entry, *LMS*, AJCP M11, SLV; LE Threlkeld to Burder and Hankey, 4 September 1826, and LE Threlkeld to Burder and Hankey, 11 September 1826, *LMS*, AJCP M11, SLV; LE Threlkeld to Burder and Hankey, 23 April 1825, *LMS*, AJCP M73, SLV.
26   LE Threlkeld, Mission to the Aborigines of New South Wales, extract, c1825, *LMS*, AJCP M11, SLV; LE Threlkeld, Second half yearly report of the Aboriginal mission, 21 June 1826, *LMS*, AJCP M11, SLV.
27   LE Threlkeld to George Burder and William Hankey, 10 October 1825, *LMS*, AJCP M73, SLV.

colonists without religious guidance, and suggested that ration stations and small schools would suffice. He scoffed at the Methodist hopes for Wellington Valley, insisting that the Wiradjuri people there had never shown an interest in Christianity.[28] In spite of this assessment, it was at Wellington Valley that the Church Missionary Society began their own mission work several years later, a project possibly hindered from the start by these Anglicans' neglect of the early Methodist records from the area.[29] The CMS *Missionary Register* (1831) claimed the impetus for this mission had come from the British government, hoping to avoid the vicious dispossession that had already occurred elsewhere.[30]

Like the Awabakal, the Wiradjuri people of Wellington Valley had had years of mixed experiences of colonialism, initially in penal form. They lived in a large and ecologically diverse region, which included grass plains and eucalyptus forests, where they utilised fishing and firestick farming. Convict stations had arrived in their country in Bathurst in 1815 and in Wellington Valley in 1823 (this station closed in 1830). These were small and fairly peaceable outposts. However, as Heather Goodall notes, the massive increase in sheep, cattle and settlers around Bathurst in the 1820s damaged the Wiradjuri situation radically, leading to escalating violence and a declaration of martial law by Governor Brisbane in 1824. Indigenous casualties were estimated to be large, although it is hard to say exactly how this affected the people of Wellington Valley, in whose district a direct European presence was still fairly minor.[31]

When JCS Handt and William Watson arrived in September 1832, they found the local residents already waiting for the 'Misshinir'. Their first meetings were characterised by a cordial mistrust. The women and children kept their distance at first, having been threatened by local colonists that missionaries would abduct and enslave them. At the same time, however, Wiradjuri clearly expected the missionaries to distribute gifts and food. They did chores around the missionaries' camp, heard the missionaries' assurances that they had been sent by the King to teach the people how to live like Europeans, and took an interest in the hymns and prayers.[32]

During the first few months, the mission papers recorded two particular elements of station life which would become potent and enduring, but which were handled equivocally in British publications. One was the conversational nature of evangelising. While the Wellington Valley records often complained of Wiradjuri indifference or rudeness, some religious discussions were energetic

---

28   Archdeacon Scott to Governor Darling, 1 August 1827, *BPP: Papers Relating to Australia, 1830–36*, vol 4, 1970: 165–169.
29   Roberts and Carey 2009.
30   CMS, *Missionary Register*, January 1831: 118–119.
31   Goodall 1996: 11, 30; Read 1988: 2–4, 9–12; Roberts 2003: 151–152.
32   JCS Handt, journal, 30 September 1832, *WVP*; Watson, journal, 30 September 1832, *WVP*; Watson, 1832–1833 Report, *WVP*.

and curious. Handt, for instance, recalled being asked whether God was a black fellow, and responded 'he was neither black nor white, but as bright as the sun.'[33] Watson recorded his early fascination with the claims of a young man called Oorimbildwally, who claimed to have significant dreams about the missionaries' God.[34] Also evident during the first few weeks in Wellington Valley – a sign of tensions to come – were missionaries' repeated requests for custody of children, 'to make them like ourselves'. An argument started early on when Watson tried to stop an old man, Bogin, taking a young boy, Peter, away from the station.[35]

The CMS published mixed accounts of these early developments. Between 1832–34, the *Missionary Register* and *Church Missionary Paper* described the efforts at Wellington Valley to set up a vegetable garden, distribute rations and persuade people to attend church and leave their children there to be educated. (This last task was admitted to be difficult, but details of the tensions were often left out.) Descriptions of violence towards women, infanticide and behaviour labelled as 'witchcraft' and 'godlessness' were also included. Notable, too, were the publications' mixed treatment of Indigenous voices and viewpoints. The wide array of Wiradjuri ideas and comments recorded (or hinted at) in the missionaries' diaries were barely mentioned in these formal publications, with one exception: direct quotations and detailed conversations about religion were highlighted.[36]

As in Threlkeld's papers, the Wellington Valley records showed suspicions from early on that missionary work might prove not only challenging, but impossible. In 1831, CMS secretaries Thomas Woodrooffe and Dandeson Coates wrote to the Watsons as they set out for New South Wales, wishing them energy and faith for the task ahead, and warning that they would encounter 'peculiar difficulties … arising from the wrongs and injuries inflicted on the natives by the settlers, and from the depth of degradation into which the Aborigines are sunk.' The obstacles the Watsons would encounter, they suggested, were amongst the greatest in the world. Once again, however, difficulty itself could imply a certain nobility.

> It may be given to you only to sow the seed, and reserved to another to gather in the harvest: God will, however, be glorified thereby, and in the great day of Christ 'he that soweth and he that reapeth shall rejoice together.'[37]

---

33  Handt, journal, 4 December 1832, *WVP*.
34  Watson, journal, 19 April 1833, 12 May 1833, 20 May 1833, *WVP*.
35  For instance, Handt, journal, 12 November 1832, 24 November 1832, *WVP*; Watson, journal, 14 October 1832, *WVP*.
36  CMS, *Church Missionary Paper*, no LXXV, Michaelmas Day 1834; CMS, *Missionary Register*, May 1833 – October 1833: 238, 455–458; CMS, *Missionary Register*, February 1834: 114–119; CMS, *Missionary Register*, March 1834: 133, 151–154.
37  Thomas Woodrooffe and Dandeson Coates to Mr and Mrs Watson, 7 October 1831, *BPP: Correspondence and Other Papers Relating to Aboriginal Tribes in British Possessions*, 1834: 151–152.

In Good Faith?

Fig 2. During the 1830s, the Church Missionary Society published tales of bush life, cultural clashes and missionary work at Wellington Valley. As the picture indicates, many aspects of traditional Wiradjuri life were continuing, to the fascination and concern of the missionaries.

*Missionary Register*, September 1834, L & G Seeley, London. National Library of Australia, N266.3CHU.

Concerns about Australian prospects did not remain in-house either. Along with early, relatively optimistic accounts from Wellington Valley, the *Missionary Register* (1832) published Handt's description of a Sydney native feast, where he described the Indigenous people there as degraded and rapidly vanishing.[38] In early 1834, the journal mentioned explorers' depictions of Indigenous Australians as being 'at the very bottom of the scale of humanity'. It also approved the exile of the Tasmanian people to Flinders Island, on the grounds that they were too ferocious to live elsewhere.[39]

This Tasmanian situation had particular meanings for missionary work in the 1830s. Christian evangelising had been introduced to these people, exiled first to Bruny Island, Gun Carriage Island and finally Flinders Island in 1835, where

---

38   CMS, *Missionary Register*, May 1832: 238.
39   CMS, *Missionary Register*, February 1834: 114.

coercion and institutionalisation were much greater than on other stations at the time. Catechists were employed from 1833 onwards and church services held, although commandant Peter Fisher remarked that he doubted how much of them were understood.[40] More broadly, Lyndall Ryan sees the Flinders Island experiment, promoted to other colonies by Lieutenant-Governor Sir George Arthur, GA Robinson and missionary advocates James Backhouse and George Walker, as premised on what would become a wider belief: that Indigenous people could be civilised if removed to reserves, where the young people would be trained to integrate into the lower ranks of colonial society. The failure of this approach in Van Diemen's Land was blamed not on incarceration or poverty, but rather on the social impacts of the earlier war.[41] These efforts received a mixed response in philanthropic publications. The Aborigines Protection Society's 1839 annual report mentioned with some optimism 'the actual improvement of the natives of Van Diemen's Land'. However, by the following year they seemed more equivocal, describing Robinson's optimism about Flinders Island residents learning to value money and live in permanent houses, but also publishing harrowing statistics about deaths on the island, referring to the residents as a 'poor remnant of a banished and ill-used race'.[42] Here, the prospect of Indigenous 'extinction' was apparent, and without the element of hope present in some other districts.

## 'Bye & bye white men would come': the complex rise of philanthropy and imperialism

At this time, though, there was an increasing interest in the new settlements of Port Phillip and South Australia. At first, this was due in large part to Joseph Orton, a Methodist missionary who had been previously in Jamaica, where his opposition to slavery brought him into conflict with white planters, before moving to New South Wales to coordinate regional missionary activities. In 1833, the WMMS's *Missionary Notices* included a request from Orton for more missionary assistance for Indigenous people, whom he considered degraded but capable of improvement.[43] He went on to consult with Governor Bourke and Sir George Arthur about the prospects of a Port Phillip Aboriginal mission, having visited this new settlement himself in 1836, the year it was officially annexed.[44] This was a year after John Batman's party had arrived and signed a treaty with a

---

40   Reynolds 1995: 170–173; Ryan 1981: 126, 180, 184–185.
41   Ryan 1980: 14–22; Ryan 1981: 176–178.
42   Aborigines Protection Society (APS), Second Annual Report, 21 May 1839: 7–8, 13–16, in APS, Transactions, c1839–1909, MIC/o6550, reel 1 (Records the property of Anti-Slavery International); APS, Third Annual Report, 23 June 1840: 30–32, APS, Transactions, reel 1.
43   WMMS, *Missionary Notices*, vol IV, no 215, November 1833: 366–367.
44   Meeting of the Committee, 5 May 1837: 503–509, *MMS*, AJCP M120, reel 3, SLV; Joseph Orton to Governor Bourke, 16 August 1836, *MMS*, reel 9, AJCP M126, SLV.

Woiwurrung delegation which Batman claimed ceded ownership of the district to him in return for gifts, but which the Woiwurrung probably understood as an attempt to invoke the *tanderrum* ceremony, allowing visitors temporary access to land in return for presents and conciliatory gestures.[45]

When Orton arrived, Indigenous people around Melbourne received him amicably. Translating (possibly imperfectly) through Murranguruk, also known as William Buckley, an escaped convict found living with the Wathawurrung people, he told them that 'bye & bye white men would come to teach their children to read and write'. He distributed presents and invitations to his church service, which 50 Aboriginal people attended, watching the foreign ceremonies with interest. This left Orton in an optimistic mood. When washing in the river one morning, he prayed to God to make him useful in 'this land of Barbarians', and believed it was significant when he opened his pocket Testament afterwards and saw the phrase 'and the *barbarians* shewed me no little kindness'.[46] His 1836 publication *The Aborigines of Australia* called for further mission work in Port Phillip, portraying local people as heathen, savage and violent towards each other but also 'remarkably docile' towards Europeans and receptive to missionary work.[47] This mirrored his private comments to the WMMS, where he combined evangelical enthusiasm with warnings of severe spiritual hardship. This work, he said would suit only those who sincerely believed the teaching 'In the wilderness shall waters break out and streams in the Desert', 'and the parched ground shall become a pool and the thirsty land springs of earth'.[48]

This slowly developing enthusiasm was part of a much greater mood of religious change in the 1830s. Philanthropists leaving for the Australian colonies at this time departed from a Britain in spiritual turmoil. The 1832 Reform Act[49] had enabled dissenters to enter the political process, while the 1836 Registration Act[50] took the administration of births, deaths and marriages out of the hands of the Church of England. The 1833 abolition of slavery in British dominions – a campaign spearheaded by independent backbencher Sir Thomas Fowell Buxton – was considered a triumph for Evangelical advocacy, and in turn encouraged the 1835 Select Committee on Aborigines (British Settlements), the report of which was co-authored and structured by members of Buxton's circle, who were influenced by the Clapham sect and had links to Quakers, missionary societies

---

45  Broome 2005: 10–11; Clark 1998: 82–83.
46  Joseph Orton, 21 April 1836, Joseph Orton, Journal 1832–1839 and 1840–1841 [hereafter *JOJ*], ML ref A1714–1715, CY reel 1119, State Library of NSW. See also 23, 24, 28 April 1836.
47  Joseph Orton 1836, *The Aborigines of Australia*: 7–9.
48  Joseph Orton to WMMS General Secretaries, August 1836, Joseph Orton, Letterbooks 1822–1842, ML ref A1717–A1720, State Library of NSW. Also, Joseph Orton to WMMS General Secretaries, August 1836, *MMS*, reel 9, AJCP M126, SLV.
49  The name commonly given to the Act to Amend the Representation of the People in England and Wales (1832).
50  A shortened version of the title: An Act for Registering Births, Deaths and Marriages in England (1836)

and movements for prison reform. Buxton himself networked with Evangelical Whigs and sympathetic members of the Colonial Office.[51] The report made clear that Christianity was central to their notions of protecting and elevating colonised peoples. Elizabeth Elbourne draws attention to the Committee's aim 'to secure to them [the Aborigines] the due observance of Justice and the protection of their Rights; to promote the spread of Civilization among them, and to lead them to the peaceful and voluntary reception of the Christian Religion.'[52] (The emphasis on voluntary conversion did not suggest that Christianity was non-essential, but rather implied the importance of personal, Protestant revelation.) This work was followed in 1837 by the establishment of the Aborigines Protection Society by Dr Thomas Hogkin, with Buxton as president and input from many figures who had been active on the Select Committee. The APS's earliest campaigns focused on the need for native reserves in the Canadian colonies and southern Africa and protesting against the treatment of Africans by the Boers. While supportive of missionary and anti-slavery movements, the APS was somewhat less religious and more scientific in its approach, and would become envious of the greater support available to missionary movements.[53]

As Elbourne points out, this enthusiasm was in many ways specific to the 1820s and 1830s, an era of rapid expansion of colonialism, economic liberalisation and domestic political citizenship for white men. It would become a source of controversy worldwide, when missionaries were accused of encouraging slave revolts in the West Indies, and became caught up in British settlers' land wars with Xhosa in the Cape colony and Maori in New Zealand. Missionaries, while linked in various ways to the colonial state, nonetheless tended to contrast their model of civilisation with those of British officials and settlers from different national backgrounds, whom they often accused of neglecting, corrupting or destroying the natives. This position could make missionaries' standing unpopular and precarious. (Indeed, Roberts and Carey have suggested that colonists' knowledge of such clashes in Barbados and the Cape in the 1820s was one reason why the first missionaries in New South Wales were treated so suspiciously.) Moreover, the very liberalising impulses which had helped prompt developments like the 1835 Select Committee could also prove a double-edged sword. In settler-colonies in Australia, Canada and the Cape, debates were also raging at this time over the legal, political and economic rights of settlers. The ultimate results, including responsible government for the colonies, would often prove mixed or harmful for native peoples.[54]

---

51  Armstrong 1973: 164–165; Laidlaw 2002: 82–83; Lester 2005: 65–66.
52  Elbourne 2003 (online through Project Muse).
53  Bourne 1899: 9; Laidlaw 2007: 133–161.
54  Elbourne 2003; Roberts and Carey 2009; Lester 2005: 65, 68–69, 78–80.

In Good Faith?

Given the relevance of the Select Committee to how philanthropic work was seen, it is worth considering this report in some detail. The New South Wales section drew extensively and strategically on records from Wellington Valley. CMS spokesman Dandeson Coates reported that the circumstances there were difficult and discouraging, due to disease, violence and sexual exploitation of women and children. Nonetheless, he added, there were some positive signs: children were learning to read and people were attending church services.[55] Wellington Valley aside, though, Australian missions were not prominent in this report. Due, probably, to his split with the LMS, Threlkeld's passionate views did not feature directly. Other Australasian witnesses (none of whom had much Aboriginal experience) made rather pessimistic statements. Rev William Yate did remark that Lake Macquarie and Wellington Valley had shown that Indigenous people could understand Christianity, but other commentators were less sanguine.[56] Rev John Williams, who spoke mostly about the Pacific, added that he thought Indigenous Australians 'the most degraded of any aborigines that I had met with'. While maintaining that they, like all people, were capable of salvation, he also observed that the Parramatta school had failed.[57] Archdeacon Broughton praised Threlkeld's translation work, hoped that the people on Flinders Island were better off there, and noted that the children living with Mr Cartwright in Blacktown showed some improvement. Nonetheless, he also described Indigenous Australians as idle and degraded, indifferent to property and Christianity, and especially difficult to civilise because of their unwillingness to give up their children. He concluded that they were decaying as a people and, in a short time, 'I will not say exterminated, but they will be extinct.'[58] Rev Walter Lawry of New South Wales also added that Aborigines would probably become 'extinct' soon, as a result of European vices.[59] The Committee's 1837 report concluded that Aboriginal Australians were corrupted by contact with settlers and in danger of destruction.[60]

What stands out most, in some ways, is the Committee's relative lack of interest in Indigenous Australia. Zoë Laidlaw and Elizabeth Elbourne, who have pursued more transnational approaches, emphasise the central importance of the Cape colony to this report, noting that the Committee began work following concerns from the LMS over the oppression of the Xhosa. Laidlaw suggests that Australian historians have overemphasised their country's importance to the

---

55   Dandeson Coates, John Beecham and William Ellis, evidence, 6 June 1836, *BPP: Report from the Select Committee on Aborigines (British Settlements) together with minutes of evidence, appendix and index*, Anthropology: Aborigines, vol 1, 1836: 486–490, 520.
56   William Yate, evidence, 13 Feb 1836, *BPP: Report from the Select Committee on Aborigines (British Settlements)*, vol 1, 1836: 201–206.
57   *BPP: Report from the Select Committee on Aborigines (British Settlements)*, vol 1, 1836: 675.
58   Archdeacon Broughton, evidence, 3 Aug 1835, *BPP: Report from the Select Committee on Aborigines (British Settlements)*, vol 1, 1836: 13–24.
59   *BPP: Report from the Select Committee on Aborigines (British Settlements)*, vol 1, 1836: 498.
60   *BPP: Report from the Select Committee on Aborigines (British Settlements)* vol 2, 1837: 10–13.

report; the New South Wales sections occupied a space larger than originally intended because of the removal of more controversial African material.[61] Even so, I would add, the Australian material still receives relatively minor attention, a tendency that was also evident in missionary society journals, which preferred to focus on India, southern Africa, China, the Pacific and North America. If Australia did assume a special status, it was often for having the most allegedly degraded natives or the most lamentable Indigenous record. For instance, when the *Evangelical Magazine* (issued by Calvinistic Methodists) promoted the work of the Select Committee, Australia was named among the colonies guilty of exterminating their native peoples.[62]

## 'A kind and Christian procedure'?: hopes and fears for the new settlements

Despite these concerns, philanthropists of the mid-1830s did express some hopes for missionary work in districts that had been colonised only recently. In particular, for a brief period the new colony of South Australia was singled out by British philanthropists as unusually optimistic. While European whalers and sealers had been visiting the southern coast for decades, official colonisation did not begin until the mid-1830s. Unlike its neighbours, South Australia was colonised by a commercial company, distributing land systematically to free citizens, thus appearing to provide an alternative model. Some hopes were kindled for Indigenous policy; Lyndall Ryan, for instance, suggests that Sir George Arthur influenced the Colonial Office to urge the commissioners of the Wakefield Scheme to sign a treaty with Indigenous people and establish a protectorate.[63] Certainly, missionary societies and later the Aborigines Protection Society hoped that a more civilised settlement would develop. An LMS committee, lamenting that much of Australia was in a state of 'religious destitution and moral barbarism', looked forward to a better South Australian system, 'determined upon a kind and Christian procedure'.[64] In 1838, the *Colonial Church Record* and the APS rejoiced that this colony would take no convicts, and hoped for kinder Indigenous policies, with reserves, protectorates and schools.[65] South Australian protectors were indeed appointed from 1837

---

61    Elbourne 2003; Laidlaw 2002: 79–80, 88.
62    *Evangelical Magazine and Missionary Chronicle*, vol XV, July 1837: 330–331; *Evangelical Magazine and Missionary Chronicle*, vol XVI, April 1838: 188–189.
63    Ryan 1980: 14–22; Ryan 1981: 176–178.
64    *Evangelical Magazine and Missionary Chronicle*, vol XIII, December 1834: 504.
65    APS 1838, *First Annual Report of the Aborigines Protection Society*, 16 May 1838: 23, 26 (original property of Anti-Slavery International); Colonial Church Society (CCS), *Colonial Church Record*, vol 1, no 3, October 1838: 42.

(although they were not full-time until 1839), with missions established in Adelaide in 1839 and at Port Lincoln and Encounter Bay in 1840. Protector Matthew Moorhouse also set aside several reserves in the early 1840s.[66]

However, the earliest South Australian philanthropic records are characterised less by unique optimism than by tensions, some specific to this region, other familiar from elsewhere. One was the troubling place of charity and gratitude within Indigenous welfare policies. Protector Bromley had looked forward initially to a harmonious paternalism with the Indigenous people around Adelaide, planning to teach them to 'regard us as neighbours and brethren'. However, he soon complained that they were greedy and demanding, taking his own supplies for themselves, disdainfully refusing the unappetising oatmeal and rice he offered, and begging food from colonists instead. Bromley wrote despondently 'gratitude is out of the question with them'.[67] Later, when philanthropy became more institutionalised, other conflicts emerged. Ann Scrimgeour's work on the Lutheran missionaries to the Kaurna people in the 1840s highlights the tensions between 'Christianity first' and 'civilisation first' approaches, as the missionaries disagreed with Governor Grey about whether or not the children should be taught in English and sent out as servants. Scrimgeour contrasts the missionaries' wish for 'a rarefied and idealised *Christian* civilisation', set apart from the rest of colonial life, with Grey's belief that capitalist imperialism was a force for good.[68] Moreover, hopes that South Australia would prove unusually humane were not realised. Indeed, the shocking participation of protector Moorhouse in a mass killing of Indigenous men near Lake Victoria in 1841 (his armed party had proceeded into this dangerous area to investigate attacks on settlers, despite Indigenous warnings) revealed a level of complicity with violent dispossession which arguably surpassed that of the Port Phillip protectors, for instance. As Peggy Brock points out, despite South Australia's early humanitarian rhetoric and alternative administrative models, the ultimate results for Indigenous people largely mirrored those elsewhere.[69]

Also initiated in 1837 was George Langhorne's state-sponsored mission in Port Phillip, established following discussions between Governor Bourke and Chief Justice Burton. It was located in a key meeting and ceremonial area for the Kulin nations (the site of the present-day Botanical Gardens). Langhorne distributed

---

66   State Records of South Australia 2002: 8–15.
67   Protector Bromley to Colonial Secretary, 2 May 1837, State Records of South Australia (SRSA), GRG24/1, Colonial Secretary's Office, Letters and other communications received, no 117 of 1837; Protector Bromley to Colonial Secretary, 26 May 1837, SRSA, GRG24/1/1837/152; Protector Bromley to Provincial Secretary, 1 June 1837, SRSA, GRG24/1/1837/169; Protector Bromley to Colonial Secretary, 26 June 1837, SRSA, GRG24/1/1837/206; Protector Bromley to Governor Stirling, 29 June 1837, SRSA, GRG24/1/1837/210; Protector Bromley to Colonial Secretary, 6 July 1837, SRSA, GRG24/1/1837/224.
68   Scrimgeour 2006.
69   Brock 1995: 208, 218–222; Matthew Moorhouse to Colonial Secretary, 13 September 1841, in Protector of Aborigines, *Letterbook 1840–1857*, SRSA, GRG52/7, vol 1, unit 1.

rations and tried to encourage schooling and mild labour, but claimed little success, at a time when local people could presumably see little benefit in cooperating with him.[70] He left Melbourne in 1839. This was the same time, however, as the new protectors of Aborigines were arriving, on the instructions of Lord Glenelg, Secretary of State for the Colonies, who was a well-known supporter of anti-slavery and Protestant missionary movements. (These were often grouped together in popular discourse under the heading of 'Exeter Hall', a venue in London famous for its use for massive public gatherings by these bodies.) Glenelg had become concerned about the need to recognise Indigenous Australians as subjects and protect them from destruction. Following the Select Committee report, he informed Governor Gipps of the appointment of protectors GA Robinson, James Dredge, William Thomas, ES Parker and CW Sievwright.[71] Robinson was fresh from his apparent success in Van Diemen's Land, negotiating with Indigenous peoples for their removal from the Tasmanian mainland. Of his assistants, Sievwright was a former army officer, while the others were schoolteachers. While a more secular and administrative undertaking than the earlier missions, the Port Phillip protectorate nonetheless demonstrated a number of common elements. These included the Evangelical commitments of protectors Dredge, Thomas and Parker (Dredge, in particular, was recommended for the post by influential Methodist leader Dr Jabez Bunting), the wish to learn local languages, and the brief to prepare Indigenous people for 'civilised' life and to promote 'moral and religious improvement'.[72] Another commonality with mission work was the sense of apprehension about their prospects. While missionary discourse could find a certain glory in hardship, this was less available to protectors dependent upon reluctant public funding. Michael Christie notes that Governor Gipps was never keen on the protectorate – he delayed its onset, knowing it would be unpopular, particularly at a time of financial problems – and that the majority of Melbourne's media opposed it from the start. Port Phillip superintendent CJ La Trobe was more sympathetic initially, coming from a Moravian background with family links to the Clapham sect, but his enthusiasm would ultimately wane as well.[73] Meanwhile, philanthropic publications, while more sympathetic towards the protectorate's objectives, could be equally disappointed by its outcomes. The APS's 1840 annual report concluded that this body had already shown itself unable to prevent dispossession.[74]

---

70  Michael Cannon, notes, in Cannon (ed) 1982, *Historical Records of Victoria (HRV): The Aborigines of Port Phillip, 1835–1839*, vol 2A: 191; Christie 1979: 82–84; James Dredge, 9 January 1839, in James Dredge, Diaries, Notebook and Letterbooks, ?1817–1845 [hereafter *JDD*], MS11625, MSM534, SLV; GM Langhorne to CJ La Trobe, 15 October 1839, in Cannon (ed) 1983, *HRV*, vol 2B: 508.
71  Christie 1979: 87.
72  Sir George Arthur to Lord Glenelg, 15 December 1837, in Cannon (ed) 1982, *HRV*, vol 2A: 33; Lord Glenelg to Sir George Gipps, 31 January 1838, in Cannon (ed) 1983, *HRV*, vol 2B: 375, also 365.
73  Christie 1979: 93–94, 100–103; Reece 1974: 198.
74  APS, Third Annual Report, 23 June 1840: 32–34.

Such dismissals were voiced from the very beginning of the protectors' projects. When they arrived in Port Phillip, they camped near Indigenous people outside Melbourne and distributed rations and gifts intended to demonstrate European technology and manners. One note by protector William Thomas from 1840 listed 'Presents for Natives in my possession' including tomahawks, pocket knives, knives and forks, cigars, mirrors and twine. Shortly after their arrival, the protectors staged a feast for 300 people, serving bread and mutton. Indigenous people demonstrated dancing, climbing and spear throwing, and fireworks were let off in celebration.[75] The protectors' reception from Indigenous people was friendly at first, but this would change as the land fell under settler control swiftly and intensively during the late 1830s and early 1840s. In mid-1840, for instance, protector Thomas made the controversial decision to move his station from Arthur's Seat to Narre Narre Warren, following arguments with Woiwurrung and Boonwurrung people over their insistence on living close to their country around Melbourne. Tensions around traditional land use and the protectors' complicity in expelling people from European settlements would plague the protectorate for years to come.[76]

Meanwhile, his protectors James Dredge and ES Parker moved north and north-west, to a general Indigenous welcome. When Dredge arrived at his station near Mitchellstown, he found that Daungwurrung people there seemed friendly, did chores in return for food and said they would bring their families to live nearby.[77] This was at the same time as they were beginning to respond to dispossession by attacking stations along the Goulburn River, resulting in a controversial mass arrest by Major Lettsom in 1840, in which two Indigenous men were shot dead.[78] Such early developments contributed to Dredge's sense that the protectorate was corrupt and unable to save Indigenous people from destruction.

Parker moved first to Jackson's Creek, then to the Loddon in June 1840, and in 1841 to a site near contemporary Franklinford. His work took him through the country of the Djadjawurrung and Djabwurrung people, who lived around the open plains and swamplands at the base of the Grampians and Pyrenees mountains. They had been trading European items and meeting explorers from the mid-1830s, but Parker arrived at the beginning of a rapid and devastating process of dispossession. Ian D Clark estimates that almost half of Djabwurrung country was taken by squatters by 1841, and virtually all of it by 1846.

---

75  Cannon, notes, in Cannon (ed) 1982, *HRV*, vol 2A: 434; Dredge, 28 March 1839, *JDD*, MS11625, MSM534, SLV; William Thomas to GA Robinson, 1 January 1840, William Thomas, Papers, 1834–1868 [hereafter *WTP*], ML MSS 214, reel 4, State Library of NSW.
76  Christie 1979: 97; William Thomas to GA Robinson, 26 August 1840, *WTP*, ML MSS 214, reel 4; Thomas, journal, 2 and 5 September 1840, *WTP*, ML MSS 214, reel 1, State Library of NSW.
77  Christie 1979: 94; Dredge, 21–26 August 1839, *JDD*, MS11625, MSM534, SLV.
78  Broome 2005: 31–32; Christie 1979: 65.

Nonetheless, Parker himself was received politely, greeted 'with some degree of ceremony'. They divided their camp into family sections, introduced Parker around and reminded him carefully of their previous meetings.[79]

At the same time, his colleague CW Sievwright travelled initially through Geelong and Lake Terang before moving into the tumultuous country of the Gundidjmara people at Mt Rouse. The Gundidjmara harvested the coastland and marshes and lived in eel farming villages around Portland, Warrnambool and Lake Condah. They had a history of both trading and violence with whalers and sealers along the coast, and from the early 1840s they became notorious for their attacks on Europeans around Hamilton, the Grampians and the Glenelg River. Sievwright claimed that colonists, in turn, were launching vicious retaliatory raids. This protector was amongst communities whose struggle for autonomy was ongoing and bloody.[80]

Of all the protectors, GA Robinson had the greatest number of meetings with new people, as he travelled around Port Phillip taking a census and urging people to move to the protectorate stations. These are also the main meetings to have been discussed in cross-cultural terms by historians. Jan Critchett and Vivienne Rae-Ellis focus on the anthropological value of Robinson's accounts, noting his guides' orchestration of ceremonial encounters, and his own distribution of gifts and adherence to courteous behaviour, conveying a sense of formal, rather ambassadorial meetings.[81]

As the protectors were setting out, Joseph Orton's aim of establishing a Methodist mission was being realised nearby. Missionaries Francis Tuckfield and Benjamin Hurst set up at Lake Colac, 40 miles west of Geelong and inland from Corio Bay, on land used by a number of Indigenous communities, notably the Gulidjan and Wathawurrung. The Gulidjan — apparently a small group even before colonisation — lived on compact, fertile tracts of lake country, while the Wathawurrung were fisherpeople whose country also included the open plains towards the Great Dividing Range. They had encountered explorers from the turn of the century and sealers and whalers from the 1820s, meetings profitable or violent but fairly minor in terms of land control. This changed with the arrival of permanent settlers. The Gulidjan in particular seem to have been dispossessed so quickly that by the 1840s they had few options besides mission life, station work and

---

79   Clark 1990: 94; Morrison 2002b: 204; ES Parker, Quarterly Journal, December 1840 – February 1841, Public Records Office of Victoria (PROV) VA512 *Chief Protector of Aborigines*, VRPS4410, unit 2, 1841/55 (reel 2).
80   Christie 1979: 11, 27, 97; Clark 1990: 33–34; Corris 1968: 26, 112–115; Critchett 1990: 55–61; Lourandos 1977: 208, 214.
81   Critchett 1990: 5–18; Rae-Ellis 1988: 177–179, 201–205; GA Robinson 1998, *Journals: Port Phillip Aboriginal Protectorate*, Clark (ed) vol 2: 150–155; GA Robinson 2001, 'A Report of an Expedition to the Aboriginal Tribes of the Western Interior during the Months of March, April, May, June, July and August, 1841', in Clark (ed) vol 4: 14–24.

begging.⁸² Tuckfield and Hurst wrote little about their initial meetings with Gulidjan or Wathawurrung, other than to comment that they were interested in the missionaries' ceremonies.⁸³ However, Tuckfield's journal from 1839 did describe what may have been 'Dantgurt' (Djargurdwurrung) people's first visit. A hundred people arrived, ceremonially painted and armed, and sat silently 200 yards from the buildings. They ignored Tuckfield's greetings, waiting instead for the people resident there to acknowledge and welcome them; the missionary was, at this moment, a marginalised figure.⁸⁴ This did not imply a hostile atmosphere, though; when Orton visited Buntingdale in 1839, he found the local people friendly with Tuckfield, embracing Orton affectionately when he was introduced as Tuckfield's brother.⁸⁵

Early reports from Buntingdale featured some notable elements. As Methodists, they felt somewhat isolated and apprehensive amongst the settler population; even Tuckfield's journey to the colony, on a ship full of 'high church people', was uncomfortable. (Indeed, Judith Binney has noted that missionary journeys 'out' were often experienced as disturbing transition points, exposing them to the wickedness of their fellow European travellers.⁸⁶) Also notable was their commitment – again, relevant to most south-eastern missions – to ministering to Indigenous people as far from other Europeans as possible. They stated repeatedly that only Christianity could save people, and resisted suggestions of economic integration into settler society. Benjamin Hurst, for instance, wrote to Port Phillip superintendent CJ La Trobe in 1841 that he disagreed with South Australian plans to make Indigenous people useful by training them as rural labourers. Hurst argued that Aborigines were 'useless and dangerous neighbour[s]' because their hearts were still 'desperately wicked'; they would only become peaceable and industrious when they realised they were sinners and experienced atonement.⁸⁷

Buntingdale's early records show a mixture of optimism and apprehension. In an initial memorandum for Hurst and Tuckfield, Orton described their prospective work as challenging but potentially great; 'you are engaged in an arduous and difficult mission, one that will call forth all your piety, zeal, diligence, patience, perseverance and implicit confidence in the promise of almighty God.'⁸⁸ The *Missionary Register* and the WMMS's annual report for 1840 stated

---

82  Clark 1990: 222, 277; Corris 1968: 52–53, 71, 102; Lourandos 1977: 215.
83  Francis Tuckfield, 18 August 1839, in Francis Tuckfield, Journal, 1837–1842 [hereafter *FTJ*], MS11341, Box 655, SLV.
84  Tuckfield, 14 December 1839, *FTJ*, MS11341, Box 655, SLV.
85  Joseph Orton to General Secretaries, 13 May 1839, *WMMS*, reel 1, Mp2107, NLA; Orton, 17 May 1839, *JOJ*, ML ref A1714–1715, CY reel 1119, State Library of NSW.
86  Tuckfield, 3 January 1838, 27 June 1841, 4 July 1841, *FTJ*, MS11341, Box 655, SLV; Binney 1968: 16
87  Benjamin Hurst to CJ La Trobe, 22 July 1841, *MMS*, reel 4, AJCP M121, SLV.
88  Copy of Memorandum left with the Brethren Hurst and Tuckfield by Mr Orton, June 1839, *WMMS*, reel 1, Mp2107, NLA.

that good progress in schooling, labour and linguistics had occurred there.[89] However, Hurst and Tuckfield's reports, from which this hopeful information presumably derived, betrayed greater concern, describing with horror the local depopulation, which they blamed on a combination of colonial cruelty and violence between Indigenous peoples. Hurst wrote 'But oh! how painful is the thought that perhaps in a very few years the whole of the tribes of Australia Felix will be annihilated.'[90] Tuckfield, somewhat more optimistically, reiterated the link between hardship and Christian triumph: 'surely the day of small and feeble things must not be despised. Our work is a scene of toil, difficulty and danger, but God is with us and we are happy.'[91]

If reports from these southern districts were, at best, ambivalent, those from the northern regions of New South Wales known as Moreton Bay (later to separate as the colony of Queensland) were more discomforting still. There had been a penal settlement there since 1824, initially outnumbered by Indigenous people and characterised by tumultuous but fairly localised developments: Indigenous labour, theft of crops, spread of introduced diseases, and incidents of violence. JCS Handt, having left Wellington Valley after hostilities with Watson, was posted there to preach to both Aborigines and convicts. This time, his early reports showed no optimism. In 1837, he told William Cowper of the CMS corresponding committee that his hopes were few; his supposed congregation seemed to him 'savage and cruel' and reluctant to live with him.[92] Further comments from 1838 were published in the *Missionary Register*, describing the people of Moreton Bay as 'rude and savage', treating missionaries only as a useful source of food.[93] Despite this, another German mission was being planned nearby, after New South Wales politician John Dunmore Lang lobbied the Scottish Missionary Society. Their 1837 records indicated that they lacked enthusiasm from the start. Rev Johannes Gossner, who trained missionaries in Berlin, agreed to send a party to Moreton Bay, but even he hoped the mission could be extended to New Zealand or the Pacific; he considered Indigenous Australians 'the lowest grade of humanity'. Accounts of early meetings between these German missionaries and Indigenous people are sparse and highlight the linguistic and philosophical barriers between them. Handt commented that he could barely understand what he heard about Indigenous spirituality, and doubted that his efforts to tell them about the Supreme Being's love and the punishment of sinners were understood.[94] Moreover, from the early 1840s, these

---

89  CMS, *Missionary Register*, May 1840: 230; Report of the Wesleyan Methodist Missionary Society, 1840, in WMMS, *Reports of the Wesleyan Methodist Missionary Society*: 29–31.
90  Benjamin Hurst to WMMS General Secretaries, 14 January 1840, WM Tennant Letters 1837–1883, MS12699, Box 3504/9 (1–40), SLV.
91  Francis Tuckfield to WMMS General Secretaries, 29 January 1840, MS10623, MSB281, SLV.
92  JCS Handt to William Cowper, 13 September 1837, *CMS*, reel 40, AJCP M212, SLV.
93  CMS, *Missionary Register*, August 1839: 389–390.
94  Extracts from the Minutes of the Committee of the Scottish Missionary Society, 10 May 1837, in John Dunmore Lang, Papers 1811–1887, vol 30, reel 18, mfmG24821, NLA; Johannes Gossner to Samuel Jackson, 1

small missionary efforts were eclipsed by intense colonisation, as pastoralists moved into the area and widespread violence followed. These northern districts would become notorious over much of the 19th century for their histories of bloody dispossession.[95]

## 'Docile and faithful labourers': the unusual case of Western Australia

Philanthropic reports from Western Australia during the late 1830s and early 1840s were more hopeful, although still guarded. Evangelical efforts there began when Methodist settler Francis Armstrong was employed as an Indigenous interpreter near Mt Eliza, running a small institution between 1834–38. This was followed by Louis Giustiniani's short-lived Anglican school at Guildford (established 1836), John Smithies' Methodist institutions in Perth and Gullillilup (established 1840 and 1844), and George King's small Anglican school in Fremantle (established 1842). Both King and Smithies received small amounts of government funding. Western Australia did not seem to attract the high philanthropic hopes that South Australia did, and by the mid-1830s punitive expeditions and violent racial clashes were being reported.[96] Nonetheless, Western Australia was still something of a focus for philanthropic writers concerned to avoid the excesses they had witnessed in older colonies. The Australian Church Missionary Society (thereafter the Colonial Church Society) commented in 1837 on the need to send missionaries to minister to the settlers of Western Australia, with the hope that the benefits would flow on to Indigenous people.[97] The *Colonial Church Record* also described frontier violence in Western Australia (blamed on the loss of Indigenous food sources) and asserted that only Christianity could turn Indigenous people into 'a body of docile and faithful labourers'.[98]

Like their eastern counterparts, the Western Australian institutions focused largely on children. King, setting up his Fremantle school, wrote optimistically to the United Society for the Propagation of the Gospel of how wonderful it would be to 'gain over the sons & daughters of these warriors to the holy standard of the cross', but added that their parents were too unreliable to be taught.[99] This

---

April 1837, JD Lang Papers, vol 30, reel 18; Handt, journal, 26 October 1832, 7 November 1832, 13 November 1832, *WVP*; JCS Handt to William Cowper, Annual Report of the Church Missionary Society Mission at Moreton Bay for the year 1838, Sir William Dixson, *Documents relating to Aboriginal Australians, 1816–1853*, Dixson Library, ADD 80–82, CY reel 3743, State Library of NSW.
95  See for instance Evans 1992: 7–30; Mackenzie-Smith 1992: 58–68; Reynolds and May 1995: 169.
96  George King to Ernest Hawkins, 1 January 1846, United Society for the Propagation of the Gospel, Records [hereafter *USPG*], AJCP M1222, SLV; McNair and Rumley 1981: 42–43; Toussaint 1995: 245.
97  First Report of the Australian Church Missionary Society, c1837, in Colonial Church Society (CCS), *Report of the Australian Church Missionary Society, now formed into the Colonial Church Society*, 1838–1840: 2–3.
98  CCS, *Colonial Church Record*, vol 1, no 2, September 1838: 25–29.
99  Rev George King to Rev E Hawkins, 9 Sep 1841, *USPG*, AJCP M1222, SLV; Rev George King to Rev E Hawkins, 28 Oct 1841, *USPG*, AJCP M1222, SLV.

did not necessarily mean that relations were hostile, however; as in the other colonies, some Indigenous people apparently hoped to utilise connections with missionaries. George King claimed in 1847 that people in King George's Sound, suffering greatly through dispossession, had requested a missionary, asking 'what time you make native school? boy & girl plenty go.'[100] Unlike in the east, though, the missionaries' aim here was to incorporate young Indigenous people into the labouring classes of colonial society, instead of isolating them – a policy due partly to the initial scarcity of migration and convict labour in this colony.[101]

Another element that made Western Australian philanthropists unusual was their stronger denominational competition. John Smithies complained to the WMMS that 'Romish emissaries' were trying to lure his students away to the Sisters of Mercy school. Such complaints may have had an ulterior motive; Smithies, who wanted greater funding, commented pointedly that the 'Romanists' had sent a large group of priests into the wilderness (they would later establish New Norcia mission); 'in zeal and labours, and privations, they outdo us.'[102] George King was similarly concerned about Catholic missionaries, but he was also suspicious of Smithies himself and horrified in 1846 when the government suggested merging his small Anglican school with the Wesleyan one. He wrote to the Bishop of Australia:

> This would be a sad alternative indeed: these native children have been educated under the nurture & admonition of the Church ... since they were first taught to lisp the English tongue; & now that they are able to mingle their voices with that of the people of God in the sanctuary, & to join in the responses of our beautiful liturgy ... must we now cast them off & constitute them aliens & disinherit them from the blessings & privileges of the Church?[103]

He fretted that the colonial government meant to combat Catholicism by encouraging Methodism;

> in attempting to shun the Scylla of popery, we have dashed our precious charge against the Charybdis of dissent; & thus robbed our children of the high & holy principles which we have inherited through the church, from our fathers.[104]

This rivalry may have stemmed from the greater proximity of different mission stations around Swan River, and perhaps also the greater Western Australian

---

100   Rev George King to Rev E Hawkins, 11 June 1847, *USPG*, AJCP M1222, SLV.
101   Hetherington 1992: 41, 47–48; Hetherington 2002: 34–35, 116–117.
102   WMMS, *Report of the Wesleyan Methodist Missionary Society for the year ending April 1845*, April 1848: 37–39.
103   Rev George King to the Bishop of Australia, 9 April 1846, *USPG*, AJCP M1222, SLV.
104   Rev George King to the Bishop of Australia, 9 April 1846, *USPG*, AJCP M1222, SLV.

belief that Indigenous people might prove useful members of colonial society. This is not to say, though, that the spectre of missionary failure was absent. By 1840, for example, Western Australian protector Peter Barrow was already stating that his hopes for Indigenous people were low. He called them unpredictable and treacherous, concluding 'They have no inclination for civilization and a strong dislike to be interfered with.'[105]

It has been commonplace for scholars to assess Australia's first Indigenous missions and protectorates as failures, and given philanthropists' disputes with settlers and government, their rare conversions, and their often gloomy evaluations of their own work, this is unsurprising. However, such a dismissive conclusion is problematic. These philanthropists were part of a vital, passionate conversation about colonialism, which stretched from personal encounters with Indigenous people to Evangelical publications in Britain. Furthermore, the spectre of mission failure did not emerge simply as a result of local obstacles. It was present from the start and was in many ways constitutive of Australian missionary work and Aboriginal policy-making. The prospect of spiritual failure and Indigenous doom could be interpreted by philanthropists initially as a challenge, part of a redemptive struggle, yet its long term implications were far more ominous.

---

105   Peter Barrow to Ernest Hawkins, 15 November 1840, also Peter Barrow to Ernest Hawkins, 29 July 1840, Peter Barrow to Ernest Hawkins, 10 August 1840, *USPG*, AJCP M1222, SLV.

# 'Godless political experiments': philanthropy and governance

During the 1840s, a time of great dispossession, illness and social turmoil in western Victoria, the Buntingdale Methodist mission near Geelong witnessed severe conflict between different Indigenous groups. People living in the area still adhered in many ways to traditional law, but also tried to utilise their colonial connections. In 1840, missionary Francis Tuckfield wrote anxiously to his colleague Benjamin Hurst, urging that they clarify Indigenous people's legal status. The Wathawurrung people were committing violent crimes nearby and portrayed themselves to Tuckfield as both protected by and exempt from colonial law: 'They think whatever they do whether it be to the whites, or to the blacks of any other tribe they can take shelter under the wing of the Protector of Aborigines'. He had tried to tell them that this was wrong, but they referred constantly to the local protector, CW Sievwright, who had promised them protection and guns. Tuckfield was already dissatisfied with the government in this respect. The previous year he had complained in his diary that the murder of a Gulidjan woman by Wathawurrung men had gone unpunished because the protector had no guidelines for handling serious crime.[1] Hurst endorsed his colleague's concerns, telling Port Phillip superintendent CJ La Trobe 'The Aborigines are declared to be British subjects, and it therefore appears to me are entitled to the protection of British law.'[2] These issues arose again in 1842, when the missionaries announced their intention to leave Buntingdale. When they told the residents that they were leaving because the numbers at the mission were too low, 120 people gathered to discuss the problem.

> On this very interesting occasion the Natives particularly complained of the want of protection. Intimating that as the white men had killed some of their fighting men, the great Governor ought to send them the Police to protect them from the violence and revengeful attacks of those [neighbouring] tribes.[3]

---

1  Francis Tuckfield to Benjamin Hurst, 17 January 1840, in Francis Tuckfield, Journal 1837–1842 [hereafter *FTJ*], MS11341, Box 655, State Library of Victoria (SLV). Note – Tuckfield refers to the Wathaurung as Woddrowro or Woddrowrow. Also Tuckfield, 14 December 1839, *FTJ*.
2  Benjamin Hurst to CJ La Trobe, 22 July 1841, Methodist Missionary Society, Records [hereafter *MMS*], reel 4, AJCP M121, SLV.
3  Francis Tuckfield, Report on the Wesleyan Methodist Missionary Society's Mission to the Aborigines of the Sub District of Geelong, Port Phillip, August 1843, Wesleyan Methodist Missionary Society, Archive: Australasia 1812–1889 [hereafter *WMMS*], reel 2, Mp2107 (Record ID: 133095), National Library of Australia (NLA). Note: the term 'Dantgurt' refers to the group designated Dhaugurdwurrung (elsewhere Djargurdwurrung) by Clark 1990: 177.

Several weeks later, these fears were realised vividly, when a Djargurdwurrung woman was murdered in a revenge attack. Her frightened relatives fled the station, again lamenting their lack of security.

The discourse around colonial governance in the early 19th century was shaped by an array of imperial and local developments, from revenge killings at Lake Colac to debates about British subjecthood in Exeter Hall. As John L Comaroff has observed of South Africa, missionaries contrasted their own form of governance (pious, intensive, aiming to improve all aspects of life) with the state bureaucracy and the harsh dominance of white settlers.[4] Nonetheless, philanthropic work was not easily separated from broader mechanisms of imperial authority. In Australian mission and protectorate records, discussions of government, law and subjecthood conveyed important views, not only about the place of Indigenous Australians in the empire, but also about the empire itself and missionaries' role within it. In most missionaries' proposals and a lot of protectorate practice (especially in Port Phillip), Indigenous people would be governed through a Christianity-first approach, with the aim of transforming them into equal British subjects. In practice, however, this became deeply problematic, as philanthropists struggled with legal ambiguities, cultural prejudices and their own rather weak circumstances. Also challenging was the impact of changing models of government, as the Australian colonies moved towards greater independence. While this chapter considers the subject status of Indigenous people, it also focuses on the fluid and contested nature of colonial authority itself, as debated by philanthropists and critiqued or utilised by Indigenous people. Aboriginal Australians had very little power to affect how they were governed, but as the above anecdote suggests, dialogues about governance (however partial and unequal) shaped mission life and filtered through to Evangelical debates.

## 'The rights of common humanity': imperial authority, Evangelical complexities

British Evangelical campaigners during the first half of the 19th century protested frequently against the crimes committed by white colonists around the world. However, they did not necessarily condemn British imperialism in principle. Their own patriotism and belief in their mandate to spread the Gospel, as well as, perhaps, a pragmatic awareness that the empire was the only game in town, led them to seek more creative ways to work within an imperial system. Speakers at the 1837 anniversary gathering of the Wesleyan Methodist Missionary Society stressed that colonialism need not be harmful if 'conducted on principles of honourable enterprise.' One speaker challenged the British

---

4   Comaroff 1989: 672–675.

government to legislate and enforce missionary policies in African territories soon to be colonised; Christianity alone would make these regions peaceful and pliant zones.⁵ Similarly, at a London Missionary Society valedictory service in the same year, several speakers lamented violence towards colonised people (Indigenous Australians were described as victims of extermination), but expressed high hopes for missionaries travelling the world with support from the British parliament and public.⁶ Zoë Laidlaw has noted that the Aborigines Protection Society, especially its leader Thomas Hogkin, may have been less convinced of imperialism's ultimate virtues than were most missionary societies, but even this body did not explicitly oppose British expansion, merely the 'mistaken policy' that caused it to be 'perverted' into violence.⁷ Even by 1850, after over a decade's discussion of the harm caused by empire, they continued to insist that imperialism should be a positive force to spread Christianity abroad and relieve poverty at home; 'it is not civilization and Christianity that exercise this destructive influence, but the vices that too often accompany them'.⁸ Plans to make the imperial system benign often involved calls for the expansion of British subjecthood. The APS, in particular, stressed the need to extend the rights of British subjects to colonised peoples, citing their personal, economic and intellectual entitlements:

> the rights of a common humanity, the rights of citizens, the right to possess and retain their own, the rights of protection and security to life and property, and the rights of unfettered liberty of mind, of free action and self disposal.⁹

This was not seen in wholly secular terms, however, but rather as a state of elevation to be reached through civilising projects and missionary work.

The 1837 report of the 1835–36 Select Committee on Aborigines (British Settlements) is of particular interest here. While highlighting the cruel dispossession of native peoples, the authors nonetheless praised Britain's benevolent intentions; solutions to colonial destructiveness lay in greater religious authority. The report used arguments that had been crucial to the anti-slavery movement, asserting that abuse of indigenous peoples was impractical

---

5   Wesleyan Methodist Missionary Society (WMMS), *Missionary Notices*, vol IV, no 258–9, June-July 1837: 491, also 483–484.
6   London Missionary Society (LMS), *TheMissionary Magazine and Chronicle*, vol 1, 1837: 277–286.
7   Laidlaw 2007: 136–139.
8   Aborigines Protection Society (APS), *The Colonial Intelligencer, or Aborigines' Friend*, 1849–1850, vol II: 67–68, in APS, Transactions, c.1839–1909, MIC/o6550, reel 3, (records the property of Anti-Slavery International). Also, APS, 1838, *First Annual Report, 16 May 1838*: 8 (Monash University Microfilm 4094 seg 2 item 30393 – records property of Anti-Slavery International); APS, Second Annual Report, 21 May 1839: 21, in APS, Transactions, reel 1; APS, Third Annual Report, 23 June 1840, introduction, in APS, Transactions, reel 1; APS 1841, *Extracts from the Papers and Proceedings of the Aborigines' Protection Society*, vol II, no III, April 1841: 89–90.
9   APS, Third Annual Report, 23 June 1840, in APS, Transactions, reel 1: 9.

as well as immoral, as it incited war and discouraged natives from becoming loyal, industrious subjects. Britain's power was a Providential blessing, accompanied by moral duties; 'He who has made Great Britain what she is, will inquire at our hands how we have employed the influence he has lent to us'.[10] The Select Committee's report indicated generally that native affairs were best governed at a distance, rather than by local executives who might bow to pressure from colonists, and urged that any initiatives in colonial constitutions affecting indigenous peoples should be expressly sanctioned by the Queen.[11] London Missionary Society representative William Ellis told the Committee that destruction of Aboriginal societies in New South Wales need not be inevitable; while the behaviour of settlers was deplorable, he could not comment on the impact of *government*, as he had seen so little of it.[12] The testimony of Saxe Bannister, former New South Wales attorney-general, was also interesting here. Bannister, who prided himself on his philanthropy, proposed a new superintending body of protectors ('disinterested arbitrators') across the colonies, linking back to a special branch of the Foreign Office – not the Colonial Office, which, he feared, was too loyal to colonists' interests. He claimed the need for this had become apparent in 1826, when Governor Darling sent soldiers to the Hunter River to avenge attacks on settlers, a decision Bannister termed 'cold blooded murder'. Bannister's circumstances were unusual (notably, his deep enmity with Darling), and he did not oppose martial law per se, only its unlawful application. Nonetheless, his testimony reinforced a sense that solutions to colonial problems lay in extended imperial authority.[13] This seems to support Zoë Laidlaw's claim that the Committee's work encouraged Britons to see indigenous affairs as a more singular, imperial concern.[14] Similar sentiments were expressed by the APS, who warned that the British government should incorporate all Australian territories unambiguously within the empire. As long as the reach of British sovereignty was unclear, they argued, Indigenous people would be vulnerable to abuse as enemy aliens.[15] This seems to endorse, in some ways, Elizabeth Elbourne's point, that 'despite the fact that missionaries were sometimes thorns in the side of colonial administrators and of settlers, they were also more effective advocates of loyalty to the imperial *centre* than were the less ostensibly altruistic settlers.'[16]

---

10  *British Parliamentary Papers (BPP): Report from the Select Committee on Aborigines (British Settlements) together with minutes of evidence, appendix and index*, Anthropology: Aborigines, vol 2, 1837: 76, also 4–5, 75.
11  *BPP: Report from the Select Committee on Aborigines (British Settlements)*, vol 2, 1837: 77.
12  William Ellis, evidence, 6 June 1836, *BPP: Report from the Select Committee on Aborigines (British Settlements) together with minutes of evidence, appendix and index*, Anthropology: Aborigines, vol 1, 1836: 490–491.
13  Saxe Bannister, evidence, 14 March 1837, in *BPP: Report from the Select Committee on Aborigines*, vol 2, 1837: 15–16, 21; Reece 1974: 110–113.
14  Laidlaw 2002: 79–80, 88, 91.
15  APS, First Annual Report, 16 May 1838: 23; APS, Second Annual Report, 21 May 1839: 22.
16  Elbourne 2002: 14.

However, philanthropists' place within the empire remained complicated. In one sense, missionaries can be characterised as aggressive promoters of British culture, who helped create spaces for imperial dominance and encouraged Britons back home to see themselves as bringers of civilisation with a divine mandate for global expansion. At the same time, though, as Anna Johnston notes, local missionaries' relationships with colonial authorities were mixed; 'variously mutually supportive, mutually antagonistic, or ambivalent – in short, … highly contingent on local circumstances.'[17] Settings ranged from India, where evangelising was considered subversive by the East India Company and where missionaries rejoiced at Queen Victoria's 1858 proclamation of official control, to New Zealand where missionaries arrived long before the British state, protested at settler depravity and were concerned that further colonisation would be damaging to Maori (although some of their Evangelical superiors in Britain disagreed). The Cape colony was relevant, too, where the London Missionary Society in particular had been a challenging presence in the 1820s and 1830s, as mission settlements provided Khoisan people with possibilities for autonomy and freedom from serfdom, thus incurring the resentment of white farmers. Andrew Bank, however, has stressed the growing conservatism within the Cape's liberal white population by the 1840s, where former humanitarians and even missionaries were made anxious by British wars with the Xhosa, urged a formal British takeover of 'Cafferland' and began to doubt Africans' potential for full equality.[18] The different imperial dynamics of the South Seas have been explored by Niel Gunson and Jane Samson, who observe that missionaries in this region were significant political actors yet formally instructed to avoid politics, their behaviour also varying between denominations. The Wesleyans, for instance, tended to take a more conservative political line, while the LMS was more open to dissent. These regions were affected, too, by indigenous evangelists, who were a notable presence from early days, and by missionaries' wish not for intensive state control but for their own authority to be respected and backed up by the British navy. Relevant factors here included by the rise of Evangelicalism in the officer class, missionaries' alternate mistrust of and dependence on British firepower, and the complex dynamics of class between officers, upwardly mobile 'mechanic' missionaries and European settlers, whom they accused of sinful influences.[19] Thus, while Evangelical movements may have been imperial in a broad sense, their roles within empire varied greatly according to local circumstances. This became clear in the Australian colonies.

---

17  Johnston 2003a: 72.
18  Bank 1999: 367–372; Elbourne 1997: 35–36.
19  Binney 1968: 30, 79–80; Johnston 2003a: 13–19, 75; Gunson 1978: 144–145, 172, 218–219, 280, 319; Samson 1998: 12–23, 27.

## 'Put not your trust in princes': philanthropy and colonial government

Governments played a vital role in the first Australian missions and protectorates, helping to establish and maintain them, and later to close them down. While official contributions varied, all these institutions accepted state support as their due; there was no suggestion that it was inherently undesirable or compromising. At the same time, however, relationships between philanthropists and the state were often troubled, as philanthropists accused officials of inadequate support, unreasonable demands and malignant intentions. The particular lament that governments were allowing Indigenous people to suffer and die, *without Christian guidance*, revealed not only philanthropists' horror at excesses of dispossession, but also their own curious, conflicted dependence on the state.

Financial and ideological tensions began to develop early. LMS missionary LE Threlkeld (never the most compliant man) quickly became suspicious of the New South Wales government's intentions towards his Lake Macquarie mission, writing darkly 'put not your trust in Princes. Amen. Amen.'[20] Also suspicious of *'the Established Church'*, he informed Anglican Archdeacon Scott that he could not accept any backing that might subject the mission to official interference.[21] Similarly, in 1841, Benjamin Hurst of the Buntingdale mission urged Port Phillip superintendent CJ La Trobe that authority over Indigenous wellbeing should rest with English missionary societies, arguing that this was the only way to ensure pious integrity.[22] In South Australia, Lutheran missionary Christian Gottlieb Teichelmann, requesting greater resources for his Adelaide station, made a rare reference to Indigenous people's wishes in this area: 'the natives are suspicious against Government operations for them, but not so against the missionaries: for they know very well that our designs are good, though they do not believe that the Government really wishes their spiritual welfare.'[23] Given missionaries' wish to prove their own expertise, it is perhaps unwise to place too much faith in this claim, although it is certainly possible that the Kaurna saw Teichelmann as more sympathetic than some other authority figures.

One reason for missionary mistrust of the government, particularly in its local colonial forms, stemmed from concern that state officials would not pay enough attention to the all-important role of Christian conversion. This was one reason

---

20   LE Threlkeld to George Burder and William Hankey, 5 July 1825, London Missionary Society, Records [hereafter *LMS*], AJCP M73, SLV.
21   LE Threlkeld to George Burder and William Hankey, 20 January 1826, *LMS*, AJCP M73, SLV.
22   Benjamin Hurst to CJ La Trobe, 22 July 1841, *MMS*, reel 4, AJCP M121, SLV. For other examples of calls to imperial authority, see James Dredge, *Brief Notices on the Aborigines of New South Wales*, Geelong, James Harrison, 1845: 6; Joseph Orton to Major-General Richard Bourke, 16 August 1836, *WMMS*, reel 2, Mp2107, NLA.
23   APS, Third Annual Report, 23 June 1840: 35.

why many Evangelical commentators became suspicious of the protectorate system. The place of religion in the protectorate was problematic. In their initial mandate, the South Australian protectors were urged to improve Indigenous people's morals by:

> uniting a regular system of Christian instruction ... by teaching, recommending and exemplifying the obligation of the Christian Sabbath, and by persuading them to yield a cheerful submission to the salutary restraints and moral discipline of the Christian religion, which ... is the surest instrument of effecting the *real* civilization, and of ameliorating the temporal condition, of barbarous tribes.[24]

While these instructions adhered in some ways to the 'Christianity first' doctrine, the emphasis was more on outward display of Christian ritual. Instructions to the Port Phillip protectors were even more cautious; they were to instruct people 'with elements of the Christian religion' and prepare them for later specialist teaching – presumably by missionaries, but this was not expanded upon.[25]

These limited spiritual aims were distasteful to missionary observers. As early as 1838, Threlkeld told the New South Wales Legislative Council's Committee on the Aborigines' Question that a protectorate might help stop frontier violence, but that moral improvement remained a missionary's job.[26] Methodist representative Joseph Orton was even less enthused. He declared he would not support any amalgamation of missions and the protectorate, telling Justice Burton that this might 'lead to secularities and temporalities perfectly incompatible with the character of Christian missionaries.' Orton stressed it was vital that missionaries were not 'in *any wise shackled*' in their relationship to government, and claimed that the protectorate's secular mandate for governing Indigenous people made it 'comparatively feeble'; 'it cannot save them from gradual extermination, it cannot save their precious souls'.[27]

Several of the protectors were Evangelicals, in fact, and did emphasise Christian preaching in their work, but this could serve to heighten their discomfort with the state apparatus within which they worked. Port Phillip protectors ES Parker and GA Robinson, for instance, ended up blaming the protectorate's failure partly on its secular nature, regretting that more missionary activity had not

---

24  Sir George Arthur to Lord Glenelg, 15 December 1837, in Cannon (ed) 1982, *Historical Records of Victoria (HRV): The Aborigines of Port Phillip, 1835–1839*, vol 2A: 33.
25  Lord Glenelg to Sir George Gipps, 31 January 1838, in Cannon (ed) 1983, *HRV: Aborigines and Protectors, 1838–1839*, vol 2B: 375.
26  LE Threlkeld, 21 September 1838, evidence, in NSW Parliament, Legislative Council, 1838, *Report from the Committee on the Aborigines Question, with Minutes of Evidence*: 22–23.
27  Joseph Orton to Justice Burton, 3 December 1838, Joseph Orton, Letterbooks 1822–1842 [hereafter *JOL*], ML ref A1717–A1720, State Library of NSW; Joseph Orton to General Secretaries, 5 January 1841, *JOL*, part 2.

occurred.[28] Ironically, it was a protector, James Dredge, who became the most passionate advocate for missionary work free of government interference. A devout Methodist with missionary ambitions, Dredge was disappointed in the protectorate and shocked by the harsh dispossession he witnessed in northern Victoria. He wrote angrily to British Methodist leader Jabez Bunting in 1841 that the New South Wales government was callously ignoring the destruction of Indigenous societies, treating these people as 'a grievous annoyance, and an irksome expense.' Dredge warned that the government would use missionaries as scapegoats for official failures; Indigenous people, he said, were dying or being corrupted 'while we are subjecting them to our Godless political experiments'.[29] Dredge wrote candidly to his friend, D Harding, in 1840, that the protectorate was never intended to work; it was poorly planned and undermined by Governor Gipps. He concluded furiously 'If the people of England imagine that the Government is befriending these outcasts [Aborigines] they are greatly mistaken. The Government is deriving immense revenues from the sale of their lands but they are giving them nothing in return.'[30] Without Gospel work, 'unshackled by *colonial governments*', Indigenous people would be destroyed and colonisers would face divine retribution; 'What an awful reckoning awaits these destroyers of mankind and the Government which suffers such things.'[31]

## 'My King always goes to church': Crown authority in the Evangelical encounter

Sometimes, the tensions between philanthropists and government could surface in conversations with Indigenous people themselves, which in turn fed back into Evangelical and political discourse. These discussions are interesting, as they contain hints about how Indigenous Australians were understanding and attempting to negotiate with state authority. They also illuminate local philanthropists' own ideas about governance, which were formed partly through their encounters with Indigenous people, to be reshaped in mission records and sent back to colleagues, governments and missionary societies; a complex exchange. As Jean and John Comaroff have observed of colonial authority in southern Africa:

---

28  ES Parker, Quarterly Journal, 1 June – 31 August 1842, Public Records Office of Victoria (PROV) VA512 *Chief Protector of Aborigines*, VPRS4410 unit 2, 1842/62 (reel 2); GA Robinson 2001, 1848 Annual Report, in *The Papers of George Augustus Robinson, Chief Protector, Port Phillip Aboriginal Protectorate*, Clark (ed) vol 4: 145.
29  James Dredge to Jabez Bunting, 10 May 1841, *MMS*, reel 55, AJCP 172, SLV; James Dredge to Jabez Bunting, 31 July 1840, *WMMS*, reel 1, Mp2107, NLA.
30  James Dredge to D Harding, 12 September 1840, in John Barnes, 'Annotation: A Letter from Port Phillip', in *La Trobe Journal*, no 61, Autumn 1998: 29.
31  James Dredge, 18 March 1840, James Dredge, Diaries, Notebook and Letterbooks, ?1817–1845 [hereafter *JDD*], MS11625, MSM534, SLV. Also, 28 December 1839.

> While they served as outriders of empire ... colonial evangelists did not carry a ready-made, fully realized social formation to the frontier. Rather, it was in the confrontation with non-Western societies that bourgeois Britons honed a sense of themselves as gendered, national citizens, as Godly, right-bearing individuals, and as agents of Western reason.[32]

When the first philanthropists tried to create imperial authority on the Australian frontier, they drew only partially on images of monarchy. Annual blanket distributions in South Australia were scheduled on the Queen's Birthday, presumably as a symbol of imperial benevolence, but I have not found any conversations about this with Indigenous people.[33] The only lengthy discussions of the monarchy that I have come across occurred at Wellington Valley. When those missionaries arrived in 1832, they contradicted Wiradjuri people's fear of arrest and enslavement by telling them they had been sent by the King of England to teach them about God and civilisation.[34] In 1834, missionary William Watson mentioned in his diary scolding a man called King Bobby for hunting kangaroo instead of going to church, saying 'my King always goes to church'. In response, King Bobby placated him 'Aye Aye, your King, King of England, good I believe.'[35] Similarly, the Church Missionary Society's *Missionary Register* included a conversation where a young woman called Geanil asked about a Scottish settler and was told that his country belonged to the missionaries' king. She responded 'Oh! all white masters belong to your King; King William, Sovereign Lord King William. You pray for your King every Sunday: is he a good man?' To this, the missionary responded 'Oh, yes! He prays to God, and goes to Church.' He added that Queen Adelaide was a good woman, who also prayed, read the Bible and went to church.[36] Presumably such anecdotes were published to demonstrate missionary progress. However, while the Crown may have symbolised far-off virtue, it packed little immediate punch. This would change later in the 19th century, when, as Heather Goodall, Tim Rowse and Bain Attwood have observed, the Crown became an important symbol of higher authority for Indigenous people to appeal to, particularly over land rights; reserves, for example, were referred to as guarantees from Queen Victoria.[37] However, the only example of this during the first half of the 19th century seems to have been the 1846 petition to the Queen by the people at Flinders Island,

---

32   Comaroff and Comaroff 1997 vol 2: 6.
33   For example, Matthew Moorhouse to Colonial Secretary, 14 March 1842, State Records of South Australia (SRSA), GRG24/6, no 38 for 1842.
34   JCS Handt, Journal, 30 September 1832, 24 November 1832, Carey and Roberts (eds) 2002, *The Wellington Valley Project: Letters and Journals Relating to the Church Missionary Society Mission to Wellington Valley, NSW, 1830–42, A Critical Electronic Edition* [hereafter *WVP*]: <http://www.newcastle.edu.au/wvp/>; William Watson, journal, 30 September 1832, *WVP*; Watson, Report 1832–1833, *WVP*: 1.
35   Watson, journal, 8 July 1834, *WVP*.
36   CMS, *Missionary Register*, 1836: 427.
37   Attwood 2003: 15–16; Goodall 1996: 56; Rowse 1993: 13–14.

protesting the cruelties they experienced and reminding her that they were not slaves.³⁸ The singularity of this example might be attributed to the Tasmanians' particular experience of negotiating with colonial authorities. Other than this, there are few signs at this early stage of Indigenous people asserting their rights through references to the monarchy.

Philanthropists and Indigenous people focused more commonly on the figure of the Governor. Images of the Governor as a charitable patron of Aboriginal affairs, extending limited recognition of Indigenous interests, have been traced by J Brook and JL Kohen back to the Sydney native feasts, where Governors Macquarie and Brisbane tried to demonstrate paternalistic good will and to formally acknowledge Indigenous groups (albeit in a partial, patronising way). Philanthropists' work was relevant here, most notably the parading of the Native Institution children at the feasts – although, as Penny Van Toorn has noted, such displays may have conveyed more sinister messages to Aboriginal viewers.³⁹ Governors made various other gestures towards mission residents over the years. Governor Darling, for instance, presented Threlkeld's guide and translator, Biraban (John M'Gill), with a brass plate recognising him as 'Chief of the Tribe at Bartabah' and thanking him for working with Threlkeld to translate and transcribe the Awabakal language, while Governor Gipps visited Wellington Valley and recommended offering good behaviour prizes for cooperative residents.⁴⁰ All this might be read in terms of charitable patronage to institutions and individuals, at least as much as generic state responsibility.

Philanthropists reinforced the symbolism and importance of the Governor by threatening to report Indigenous crimes to him and promising greater security and generosity on his behalf. In 1842, for instance, Wesleyan Methodist Missionary Society representative John McKenny travelled to the junction of the Goulburn and Murray Rivers and told the people he met there that he was thinking of starting a Methodist mission. Although he claimed they were unfamiliar with Europeans, they had heard of the protectorate and expressed joy when he told them 'the great Governor' had sent him to help them.⁴¹ The inclusion of such stories in papers that went back to officials or missionary societies suggests that they had a circular role. They demonstrated that philanthropists were teaching

---

38  Ryan 1981: 201–202.
39  Brook and Kohen 1991: 90–102; Van Toorn 2006: 31.
40  William Cowper to James Günther, 21 June 1841, and William Cowper to Dandeson Coates, 30 April 1841, Church Missionary Society, Records (CMS), reel 40, AJCP M212, SLV; James Günther, Journal, 8–10 November 1840, *WVP*; James Günther to William Cowper, 20 June 1841, *CMS*, reel 40, AJCP M212, SLV; Niel Gunson, 'Introduction', in Gunson (ed) 1974 vol 1: 6. Darling also served as patron for Threlkeld's 1827 work *Specimens of the Language of the Aborigines of New South Wales* and purchased a hundred copies. The missions at Moreton Bay, Buntingdale and Swan River received various official visits too, although few details about these remain.
41  John McKenny to General Secretaries, 18 July 1842, *WMMS*, reel 2, Mp2107, NLA. Also, for example, ES Parker, 30 August 1842, in ES Parker, Quarterly Journal, 1 June – 31 August 1842, PROV VPRS4410, unit 2, 1842/62 (reel 2); William Thomas to CJ La Trobe, 24 June 1840, PROV VPRS10, unit 2, 1840/569 (reel 1).

Indigenous people about the benevolent authority of the state, while also serving as an implicit reminder to the state to do its duty, and to missionary societies to lobby for this. The personification of the state in the figure of the Governor no doubt occurred partly for pragmatic reasons, as the simplest way of explaining British government. The use of a figure of appointed authority, representing the Crown, might also be linked back to a certain philanthropic wish for Aboriginal affairs to be governed through imperial, rather than colonial, power.

The figure of the Governor in Indigenous-missionary relationships could also take on uncomfortable meanings, however, when used by Indigenous people and by other colonists to represent an alternative to philanthropists' authority. At Wellington Valley in 1833, Watson recorded his frustrated arguments with Wiradjuri men, who had heard of the arrival of blankets from the Governor. A group of men made a formal demand for the blankets, 'saying they did not belong to me, they had been sent up for them and they must have them'. When Watson disagreed – planning instead to distribute the blankets to the neediest and most hard-working – a furious argument broke out and Watson feared his house would be robbed. The situation calmed down when he distributed some of the supplies, but the issue simmered. Two months later, Watson recorded another argument with a man called Narrang Jackey, who wanted a new blanket. When Watson scolded him for giving the last one away, Narrang Jackey retorted 'O never you mind that, all about blankets Governor sent for Black fellow don't belong at all to Parson, white fellow all about say so.'[42] Protector William Thomas had a similar experience of Indigenous men demanding control over flour distribution, threatening to complain to the Governor that Thomas was not feeding them properly, and Threlkeld, Dredge and Parker were all frustrated when people left their stations and travelled to urban areas because they had heard the Governor was distributing presents there.[43] These stories, while illustrating philanthropists' frustration, are also suggestive of Indigenous people's attempts to negotiate their way through a colonial hierarchy which philanthropists themselves had helped to construct.

## 'Unhappy victims of misrule': making Indigenous subjects

Aboriginal peoples' status as subjects of empire has attracted recent scholarly interest, notably from Julie Evans, whose work explores the political and legal complexities of subjecthood, and how it was used alternately to include and

---

42  Watson, journal, 24 August 1833, 7 October 1833, *WVP*.
43  Dredge, 28 October 1839, 29 October 1839, *JDD*, MS11625, MSM534, SLV; ES Parker, 15 March 1841, in ES Parker, Quarterly Journal, 1 March – 31 May 1841, PROV VPRS4410, unit 2, 1841/61 (reel 2); Thomas, 2 May 1840, 20 May 1840, William Thomas, Papers, 1834–1868 [hereafter *WTP*], ML MSS 214, reel 1, State Library of NSW; LE Threlkeld to London Missionary Society, May 1827, in Gunson (ed) 1974 vol 2: 227.

exclude colonised peoples from the legal system and to extend protection and dominance.[44] The key subjecthood issue in the early Australian colonies was Aboriginal people's legal status, an issue which has been explored in detail by Laura Benton, Susanne Davies, Ann Hunter and Russell Smandych.[45] During this period, the legal position of Indigenous Australians was contested and unclear. Examples of this uncertainty included enactments of martial law by Governors Brisbane and Darling (implying disorder amongst subjects, but understood by some colonists as a war against enemies), arguments over whether Indigenous people could give evidence in court or be subject to summary justice, and the contradictory rulings in the Murrell and Bonjon cases (1836 and 1841) about whether British law applied to Indigenous Australians.[46] In general, Laura Benton and David A Roberts have characterised the first half of the 19th century as a time of ad hoc approaches to Indigenous legal status, acknowledging neither true plurality nor full civil equality. Roberts suggests this fed into an implicit understanding that Aboriginal people's status was not important enough to define, perhaps because colonists saw them as having no real future.[47]

British philanthropists engaged with these issues to some extent, stressing the need to clarify Aboriginal people's legal position, often with the aim of addressing frontier violence. This was emphasised in the Select Committee's 1837 report and in the Aborigines Protection Society's lobbying of the Colonial Office in 1839 to allow Indigenous people to give evidence. (Justice Burton appears to have dissuaded the Office from this, advising that Aboriginal evidence was too problematic.[48]) This legal focus was perhaps unsurprising, given British philanthropists' strong interest in issues relevant to the Cape colony, where questions of legal equality had great importance to the slave-like living conditions of many San and Khoekhoe people.[49] However, its meaning in an Australian context was problematic. There were occasional acknowledgements that the inequalities and dispossession fundamental to settler-colonialism may have made true equality impossible. Pacific missionary William Yate commented to the Select Committee that whatever rights Aboriginal Australians theoretically possessed, their lowly status meant they had little real hope of being taken seriously.[50] Similarly, a scathing article in the APS's 1840 report stated that the

---

44   Evans 2004: 69–82; Evans 2002a: 175–198; Evans 2002b: 165–185; Evans et al 2003.
45   Benton 2002; Davies 1987: 313–335; Hunter 2004: 215–236; Smandych 2004.
46   Hunter 2004: 218–219, 228–229; Reece 1974: 110–113; Roberts 2006: 24–25; Smandych 2004: 237–283. For Threlkeld's mixed descriptions of frontier war, see LE Threlkeld to George Burder and William Hankey, 11 September 1826 and LE Threlkeld to Burder and Hankey, 4 September 1826, *LMS*, AJCP M73, SLV.
47   Roberts 2006: 21. Also, Benton 2002: 205.
48   Dandeson Coates, evidence, 6 June 1836, *BPP: Report from the Select Committee on Aborigines (British Settlements)*, vol 1, 1836: 487; *BPP: Report from the Select Committee on Aborigines (British Settlements)*, vol 2, 1837: 121–141; Smandych 2004: 250–251.
49   Elbourne 2003 (online through Project Muse).
50   Rev William Yate, evidence, 13 February 1836, *BPP: Report from the Select Committee on Aborigines (British Settlements)*, vol 1, 1836: 202.

Port Phillip protectors' task of keeping peace between impoverished Indigenous people and colonists determined to protect their property was virtually impossible: 'This is the state of things brought about by a system of colonization, which presents the alternative of famine or murder to the natives.'[51] However, these more radical objections were rarely pursued further.

A study of philanthropic writings produced in the colonies makes a useful addition to this historiography of subjecthood. Many philanthropists were distinguished by their passionate opposition to the arbitrary cruelties committed in the name of law and order. However, they were also notable for their mixed efforts to situate Indigenous people within a firmer and more coherent system of government, expanding both protection and control. Their records are valuable, too, in providing insights into some of the first detailed exchanges recorded with Indigenous people about their subject status. Such conversations could be notable at local levels, whilst having mixed (and ultimately inadequate) effects on broader imperial thinking. British publications only occasionally mentioned the feelings of local missionaries about native subjecthood in Australia, while ignoring the opinions of Indigenous people themselves. This indifference was in some ways unusual; these societies paid more attention to the opinions of other native peoples. In 1836, for instance, the London Missionary Society gave an enthusiastic description of an Exeter Hall meeting featuring 'the Caffre Chief [Jan] Tzatzoe' and 'Andries Stoffles, the Hottentot'. These African delegates, speaking in the wake of the British war against the Xhosa and controversies over the quasi-slavery of African indentured labourers, praised mission work and expressed hopes that British subject status would help protect them from violence and educate their children.[52] Similarly, the APS published an address from the General Council of Chiefs in British North America in 1840, complaining to the Governor and the Queen about poverty and dispossession but also declaring imperial loyalty. No equivalent Australian issues were mentioned.[53] Thus, when considering ideas about subjecthood in Australian philanthropic records, it must be acknowledged that their international influence was minor; their value lies partly in illuminating unrealised or neglected visions of governance. At the same time, however, examining missionaries' day-to-day attempts to 'train' Indigenous people for subjecthood enables us to trace this history beyond legal and policy debates, to a setting where governance and subject status were shifting, conflicted and personal.

Upon arriving in New South Wales in 1838, protector James Dredge was outraged by the initial verdict of 'not guilty' for the Myall Creek killers, 12 white men arrested for the massacre of perhaps 30 Aboriginal people in the

---

51  APS, Third Annual Report, 23 June 1840: 33.
52  LMS, *Missionary Magazine and Chronicle*, vol I, no IV, September 1836: 54–58.
53  APS, Third Annual Report, 23 June 1840: 18–19.

Liverpool Plains district. Describing it as the worst travesty of justice he had ever encountered in an English court, he blamed it on the hatred felt for Aboriginal people by 'the depraved of the community', encouraged by 'a corrupted portion of the colonial press'.[54] Philanthropists' papers provide some of the angriest accounts of a justice system which functioned to reinforce discrimination and dispossession. Dredge, for instance, also protested that soldiers and police threatened Aboriginal people and solicited the women, and that Aboriginal prisoners were dying in gaol.[55] One incident in 1840 was particularly distressing. A large group of Daungwurrung people from northern Victoria were arrested for attacking squatters' stations, and during the skirmish several of them were shot by the police. Dredge lamented in his diary that their imprisonment was unlawful, but that he could not help them; 'They are the unhappy victims of misrule.'[56] Meanwhile, his colleague protector William Thomas felt disgusted when men were arrested and convicted almost at random for sheep theft, on the grounds that one Aboriginal prisoner was as good as another. He worried, too, that sexual assaults on Indigenous women were unlikely to be taken seriously by the courts.[57] Similarly, in 1841, people at protector ES Parker's station told him that a squatter, Mr Francis, had murdered several people, but Parker concluded that the bar on Indigenous evidence made a trial unlikely.[58]

Philanthropists complained that these violations stemmed from a system of policing which was unsystematic and violent. This is not to say that philanthropists were strangers to ad hoc policing themselves, however; there were occasions when missionary and protectorate authority was enforced with scant regard for the law. Sometimes this resulted from uncertainty and a wish for clemency. Port Phillip Chief Protector GA Robinson, for example, told the other protectors in 1839 that they should avoid using their magisterial powers against Indigenous people unless absolutely necessary, while Dredge and Thomas argued over whether it was fair to prosecute impoverished people for stealing food.[59] On a sterner note, South Australian protector Matthew Moorhouse hoped the shady legal circumstances of Aboriginal prisoners would encourage compliance with 'civilising' regimes. He advised missionary Clamor Schurmann to tell the relatives of a prisoner from Port Lincoln that his sentence would be reduced if they behaved obediently.[60]

---

54  Dredge, 15 November 1838, *JDD*, MS11625, MSM534, SLV.
55  Dredge, 2 September 1839, 23 September 1839, 17 October 1839, *JDD*; James Dredge to Jabez Bunting, 10 May 1841, *MMS*, reel 55, AJCP M172, SLV.
56  Dredge, 10–13 October 1840, *JDD*, MS11625, MSM534, SLV.
57  For instance, William Thomas to GA Robinson, 19 October 1839, f29–31, *WTP*, ML MSS 214, reel 7; William Thomas to GA Robinson, 29 February 1840, PROV VPRS4410, unit 3, 1840/66 (reel 2); Thomas, 27 September 1840, *WTP*, ML MSS 214, reel 1; William Thomas to GA Robinson, 5 June 1843, PROV VPRS4410, unit 3, 1843/76 (reel 2); William Thomas to GA Robinson, 31 November 1844, PROV VPRS4410, unit 3, 1844/82 (reel 2); Thomas, 17 September 1845, *WTP*, ML MSS 214, reel 3, State Library of NSW.
58  ES Parker, Quarterly Journal, 1 March – 31 May 1841, PROV VPRS4410, unit 2, 1841/61 (reel 2).
59  Dredge, 31 October 1839, 22 November 1839, *JDD*, MS11625, MSM534, SLV.
60  Matthew Moorhouse to Clamor Schurmann, 19 October 1842, Protector of Aborigines, *Letterbook, 1840–1857*, SRSA, GRG52/7, vol 1, unit 1.

However, ad hoc use of power was more commonly punitive, sometimes relating to sexual propriety and control over children. Protector Thomas took part in police searches for women who had left their husbands, and threatened people with arrest for stealing food from his stores, linking this to contests over child custody, so that families wishing to avoid the police agreed to leave their children with him.[61] More disturbing examples of philanthropists taking the law into their own hands occurred at Moreton Bay in 1840, when the German missionaries shot at some Indigenous men who were robbing their vegetable garden, and in South Australia in 1841–42, when protector Moorhouse took part in armed expeditions to capture people accused of murder and sheep theft. This ended, on one occasion, in a violent clash where at least ten Indigenous men were shot. (These ugly confrontations also demonstrated how models of 'protection' could vary dramatically according to local circumstances and personalities; the German missionaries had comparatively minor, suspicious relationships with Indigenous people, while Moorhouse seemed unusually keen on implementing colonial dominance through military might.[62]) Such accounts are suggestive of Julie Evans's argument that the establishment of law and order in the colonies depended on its initial breaching through the violent oppression of Indigenous people, in order to create a 'normal' order of white domination; 'in suspending itself, the rule of law maintained itself.'[63]

However, on the whole, philanthropic records showed a wish to make the legal system more systematic and consistent – and in some ways more powerful – in its dealings with Indigenous people. This was particularly evident in Western Australia, where instructions to the protectors stressed the need to enforce public order and teach people to obey British law.[64] Similar aims were also apparent elsewhere. LMS spokesmen Daniel Tyerman and George Bennett urged LE Threlkeld in 1825 that his Lake Macquarie mission must educate Awabakal people about 'the duties which they owe to the Government of this country, and mankind in general'.[65] Here, the legal position of subjects could be illustrated dramatically and alarmingly; in 1835, Threlkeld remarked that it was good for Indigenous people to watch executions, as this taught them the severity of

---

61  Thomas, 15 November 1839, *WTP*, ML MSS 214, reel 1, State Library of NSW; Thomas, 24–25 August 1844, *WTP*, ML MSS 214, reel 3; William Thomas to GA Robinson, 1 December 1847, PROV VPRS4410, unit 4, 1847/102 (reel 2).
62  Lieutenant O Gorman to Colonial Secretary E Deas Thomson, 30 March 1840, in JG Steele (ed) 1975: 268; Le Couteur 1998: 148; Matthew Moorhouse to Colonial Secretary, 13 September 1841, and Matthew Moorhouse to A Mundy, 30 June 1842, in Protector of Aborigines, *Letterbook*, SRSA GRG52/7, vol 1, unit 1.
63  Evans 2004: 78.
64  Instructions to the Protectors of Aborigines of Western Australia, enclosed in Governor Hutt to the Marquis of Normanby, 11 February 1840, in *BPP: Papers Relating to Australia, 1844*, Colonies: Australia, vol 8, 1969: 371–372; Charles Symmons to Peter Brown, 31 December 1840, in *BPP: Papers Relating to Australia, 1844*, vol 8: 388–390.
65  Rev Daniel Tyerman and George Bennett to LE Threlkeld, 24 February 1825, *LMS*, AJCP M73, SLV.

violent crime.⁶⁶ Similarly, in 1842, Indigenous people around Adelaide were summoned by the protectorate to watch a public flogging, to learn the penalty for theft.⁶⁷

Protector William Thomas made milder but more consistent efforts to educate people about legal subjecthood. He often took them to watch trials and tour the Melbourne Gaol, so that they could witness the treatment of criminals and the law's supposed impartiality – 'black & white identical in crime mingled together'.⁶⁸ Thomas wished to depict the law as colour blind, despite his own awareness to the contrary. He complained, for instance, about what he considered an excessively harsh sentence for an Indigenous prisoner in 1841, given ten years' transportation for armed robbery. Thomas found this ruling especially unfortunate because looked racially biased to Indigenous viewers.⁶⁹ He also warned people about the death penalty and told them – again, not wholly truthfully – that any violence towards one another would be punished, so 'Black fellows no more kill, but shake hands with each other like white men'.⁷⁰ Thomas's efforts to encourage Aboriginal compliance with colonial law are intriguing. Aware of Indigenous people's general lack of power, he nonetheless believed that making people subjects must involve a certain acceptance on their part of the law's basic fairness and their own engagement with it.

However, when trying to construct Indigenous people as subjects of empire, philanthropists often found themselves playing an awkward double role; alternately enforcing colonial power and pleading for mitigation. This was evident in their work as translators and advocates for Aboriginal prisoners. Threlkeld had stated in his deposition on the Murrell case that he wished to see Indigenous laws replaced by the British system, as he considered many forms of traditional authority cruel and no longer workable. However, he also had ongoing concerns about the British system itself. He urged elsewhere that Indigenous people receive proper legal representation, and hoped that his efforts to translate the Awabakal language would help ensure that innocent people were not convicted at random, a scenario 'unbecoming the profession of a Christian character'.⁷¹ Similarly, Wellington Valley missionary James Günther stated during a case in 1838 that he was not opposed to Indigenous criminals

---

66 LE Threlkeld to Colonial Secretary, 5th Annual Report of the Aboriginal Mission at Lake Macquarie, 2 December 1835, in LE Threlkeld, 'Memoranda', in Gunson (ed) 1974 vol 1: 122.
67 Matthew Moorhouse to the Sheriff, 3 August 1842, Protector of Aborigines, *Letterbook*, SRSA GRG52/7, vol 1, unit 1.
68 William Thomas to GA Robinson, 1 March 1847, PROV VPRS4410, unit 4, 1847/93 (reel 2).
69 William Thomas to GA Robinson, 1 March 1841, PROV VPRS4410, unit 3, 1841/68 (reel 2).
70 Thomas, 19 May 1844, *WTP*, ML MSS 214, reel 3, State Library of NSW. Also, 27 August 1844.
71 LE Threlkeld, Second half yearly report of the Aboriginal mission supported by the London Missionary Society, 21 June 1826, *LMS*, AJCP M73, SLV; LE Threlkeld to Chief Justice Sir James Dowling, 8 March 1841, Sir William Dixson, *Documents relating to Aboriginal Australians, 1816–1853*, Dixson Library, ADD 80–82: CY reel 3743, State Library of NSW. Also,Elbourne 2003.

being punished severely, but expressed concern that they were subjected to British laws whilst unable to give evidence. He remarked to the court this was unjust, when so little was done to 'civilise' them, and repeated this complaint in his 1841 annual report (forwarded to Governor Gipps and Lord Stanley).[72] In his diary, Günther wrote that settlers treated Indigenous people worse than animals, while the legal system did nothing to prevent this.

> 'Oh Black fellow' as he is only deemed worthy to be called, if he injures a White man is soon seized & proceeded against, but his complaints are by no means eagerly heard or his cause taken in hand & defended.[73]

Protectors Thomas and Dredge also raised concerns about the bar on Indigenous evidence and the denial of legal protection. Dredge remarked 'While they are held amenable to our laws and are punished for the violation of them, [they] are considered incompetent to tell their own tale of woe.'[74]

Such philanthropic arguments could be ignored or coopted by the state, however. In New South Wales, Governor Gipps did try to persuade the British parliament to allow laws recognising Aboriginal testimony, but he was concerned primarily with expanding the legal system's power to pursue Indigenous offenders. By the time British objections to accepting the evidence of non-Christians had been overcome, political power had begun to shift to local colonists, and the New South Wales legislature repeatedly rejected Gipps' evidence bills, motivated, Russell Smandych claims, by racial contempt towards Indigenous witnesses. (Ironically, in Western Australia, where the government was more active in recognising Indigenous evidence, this stemmed from a wish to keep order in Perth and supervise Aboriginal labourers; philanthropists do not seem to have been key advocates here.[75])

Indigenous people themselves exercised hardly any power in this area, but they did appeal to missionaries and protectors for aid, knowing these philanthropists held some legal influence. The introductory anecdote from Buntingdale, for instance, showed Indigenous pleas to and rejections of European power, suggesting a strategic use of the colonial system but also relationships of reciprocity with white authority figures. It is probable that the relatives of the murdered man in the Murrell case, who appealed to Threlkeld for help, were also trying to situate themselves more strongly within colonial law, as well as drawing on personal connections with the missionary.[76] Such connections were relevant

---

72  Günther, Journal, 17 May 1838, *WVP*; James Günther, Annual Report of the Mission to the Aborigines at Wellington Valley, 1841, enclosed in Sir George Gipps to Lord Stanley, 11 March 1842, in *BPP: Papers Relating to Australia, 1844*, vol 8: 157–158.
73  Günther, Journal, 9 April 1838, *WVP*.
74  Dredge, 8 December 1839, *JDD*, MS11625, MSM534, SLV. Also, 6 January 1841; William Thomas to Sir George Gipps, 23 June 1841, PROV VPRS10, unit 3, 1841/909 (reel 1).
75  Hunter 2004: 228–229, 235; Smandych 2004: 251–261.
76  Elbourne 2003.

around Melbourne too, when Woiwurrung leader Billibellary cooperated with protector Thomas in locking up drunk men whose behaviour was disruptive and violent, and when people asked Thomas for more information about 'white man's laws of murder.'[77]

However, philanthropists' legal help was not always strong. Despite their pleas, the Daungwurrung people imprisoned in Melbourne in 1840 did not receive much assistance from the protectors, who emphasised (perhaps overemphasised) their own helplessness.[78] Similarly, when a man called Baggama was arrested at the Bogan River in 1835 for the murder of colonial botanist Richard Cunningham, he begged the Wellington Valley missionaries for help, but their response was lukewarm; they gave him a blanket and a lecture on God. William Watson recalled 'He asked me many times over, "if they would hang him?" and said "I believe you send book (or Letter) to Governor and tell him not to hang me."'[79]

Indigenous people drew philanthropists' attention to glaring discrepancies in colonial law, an experience probably embarrassing for philanthropists at the time, but which also functioned in their records to emphasise the need for more consistent governance. Watson, for instance, complained to Governor Fitzroy in 1844 that little was done to prosecute Indigenous people for violence against their enemies; he claimed they taunted him 'Governor and Magistrates won't interfere with Black fellow.'[80] Thomas, similarly, commented in 1847 that he found it hard to convince people that British law took violence against women seriously, after a man received one day in gaol for beating up his wife. Observers remarked 'black touch em constable nanbo kodungunnu Jail (long time stop in jail) but big one beat em lubra no sulky.'[81] When a drunken bullock driver crashed his animals into the camp, demolishing people's shelters, Thomas was angry, but did not record how he responded to the residents' furious demand 'we knock at white man's house & take Blk to jail, why no take white man?'[82] Chief protector Robinson also failed to record his response when people answered his lecture against sheep theft by saying:

> Long time ago, they had plenty of kangaroo, Parm-pun, Tuerer-corn (roots eaten by the Natives); and then they were not hungry and did not take sheep. Kangaroo all gone, jumbuc (sheep) eat the roots ... what for sulky; shoot too much blackfellow; no sulky blackfellow no spear white fellow take it kangaroo. What for no put white fellow gaol?[83]

---

77  Thomas, 19 May 1844, 27 August 1844, 19 April 1845, *WTP*, ML MSS 214, reel 3, State Library of NSW.
78  Thomas, 26 October 1840, *WTP*, ML MSS 214, reel 1, State Library of NSW.
79  Watson, Journal, 1 December 1835, *WVP*.
80  William Watson to Governor Charles Fitzroy, 31 December 1849, Dixson, *Documents relating to Aboriginal Australians*, Dixson Library, ADD 80–82, CY reel 3743.
81  William Thomas to GA Robinson, 1 March 1847, PROV VPRS4410, unit 4, 1847/93 (reel 2).
82  Thomas, 14 November 1839, *WTP*, ML MSS 214, reel 1, State Library of NSW.
83  George Augustus Robinson, 'A Report of an Expedition to the Aboriginal Tribes of the Interior during the months of March, April, May, June, July and August 1841', in Clark (ed) 2001 vol 4: 27.

Philanthropists recorded such fragments of Indigenous opinion for the benefit of their superiors, or for posterity, but their inadequate recounting of their own responses points to their tricky dual role as colonial authority figures and Aboriginal advocates. Meanwhile, Indigenous people's comments and actions, while carrying no political power, could become a disruptive presence in philanthropic texts, drawing attention to the shortcomings of the colonial justice system and to the fact that these injustices were visible and contentious to colonised people themselves.

Complexities of governance and subjecthood became particularly apparent when philanthropists tried to deal with divisions and hostilities between Indigenous societies. Some missionaries were impatient with these conflicts, citing them as evidence of Indigenous people's supposed 'savagery'. At the Moreton Bay German mission in 1841, missionary Peter Nique described his efforts to play off the 'Toorbul' people against the 'Bonya' ones, threatening to go and live with the second group if the first would not engage in farming.[84] Similarly, when Karl WE Schmidt reported on his expedition to the Bunya Mountains in 1842, he mentioned that violent hostilities existed between the Moreton Bay people and the 'wild mountain tribes'. In fact, Schmidt's Indigenous guides seem to have been carefully diplomatic during their travels, negotiating with local peoples and distributing gifts. However, the missionaries rarely appreciated this, and reacted irritably, threatening to cut off ties to their guides, when the guides were reluctant to travel further. Nor did the missionaries properly differentiate between the communities involved; the impression created was one of querulous but ultimately generic 'blacks'. This error may not have been wholly innocent; the German missionaries were seeking support to move their station to another district, a task which might have seemed more problematic had Indigenous differences been fully acknowledged.[85] Similarly, in South Australia, Lutheran missionary Clamor Schurmann urged the government in 1844 to concentrate Indigenous groups at a single Port Lincoln station. He dismissed any suggestion of negotiating with Indigenous leadership or cultural identities, asserting confidently 'they will give way to a determined and lasting impulse.'[86]

In other districts, however, philanthropists developed a different view; they began trying to recognise, negotiate and to some extent re-shape Indigenous divisions. In 1840, James Dredge wrote to a friend that Indigenous societies were often dangerously unfriendly towards one another, and advised Methodist leader Jabez Bunting that governance must take into account 'the civil relations

---

84  P Nique, 'Aborigines: diary of Messrs Nique and Hartenstein of the German Mission to the Aborigines, at Moreton Bay, during a journey to Toorbal, a district of country to the northward', in *Colonial Observer*, vol 1, no 4–5, 1841.
85  Karl WE Schmidt, 'Report of an Expedition to the Bunya Mountains in search of a suitable site for a mission station', Accession: 3522, Box 7072, SLQ: 1–2, 5–6, 9–10, 12–15.
86  Clamor Schurmann, in Matthew Moorhouse to Colonial Secretary, 17 May 1844, SRSA GRG24/6/1844/488.

of the different Tribes'. He suggested working with groups individually instead of forcing them together. These ideas were repeated in his 1845 work *Brief Notes on the Aborigines of New South Wales*, sections of which were reproduced in the APS journal *Colonial Intelligencer*.[87] Similar remarks were made by Dredge's protectorate colleague, Parker, who reported to government the hostility of Djadjawurrung people on his station towards Djabwurrung visitors, claiming they were too foreign.[88] Protector Thomas also advised Governor Gipps that certain communities would require separate stations. He particularly commented that the 'coastal tribe' (unnamed) disliked staying in Boonwurrung country and upbraided Thomas for not living with them instead.[89]

However, while these philanthropists were taking into account Indigenous views, they were not just recognising Indigenous territoriality; they were also trying to recreate it. This was ironically apparent in their wish to restrict Indigenous people from travel in order to preserve what they believed to be traditional boundaries. In 1843, South Australian protector Moorhouse attempted to keep order in Adelaide by denying blankets to people from the Murray district who visited the town, asserting they had 'no proprietary right here' and might drive away the Kaurna people, 'the true proprietors of the soil'.[90] In Port Phillip, Thomas recommended banning colonists from taking Indigenous people into foreign districts without protectorate permission, as some people travelling outside their country with Europeans had been murdered by their enemies.[91]

Once again, Buntingdale became a centre for particular concern. The site of this mission had been chosen because of its proximity to different communities, but this quickly became problematic, with hostilities occurring between Gulidjan, Wathawurrung and Djargurdwurrung ('Dantgurt') people. While the violence may have had origins more complex than physical proximity, the missionaries came to believe their location was disastrous. They reported to La Trobe that the small and vulnerable Djargurdwurrung community were especially victimised by white and black enemies, and urged that the law intervene to overcome traditional violence and protect mission residents. This wish to incorporate Indigenous people as subjects was qualified, however, by an emphasis on particularity and difference; these missionaries advocated separating Indigenous groups, with a missionary for each, treating them as

---

87   James Dredge to D Harding, 12 September 1840, *La Trobe Journal*, no 61, Autumn 1998: 29; James Dredge to Jabez Bunting, 10 May 1841, *MMS*, reel 55, AJCP M172, SLV; APS, *Colonial Intelligencer, or Aborigines' Friend*, 1847–48: 42–44.
88   ES Parker, Quarterly Journal, 1 June – 31 August 1842, PROV VPRS4410, unit 2, 1842/62 (reel 2). Parker refers to them as Bolokepar, which Clark classifies as Djab wurrung clans from Lake Bolac. See Clark 1990: 114.
89   William Thomas to Sir George Gipps, 23 June 1841, PROV VPRS10, unit 3, 1841/909 (reel 1).
90   Matthew Moorhouse to Colonial Secretary, 4 April 1843, and Matthew Moorhouse to Private Secretary, 25 April 1843, in Protector of Aborigines, *Letterbook*, SRSA GRG52/7, vol 1, unit 1.
91   William Thomas to Sir George Gipps, 23 June 1841, PROV VPRS10, unit 3, 1841/909 (reel 1).

'small independent communities'.[92] When this was attempted in practice, the people now excluded from Buntingdale were resentful; they continued to travel in the area and urged mission residents, especially the young men, to leave with them. This is suggestive of ceremonial obligations, but the missionaries judged such behaviour as simply rebellious.[93] Their complaints suggest how philanthropists were not merely observing social distinctions, but attempting to remake them, flattening out complexities of relationships to neighbours and country. This strategy may have also reflected the wish of some philanthropists to consolidate their own position as benign patriarchs. Buntingdale missionary Francis Tuckfield mused that if only every community had a missionary, 'he would be able to sit down with his little nation gathered around him without fear of having the peace and security of their homes broken in upon by other tribes.'[94]

In British philanthropic publications, though, the intricacies of Indigenous identity were taken less seriously. During the 1840s, the WMMS's annual reports and *Missionary Register* featured stories from Buntingdale about the 'superstitions', 'prejudices', 'feuds and deadly animosities' that made mission life so dangerous. The missionaries' policy of separation was praised for its (initial) effectiveness, but was couched in terms of countering savage disruption rather than negotiating genuine concerns.[95] The mission's collapse and a general lack of Evangelical enthusiasm for Australia worked against any greater understanding. By 1848, the WMMS's *Papers Relative to the Wesleyan Missions, and to the State of Heathen Countries* was blaming the apparent failure of Buntingdale on hostilities between different groups. The impression created was not one of social complexity – or, indeed, social breakdown – but rather of a

---

92  Benjamin Hurst to CJ La Trobe, 22 July 1841, *MMS*, reel 4, AJCP M121, SLV; Minutes of the Annual Meeting, Australian District, 30 July 1846, *MMS*, reel 5, AJCP M122, SLV; Minutes of the 23rd Annual Meeting of the Australian District, Sydney, 15 September 1842, and Minutes of the 24th Annual Meeting of the Australian District, Sydney, 27 July 1843, in WMMS, *Synod Minutes, 1822–1855*, 1980; Joseph Orton to John Waterhouse, 24 June 1839, *JOL*, part 2; Joseph Orton to General Secretaries, 2 September 1841, *JOL*, ML ref A1717–A1720, State Library of NSW; Report of the Aboriginal Work on Bunting Dale Station, Geelong, for the Year ending June 1844, *MMS*, reel 5, AJCP M122, SLV; Francis Tuckfield, Report on the WMMS's mission to the Aborigines of the Sub District of Geelong, Port Phillip, August 1843, *WMMS*, reel 2, Mp2107, NLA.
93  Francis Tuckfield to General Secretaries, 1 January 1844, *WMMS*, reel 2, Mp2107, NLA; WMMS, *Report of the Wesleyan Methodist Missionary Society for the year ending April 1846*, 1846: 28–29; Minutes of the Annual Meeting, Australian District, 30 July 1846, *MMS*, reel 5, AJCP M122, SLV; Minutes of the 26th annual meeting of the Australian District, 30 July 1846, WMMS, *Synod Minutes*.
94  Francis Tuckfield to General Secretaries, 1 January 1844, *WMMS*, reel 2, Mp2107, NLA.
95  CMS, *Missionary Register*, May 1843: 238; CMS, *Missionary Register*, April 1844: 227; CMS, *Missionary Register*, May 1845: 210; CMS, *Missionary Register*, May 1846: 210; WMMS, *The Report of the Wesleyan Methodist Missionary Society for the year ending April 1842*, 1842: 45; *The Report of the Wesleyan Methodist Missionary Society for the year ending April 1843*, 1843: 41; *The Report of the Wesleyan Methodist Missionary Society for the year ending April 1845*, 1845: 30–31.

brutal absence of social organisation. This appeared amidst broader descriptions of Indigenous Australians as degraded, cannibalistic and dying.[96] It was this image that would endure the most in the imperial and colonial imagination.

## 'What national blessings would rebound': Aboriginal policy and the rise of self-government

The future treatment of Indigenous Australia would also be affected – and not always benignly – by the growth of settler government. While the 1830s saw some humanitarian highpoints, this era was also marked by an expansion of white male citizenship and general colonial growth. Under a Whig government in Britain, power was shifting towards the House of Commons, while the political privileges of the Church of England were being eroded through the Reform and Registration Acts, and, in New South Wales through Governor Bourke's 1836 Church Act, which provided state support for salaries and infrastructure across different denominations.[97] The expansion of a new sort of Australian society was also apparent in the sale of Crown land from 1831 to finance further migration, the recognition by the 1836 Squatting Act of settlers' expansion beyond official limits,[98] and the decision to abolish transportation to New South Wales following the damning Molesworth Committee report. All of this was linked to the arrival of tens of thousands of free immigrants, with expectations of political participation and some awareness of self-determination movements in other settler colonies. The 1839 Durham Report, commissioned by the British government in response to serious unrest in Upper and Lower Canada, occupied a significant place here. It examined Britain's role in political and social conditions in North America, especially in the relations between British and French colonists, and advised granting colonists gradual political autonomy and locally elected legislatures whilst maintaining British dominance over their foreign policy and defence, in order to avoid any American-style revolutions. Thus, a gradual picture was emerging of a colonial future, moving away from a convict system and towards free immigration and more liberal-democratic government. Such progress rested in many ways on the ongoing seizure, division and sale of Aboriginal land.

By the 1840s, moreover, British philanthropists themselves were losing interest in the Australian colonies; indeed, Alan Lester and Elizabeth Elbourne have traced a general weakening of philanthropy during this decade. Lester attributes this partly to developments at home (the political losses of TF Buxton and

---

96   WMMS, *Papers Relative to the Wesleyan Missions, and to the State of Heathen Countries*, no CXI, March 1848.
97   Its full title was: 'An Act to promote the building of Churches and Chapels, and to provide for the maintenance of ministers of Religion in New South Wales', 29 July 1836.
98   Its official title was the 'Act to restrain the unauthorised occupation of Crown Lands', 29 July 1836.

Lord Glenelg, for instance) and partly to disappointments overseas – notably, the economic and social turmoil following the emancipation of Jamaican slaves – while Elbourne points to the growing conservatism of Evangelicals as their movement became socially mainstream and lost the unifying drive of the abolition cause.[99] However, the humanitarian decline was also affected by the growth of colonial legislatures. The influential Durham Report voiced no concern for First Nations people,[100] while tensions were already developing in the Australian colonies. As I have explored elsewhere, settlers in Port Phillip linked the unpopular Aboriginal protectorate to their resentful dependence on the distant Sydney government, while commentators in New South Wales and Moreton Bay linked Aboriginal philanthropy discursively to complaints about the government being unrepresentative, remote and incompetent.[101]

Philanthropic work would decline further as colonial self-government approached. The New South Wales Legislative Committee held its first elections in 1843, the same year Gipps slashed the protectorate's budget, under some pressure from the Legislative Council. By the end of the decade, Governor Fitzroy was reporting to Earl Grey, with strong endorsement from the executive, that efforts to improve Indigenous conditions had proven almost totally useless. The legislature assented partially to Grey's recommendations for Aboriginal reserves, but all the while stressed the extreme difficulty of doing anything at all for Aborigines. A related attitude appears to have prevailed in Western Australia. This colony did not obtain self-government until 1890, with British authority over Aboriginal affairs retained till 1898 – a lingering sign of imperial unease. There was, nonetheless, a comparable decline in Aboriginal policy. In 1849, protector Charles Symmons was retitled pointedly Guardian of Natives and Protector of Settlers, and this protectorate, which in any case had long been more of a policing operation, was phased out as Symmons assumed other official roles.[102]

It is not easy to say how the first missionaries and protectors viewed the rise of colonial self-determination; they rarely mentioned it and most of them had given up before the 1850s. There are clues, though, about the opinions of broader Evangelical networks. Missionary societies' responses to self-government were interestingly mixed and rarely focused on Indigenous Australia, highlighting settler issues instead. One speaker at the WMMS 1837 anniversary expressed a hope that the tumultuous Canadian districts would remain under British

---

99 Elbourne 2002: 287; Lester 2006: 237.
100 Evans et al 2003: 34–36.
101 Mitchell 2009a, 2009b, 2009c.
102 Governor CA Fitz Roy to Earl Grey, 12 November 1849, *BPP: Papers Relating to Australia, 1850*, Colonies: Australia, vol 12, 1969: 59; Extract from minutes, 15 October 1849, in Governor CA Fitz Roy to Earl Grey, 12 November 1849, *BPP: Papers Relating to Australia, 1850*, vol 12: 60–61; Sir George Gipps to Lord Stanley, 21 March 1844, *HRA*, 1920, series 1, vol xiii, July 1843 – September 1844: 498; Harris 1990: 278–295; Hasluck 1970: 79–80.

control, arguing that the endurance of slavery in the United States demonstrated the superiority of British constitutionalism over American republicanism. However, he said of Canada, 'If, when like a ripe apple, it falls from the parent stem naturally, – so be it.'[103] Similarly, the Church of England's Colonial Church Society, which focused on white colonists, looked forward to using missionary work to help British Protestants build strong colonies with self-government and ongoing imperial loyalty.

> Let the colonies be neglected, and such results as they had seen in Lower Canada might be expected elsewhere; but if they received churches and schools and pastors from this country ... their attachment to it would last, even should their political connexion with it ever be dissolved, and Great Britain would have them for allies, when they had ceased to be dependents.[104]

Similarly, the Colonial Church Society urged that Western Australian colonists were entitled to have their 'English' habits and faith supported through further missionary work; this would promote imperial unity.

> What NATIONAL BLESSINGS WOULD REBOUND to us did we thus, as a nation, seek the spiritual welfare of our colonies ... Thus should we have a hold upon our Colonies that nothing else could give, and which, should they ever be politically severed from us, would yet endure and unite us.[105]

Such comments suggest these Evangelical writers were cautious about self-government but obliged to accept it as a political reality, with missionary work seen as a unifying force. Elsewhere, they had promoted missions in order to create Indigenous subjects; here, it was white subjects who needed to be strengthened and retained.

Some Evangelical writers did consider what self-government could mean for colonised peoples. Raymond Cooke (one of the few historians to discuss this) has argued with reference to New Zealand that Evangelicals were reluctant to endorse self-government immediately, because of their concern at colonists' treatment of indigenous peoples.[106] The most detailed response to this issue came from the Aborigines Protection Society, who lobbied Lord John Russell in 1850 to discuss his introduction into Parliament of a draft Bill extending constitutional institutions to Australia. The society expressed general support for the Bill, believing it would enhance colonists' liberties, but warned that it must include

---

103  WMMS, *Missionary Notices*, June-July 1837, no 258–9: 485.
104  Colonial Church Society (CCS), *Colonial Church Record*, no 1, vol 1, August 1838: 10–11.
105  CCS, *Report of the Australian Church Missionary Society, now formed into the Colonial Church Society*, 1839: 21, also 2–3, 9, 13, 18–19.
106  Cooke 1965: 129–133, 138.

'imparting to the Natives the privileges enjoyed by British subjects'. Again, the United States was mentioned as a warning example of a supposedly democratic country guilty of slavery and cruel dispossession – a link to republicanism may have been implied. Taking an interestingly global focus, the deputation protested the exclusion of Maori and First Nations people from political participation, claiming this weakened their loyalty to empire. In contrast, the possibility of Indigenous Australians participating in government was ignored. Instead, they were singled out as especially degraded, needing particular 'paternal care'. The APS suggested the Bill include statements about racial equality, the need to rescind discriminatory laws, and the importance of allowing Indigenous people to give evidence in court and enjoy fair trials. The protectorate was described as a failure, but further missionary work was urged. These suggestions were not well received. The Colonial Office responded that Indigenous people were already (technically) subjects, and Australia's new constitutions contained no statements of human equality or Aboriginal entitlements.[107] What is notable about the APS submission and similar documents, however, is not only their lack of success but also the fact that their focus on self-government and native affairs was a general one; Indigenous Australians still received relatively little attention.

Such neglect often surrounded Aboriginal issues within the development of Australian government. Ann Curthoys, for instance, has contrasted the general silence of New South Wales colonial sources on this topic with the extensive discussions occurring in New Zealand, in a context of vigorous Maori struggles for political power.[108] Perhaps because of this absence, references to the relationship between self-government and Indigenous affairs have been rare in Australian political history-writing, even amongst scholars who have explored Aboriginal issues elsewhere. While Indigenous oppression is mentioned briefly in histories of government by John Hirst, MMH Thompson and Terry Irving, it is not integrated strongly into their overall frameworks, and other comparable works barely touch on the issue at all.[109] Presumably disciplinary divisions were relevant here, as well as the systemic exclusion of Indigenous people from the political realm from earliest days. This proved so strong that it is, perhaps, difficult for political historians to write around.

However, it is equally clear that self-government issues have been absent in histories of the Indigenous past, suggesting a certain neglect of the British

---

107  APS, *The Colonial Intelligencer, or Aborigines' Friend*, 1849–1850, vol II: 403–409; Evans et al 2003: 64–69.
108  Ann Curthoys, 'Self-Government and Indigenous Dispossession: Linked fates, separate histories, long shadows', conference paper, *Governing by Looking Back*, 14 December 2007, Research School of Social Sciences, Australian National University: 6.
109  Hirst 2002: 6, 24–25, 72–73; Irving 2006: 14, 130; Thompson 2006: 37–38. Examples of the latter include, Atkinson 1994: 85–102; Cochrane 2006; Oldfield 1999.

empire. I am indebted to the work of Julie Evans, Patricia Grimshaw, David Phillips and Shurlee Swain, *Equal Subjects, Unequal Rights*, which examines how developing models of Australian government treated Aboriginal people with theoretical indifference and practical exclusion, a situation which the authors contrast to the debates over native franchise and constitutions occurring in Canada, New Zealand and South Africa. This is a rare example, however. A few other, brief discussions of the issue have placed self-government within a history of Aboriginal disenfranchisement, suggesting that the growth of male settler liberties also meant a consolidation of colonialism. In Lyndall Ryan's history of Aboriginal Tasmania, she notes the strong colonial opposition that greeted the 1847 removal of Indigenous survivors from Flinders Island to Oyster Cove; this move was seen as undermining self-government, as British financial support was needed for the proposed Aboriginal institution and self-sufficiency was a precondition of self-government. Ryan observes, too, that Indigenous complaints of mistreatment were ignored more thoroughly than ever after self-government, when the absence of Aboriginal people became seen as a sign of Tasmania's maturity.[110] Meanwhile, Henry Reynolds has suggested that racial hostilities made the Colonial Office reluctant to allow colonists complete control, fearing the results of settler government for Indigenous people. In their Queensland study, Reynolds and Dawn May note the humanitarian decline that accompanied the growth of self-government; 'Each shift of power – from Downing Street to Sydney and from Sydney to Brisbane brought government closer to the frontier – politically, intellectually and morally'.[111]

Ultimately, governing Indigenous Australia became a problematic subject for philanthropic commentators. At missions and protectorate stations, attempts were made to situate Indigenous people inside colonial law, prioritising regulation, protection and evangelising. Missionaries were, in many cases, motivated by genuine compassion and concern, but the increased powers of church and state they advocated would, over subsequent decades, often come to function as mechanisms of oppression. The impact of their argument on British audiences was questionable at this time. While they contributed in a broad sense to campaigns to expand imperial power and protection, British interest in Australian Aboriginal subjecthood was never sufficiently strong, and it would diminish all the more with the rise of colonial self-government. Such points of imperial weakness invite further exploration. As Elizabeth Elbourne has commented 'The great Australian silence has been much discussed; one is driven to wonder about the more deafening great British silence regarding Australia.'[112]

---

110   Ryan 1981: 209–210.
111   Reynolds and May 1995: 171. Also, Reynolds 1996: 9–11.
112   Elbourne 2003.

# 'All white masters belong to your King': race, identity and empire

On Western Australia's Foundation Day in 1841, Methodist missionary John Smithies caused a minor public controversy, when he decided to prevent the Indigenous children in his custody from taking part in official celebrations to mark the young colony's progress. These festivities, which included boat regattas, horse races and balls, he described as 'scenes of evil'. The *Perth Gazette* criticised Smithies' decision, complaining that such isolation and judgement might prove subversive, encouraging Aboriginal servants to see their white employers as sinners. Smithies retorted that no disrespect or insubordination was intended, but he had a religious duty to protect the children, especially from gambling. The prominence of Indigenous people at the official festivities – which traditionally involved races and spear-throwing contests between Aboriginal men – may have also been a factor in the missionaries' decision; Perth's celebrations were, in a sense, both too white and too black. Smithies chose instead to hold a separate feast and cricket match for the mission children, so that they could celebrate their (alleged) loyalty to empire without being exposed to corruption.[1] Such anecdotes are suggestive of the ambiguities and rifts of the 'civilising' process; loyalty to empire was vital, but could be experienced best apart from Europeans, and contact with colonists could encourage either virtuous labour or depravity. Meanwhile, the question of who should envisage and define a suitable future for Indigenous and colonial Australia was a deeply contested one.

Australia's first missionaries and protectors devoted most of their writings to their efforts to 'civilise' Indigenous people. Yet, one of the most valuable functions of these records is in illuminating how Evangelical philanthropists saw themselves, including in areas of race, class and nation. As Catherine Hall has observed in her study of missionaries and the anti-slavery movement in Jamaica, 'These texts explicitly concerned the category black, what it had meant and what it could mean; implicitly they suggested a preoccupation with whiteness, a category that was masked because it was seen as normal.'[2] Of particular importance to this discussion was the contested nature of British authority in the colonies, the sense philanthropists often expressed of being threatened by a depraved colonial population. As Methodist missionary Joseph Orton lamented in his journal in 1840, after touring the newly-invaded Port Phillip, 'wherever our countrymen go they seem to carry with them a moral pestilence – they are

---

1 McNair and Rumley 1981: 56–57; *Perth Gazette*, 3 June 1837, 5 June 1841, 19 June 1841.
2 Hall 1992: 211–212.

the greatest hindrance to Aboriginal instruction and improvement'.[3] Notions of colonial sin were inextricably connected to discourses of social class; nationality was also relevant but in some ways oddly subdued. Efforts to define what it meant to take part in a colonising project which philanthropists both supported and mistrusted raised troubling questions about whether sin, violence and destruction were marginal or intrinsic to empire.

## 'The Lord's enemies in the camp': class, race and criminality

In missionaries' and protectors' accounts of colonial life, divisions between black and white appear as fundamental on the frontier. Cultural theorist Richard Dyer has observed the importance of ideas of whiteness in unifying immigrant nations (he focuses particularly on the United States), noting 'Whiteness has been enormously, often terrifyingly effective in uniting coalitions of disparate groups of people.' However, he adds, 'whiteness as a coalition also incites the notion that some whites are whiter than others.'[4] Whiteness, as a concept, is both useful and problematic when examining sources from early 19th century Australia. Notions of racial difference were clearly a crucial aspect of dispossession, and yet the language of explicit, systematised, quasi-scientific racism that would become so crucial to Australian public life in later decades was less apparent. What emerges instead in philanthropic writings is a sense of imperial authority as contested and under threat from within, as philanthropists accused other colonists of undermining their work. This sense of civilisation under siege was understood through a powerful discourse of class difference.

Concerns about bad influences on Indigenous people were raised in various districts. In South Australia and Western Australia, philanthropists became caught up in disputed policies of isolation and (unequal) integration. These were settlements where Indigenous labour was more appealing to colonists, given the absence of a convict system and (in the case of Western Australia) the scarcity of free migration. The Methodist missionaries in Western Australia had a mandate from the start to teach both black and white children, and they encouraged Indigenous youths into domestic labour. However, as mentioned earlier, they were also anxious about their pupils being exposed to 'frivolities' and immoral influences.[5] Meanwhile, in South Australia, the Evangelical wish to shield Indigenous people from corruption (articulated by Lutheran missionary Clamor

---

3   Joseph Orton, 27 November 1840, Joseph Orton, Journal 1832–1839 and 1840–1841 [hereafter *JOJ*], MF302, Australian Institute of Aboriginal and Torres Strait Islander Studies (AIATSIS).
4   Dyer 1997: 19.
5   For example, John Smithies to General Secretaries, 25 October 1843, Wesleyan Methodist Missionary Society, Archive: Australasia 1812–1889 [hereafter *WMMS*], reel 2, Mp2107 (Record ID: 133095), National Library of Australia (NLA). See also, Hetherington 1992: 41, 47–48; Hetherington 2002: 34–35, 116–117.

Schurmann, Methodist advocate John Weatherstone and the first protector Bromley) came into conflict with Governor Grey's initiative to encourage the use of Aboriginal servants.[6]

However, these concerns were minor compared to those expressed in New South Wales, where the threat posed by 'degenerate' white colonists was linked explicitly to the penal system. It was in relation to these districts that philanthropists made their strongest calls for Indigenous people to be totally isolated from colonists. Scholars are continuing to debate the nature of relationships between Indigenous people and convicts. Jan Kociumbas, for instance, has highlighted how racial and convict stereotypes have hindered historical understanding. She warns of the danger of uncritically accepting missionaries' descriptions of convicts as brutal and sexually violent towards Indigenous people, noting how blaming – and to some extent displacing – violence onto convicts served to reinforce Evangelical ambitions for a more bourgeois colony of free workers.[7] However, while Kociumbas's critique is valuable, further discussion is needed. A more imperial focus demonstrates that these Australian arguments were, in fact, part of a much broader Evangelical conversation. Furthermore, while British publications tended to place violence and sin on the peripheries of the imperial world, this contrasted with the writings of local missionaries and protectors, whose approach to class and criminality could be more complex. My use of these records is intended not so much to illuminate Indigenous-convict relationships (although that topic is certainly important), but rather to consider the insights provided into philanthropists' views about class and authority.

The main relevant British publication in which race, class, gender and sin were discussed together was that of the 1835–37 Select Committee on Aborigines. Archdeacon Broughton and Rev William Yate warned the Select Committee about degrading white influences on Indigenous Australians. In response to a rather leading question, Yate stated that he did not believe urban colonists approved of violence against Indigenous people, but added 'the stockkeepers are convicts in the employ of the farmers, and perhaps at 100 miles distance, and they are quite out of their reach and control.' Unsurprisingly, Yate replied in the affirmative to the subsequent question, 'Is it your opinion that the introduction of a convict population amongst uncivilized and unchristianized tribes must be attended with very serious consequences, in obstructing the efforts of those who are endeavouring to inculcate the truths of Christianity?'[8] Former New South

---

6  Protector Bromley to Colonial Secretary, 2 May 1837, State Records of South Australia (SRSA), GRG24/1, Colonial Secretary's Office, Letters and other communications received, no 117 of 1837; John Weatherstone to Colonial Secretary, 29 August 1843, SRSA, GRG24/6, Colonial Secretary's Office, Correspondence files, no 1017 of 1843; Clamor Schurmann, quoted in Matthew Moorhouse to Colonial Secretary, 17 May 1844, SRSA, GRG24/6/1844/488; Scrimgeour 2006: 35–46.
7  Kociumbas 2001: 28–54.
8  Archdeacon Broughton, evidence, 3 August 1835, and Rev William Yate, evidence, 13 February 1836, *British Parliamentary Papers (BPP): Report from the Select Committee on Aborigines (British Settlements)*

Wales attorney-general Saxe Bannister's brief Australian discussion focused mainly on the need to end convict transportation, while statements from Pacific missionary Rev John Williams and acting Western Australian Governor Irwin asserted that Indigenous people were treated well by most colonists, except the 'lower orders'.[9] However, the most in-depth discussion occurred in the section on Wellington Valley by Church Missionary Society secretary Dandeson Coates. Using excerpts from William Watson's journals, Coates described prostitution, infanticide, venereal disease and the sexual abuse of children. Stockmen were the main culprits, he claimed, and he particularly mentioned abusive behaviour by ticket-of-leave men and Irishmen.[10]

The Select Committee's final report concluded that Indigenous Australians were being degraded by settlers beyond their (supposed) original savagery. Singled out for particular condemnation were cedar-cutters, convict stock-keepers, military parties on punitive expeditions, and remote free settlers. More broadly, the report blamed runaway convicts, sailors, traders and whalers for spreading violence and vice in New Zealand and the Pacific, while Dutch settlers were identified as key perpetrators of destruction in southern Africa.[11] This fit within a general discourse of suspicion about white colonists, in contrast to whom the Evangelical self could be defined more clearly. Jane Samson, for instance, points to missionary discussions about the Pacific, where working class whites (notably escaped convicts) were blamed for corrupting islanders; missionaries, she argues, were influential in shaping the popular stereotype of the dissolute beachcomber.[12] Meanwhile, Catherine Hall's study of abolitionist writings about Jamaica explores how Evangelical philanthropists attempted to recreate whiteness and Christian bourgeois normality in terms of pity, care and compassion, in contrast to the depravity of plantation owners.[13] The outrages being observed were undoubtedly horrifying, and it should be noted that the Select Committee voiced a wide variety of concerns about global imperialism. Nonetheless, the emphasis on crimes committed by marginalised white figures could imply that Indigenous destruction was largely a result of the spread of criminal working class men beyond state and church authority. This could work to obscure the wider destructive implications of settler-colonialism itself.

---

*together with minutes of evidence, appendix and index*, Anthropology: Aborigines, vol 1, 1836: 15, 18, 21, 201, 204.
9   Saxe Bannister, evidence, 19 August 1835, *BPP: Report from the Select Committee on Aborigines (British Settlements)*, vol 1, 1836: 177–178; Acting Governor Irwin to Viscount Goderich, 10 April 1833, *BPP: Report from the Select Committee on Aborigines (British Settlements)*, vol 2, 1837: 135; Rev John Williams, evidence, *BPP: Report from the Select Committee on Aborigines (British Settlements)*, vol 1, 1836: 675.
10  Dandeson Coates, evidence, 6 June 1836, *BPP: Report from the Select Committee on Aborigines (British Settlements)*, vol 1, 1836: 486–489.
11  *BPP: Report from the Select Committee on Aborigines (British Settlements)*, vol 2, 1837: 10, 14–29.
12  Samson 1998: 9, 25–29.
13  Hall 1992: 211–213.

These limitations were also apparent in publications by the Aborigines Protection Society and missionary societies. In 1838, for instance, the APS and the *Colonial Church Record* expressed relief to hear that South Australia would take no convicts, believing 'fearful profligacy and ungodliness' would thus be avoided.

> Let us strive to make the settlement of Europeans on the shores of South Australia a blessing to all the native tribes ... a barrier to the enormous mischiefs which the worst part of the convict population of the eastern coast ... more ferocious than the Saracens or the Vandals of former days, may inflict upon the defenceless heathen ... South Australia may be the New England of the East.[14]

This relief served (perhaps inadvertently) to conceal local realities; in fact, South Australia's free settlers, protectors and more systematic land distribution proved no barrier against dispossession in the long term.[15] The implication of more respectable colonists in outrages was not completely ignored; in their 1839 annual report, the APS expressed deep concern about abuses of Indigenous people on Australia's southern coast by 'sealers, whalers, barkers, stockmen, and ... *men from whom a different line of conduct might have been expected.*'[16] However, these publications often implied that white cruelty was, or should be, peripheral to empire. The APS, for instance, accused the Oragon, Puget's Sound and Hudson Bay companies of exploiting First Nations people in North America and also failing to properly cultivate the earth. It was, the society commented, 'awfully sad and solemn to think that the pioneers of civilization – the *outriders* of the whites – are generally the most degraded of their race.'[17] This could make it difficult to acknowledge the wider violence of settler-colonialism itself.

If we shift focus to local missions and protectorates in the Australian colonies, however, a similar but more conflicted picture emerges. In the south-east, working class colonists, particularly those connected to the convict system, were often described by missionaries in vitriolic terms. This occurred most passionately at Wellington Valley, the site of an old convict station. JCS Handt described their white neighbours as the 'very scum of human society', James Günther called them 'an ungodly rotten set', and Watson labelled them 'emissaries of Satan'.[18] The threat of a convict influence was described frequently in terms of siege, attack or infection.

---

14 Colonial Church Society (CCS), *Colonial Church Record*, vol 1, no 3, October 1838: 45. Also, Aborigines Protection Society (APS), *First Annual Report, 16 May 1838*, (Monash Microfilm 4094 seg 2, item 30393): 24.
15 Brock 1995: 208, 214, 222.
16 APS, Second Annual Report, 21 May 1839: 7, APS, Transactions, c.1839–1909, MIC/o6550, reel 1 (Records the property of Anti-Slavery International).
17 APS, Third Annual Report, 23 June 1840, APS, Transactions, reel 1.
18 James Günther, journal, 8 July 1838, in Carey and Roberts (eds) 2002, *The Wellington Valley Project: Letters and Journals Relating to the Church Missionary Society Mission to Wellington Valley, NSW, 1830–42, A*

Here, it is useful to consider Joy Damousi's exploration of the role of gender in how Australian convict 'pollution' was imagined. She focuses on allegations of convict women's depravity and its threat to British identity and colonial respectability. She notes that while these women were compared to savages they were generally considered more threatening than Indigenous women, as convicts represented the enemy within, the possibility of British degeneration.[19] Elements of this thinking certainly emerged in some missionary writings. When Watson and Handt first travelled to Wellington Valley, they were offended when their wives were forced to ride in a dray with two convict women, who made 'loose and abusive' conversation.[20] Their colleague Günther was similarly disgusted when his convict servant got drunk in Bathurst, in the presence of Wiradjuri men sent from the mission to escort her. Such women were unwelcome in Günther's household. While he complained about having to do domestic chores when his wife, Lydia, was pregnant and unwell (a scenario that undermined his masculine missionary work, literally and symbolically), he nonetheless added that it would be 'preposterous' to accept another servant from the Bathurst factory – 'they are the outcasts of the outcasts.' He was particularly irritated when one convict woman told a Wiradjuri girl, whom Lydia Günther was training as a servant, not to fuss too much about the housework, scoffing 'Well, if that will not please Mrs G, let her do it herself.'[21] This notion that convict women were a disgrace to white femininity and an unruly force within the home was unsurprising, given missionaries' emphasis on how their free industrious families and pious wives represented the pinnacle of civilisation.

However, for the most part, it was not convict womanhood that most disturbed the missionaries. While Damousi has illustrated how convict women represented fears of pollution *within* white colonial society, a different set of issues emerges when the focus shifts to a racial frontier. For many missionaries, operating in rural districts with a predominantly male white population, it was convict men who threatened the most dire contamination – of Christianity, of Aboriginal people, and of empire. As Elizabeth Elbourne notes in her discussion of the Select Committee, the colonies were portrayed as:

> sites of peculiarly unchecked white male sin, indeed, of an almost exaggerated hyper-masculinity, as men indulged in unrestrained appetites to have sex, to exploit resources and to kill. Only Christian men stood between such undomesticated men and their female victims.[22]

---

*Critical Electronic Edition* [hereafter *WVP*]: <http://www.newcastle.edu.au>; JCS Handt, journal, 28 October 1834, *WVP*; William Watson, journal, 4 December 1832, *WVP*.
19  Damousi 1997. See especially 53–55.
20  Handt, journal, 23 August 1832, *WVP*; Watson, journal, 23 August 1832, *WVP*.
21  Günther, journal, 23 February 1838, 12 May 1838, *WVP*; James Günther to William Cowper, 19 May 1838, Church Missionary Society, Records [hereafter *CMS*], reel 40, AJCP M212, State Library of Victoria (SLV).
22  Elbourne 2003 (online through Project Muse).

The notion that convicts and other dubious colonial characters were a worse threat to civilisation than 'ignorant' Indigenous people was implied by protector William Thomas, when he wrote in his journal about travelling through Port Phillip in 1840 with two Woiwurrung men. He recalled, 'I slept soundly under a Gum tree with 2 armed savages about me, I am sorry to say with more apparent safety than with 2 of my own colour so arm'd.'[23] Anxiety about the convict presence was, however, most prevalent at Wellington Valley, where the missionaries complained that their white neighbours encouraged laziness, swearing, atheism and sexual depravity amongst Wiradjuri people. Günther remarked that he scarcely knew whether their black or white neighbours were more indifferent to Christianity.[24] The mission's own assigned servants caused the greatest distress, though, particularly when it emerged that they had had sex with Wiradjuri women and girls. Günther wrote in his journal in 1838 'The idea of convicts, these wretched characters on a Christian mission, is, I cannot forbear to say it, revolting to my mind.'[25] In tones of despair, he described being under moral attack:

> But alas! alas! it is not enough, that we are surrounded on all sides with neighbours that prove a snare to the Native females; we are obliged to have these shameless & voluptuous fellows on our very Establishment ... we have thus at once sowed the seed of destruction and have the enemy strength in the very heart of our Establishment.[26]

He implored the Church Missionary Society in 1841, 'Let us never again engage in a warfare, and have *knowingly* the Lord's enemies in the camp.'[27] Such comments also served as a veiled rebuke to the CMS for refusing to increase mission funding and provide the free, married and pious employees the missionaries had repeatedly requested.[28]

Philanthropic objections to convict transportation were not limited to criticisms of convicts themselves; they encompassed the whole system, sometimes with particular emphasis on how it degraded the powerful as well as the powerless. LE Threlkeld commented in his 1838 annual report that penal labour not only set bad examples to Indigenous people, it also degraded white society; 'the once kind, generous, English character, sinks into that of the merciless slaveholder'. He added that while convicts in isolated circumstances could perhaps be excused for seeking out relationships with Aboriginal women, there could be no excuse

---

23  William Thomas, journal, 4 August 1840, William Thomas, Papers, 1834–1868 [hereafter *WTP*], ML MSS 214, reel 1, State Library of NSW.
24  Günther, journal, 3 December 1837, *WVP*.
25  Günther, journal, 2 February 1838, *WVP*. See also Watson, journal, 10 August 1835, *WVP*.
26  Günther, journal, 23 April 1838, *WVP*.
27  James Günther to William Cowper, 18 June 1841, *CMS*, reel 40, AJCP M212, SLV.
28  For example, William Porter to William Cowper, 19 July 1841, *CMS*, reel 40, AJCP M212, SLV; Watson, journal, 6 September 1835, *WVP*.

for the 'White Gentlemen' who did the same thing.[29] Port Phillip chief protector GA Robinson also complained that some of the 'ruffians' who mistreated Indigenous people had learned their behaviour from 'men of education', whom, he believed, should have known better.[30] Such remarks played on expectations of degenerate convict behaviour to demonstrate how sin actually pervaded the whole colonial system.

Such concerns were, again, most prominent at Wellington Valley. Here, missionary correspondent Richard Taylor described to the Church Missionary Society his 1839 visit to the region, commenting with concern at the sinful behaviour of neighbouring Europeans and adding 'This description, I fear, too equally applies to the highest as well as the lowest – from the ruler to the ruled.'[31] The local missionaries often complained that white servants' relationships with Wiradjuri women were condoned by their employers. Watson, for instance, was horrified by the promiscuous mix of gender, class and race he witnessed in 1836, when he travelled to a neighbouring station to visit a female servant who was ill. He found her sharing a tiny hut with several people, including an Indigenous woman who lived with one of the white men. This man replied to Watson's rebukes by saying 'the master sees and knows, and if he allows it, nobody else has ought to do with it.'[32] Watson and Günther complained that virtually none of their neighbours – convicts, emancipated, overseers or masters – were fit to live in a Christian society.[33]

The laziness, viciousness or greed of some settlers of high standing may have been particularly irksome to missionaries and protectors, who were mostly men of lower middle class or artisan backgrounds hoping for upward mobility through their work. Threlkeld told the London Missionary Society's secretary George Burder and treasurer William Hankey in 1825 that he was disturbed that 'publick characters', who ought to take the lead in protecting Indigenous people, seemed indifferent to the racial violence around them.[34] Protector James Dredge was similarly distressed by stories from Daungwurrung people in 1839 about Mr Mundy's men murdering Aboriginal people. He wrote in his journal 'This is another instance of the savage barbarity of *"white Gentlemen"*.'[35]

---

29    LE Threlkeld, Annual Report, 31 December 1838, *WMMS*, reel 2, Mp2107, NLA.
30    GA Robinson 2001, '1848 Annual Report', in *The Papers of George Augustus Robinson, Chief Protector, Port Phillip Aboriginal Protectorate*, Clark (ed) vol 4: 155.
31    Richard Taylor to William Cowper, 6 February 1839, *BPP: Papers Relating to Australia, 1844*, Colonies: Australia, vol 8, 1969: 46.
32    Watson, journal, 12 May 1836, *WVP*. See also 16 September 1835.
33    Günther, journal, 23 April 1838, *WVP*; William Watson to William Jowett, 17 January 1837, *WVP*.
34    LE Threlkeld to G Burder and WA Hankey, 13 October 1825, in Niel Gunson (ed) 1974 vol 2: 187.
35    James Dredge, 8 December 1839, in James Dredge, Diaries, Notebook and Letterbooks, ?1817–1845 [hereafter *JDD*], MS11625, MSM534, SLV.

Perhaps the most provocative comments on class and racial violence came from the Methodist missionaries at Buntingdale in western district of Port Phillip during the early 1840s. While they made reference to the penal system, their comments also hinted at a white brutality that could not be contained easily within convict stereotypes. They voiced opposition to Governor Grey's plans to encourage South Australian settlers to hire Indigenous labourers, claiming bad influences would be unavoidable; the free status of these settlers was, apparently, not enough to allay their fears. Missionary Benjamin Hurst insisted that Indigenous people needed to be isolated from 'the body and soul destroying influence of our ungodly and avaricious fellow countrymen'.[36] He caused particular controversy when he publicly accused some of his neighbours of assaulting and murdering Indigenous people. Here, his class discourse seemed to cause almost as much offence as did the accusations themselves. In 1840–41, Hurst informed the Wesleyan Methodist Missionary Society and Port Phillip superintendent CJ La Trobe that local colonists were undermining the mission. He added that while many of the culprits were servants and labourers ('the refuse of the Van Diemen's Land prison population'), this was not always the case. Some settlers, 'who would deem it an insult to be classed with shepherds and hut keepers', pursued Indigenous women just as outrageously. Offended by this, the local police magistrate, J Blair, assured La Trobe that the district was no longer populated by convict types, but rather by recent emigrants – 'gentlemen of education and family' and respectable labourers. La Trobe agreed, adding that while 'older hands' might have once committed disgraceful crimes, the recent arrival of gentlemen and a better class of servants guaranteed a more peaceful, law-abiding future. Hurst found himself socially ostracised, and left the district soon afterwards.[37]

Few missionaries or protectors took their concerns as far, or as publicly, as Hurst did, and their complaints about colonists did not necessarily discourage them from supporting further immigration. Here, the emphasis was on making white society more respectable, with occasional mentions of positive side effects for Indigenous people. Günther, longing for more useful and obedient servants, commented 'Oh! what an acquisition a few pious people of the labouring class would be!'[38] Dredge, lamenting the sinful climate of New South Wales in 1838, hoped that convicts would soon be replaced by free settlers; 'Emigration is

---

36  Benjamin Hurst to Rev John McKenny, 8 March 1842, *WMMS*, reel 2, Mp2107. Also, Francis Tuckfield to General Secretaries, 30 October 1841, *WMMS*, reel 2, Mp2107, NLA.
37  J Blair to CJ La Trobe, 15 January 1842, *BPP: Papers Relating to Australia, 1844*, vol 8: 185, 191; Benjamin Hurst to General Secretaries, 22 September 1840, *WMMS*, reel 2, Mp2107, NLA; Benjamin Hurst to CJ La Trobe, 22 July 1841, Methodist Missionary Society, Records [hereafter *MMS*], reel 4, AJCP M121, SLV; CJ La Trobe to Colonial Secretary, 19 February 1842, *BPP: Papers Relating to Australia, 1844*, vol 8: 204; Francis Tuckfield to General Secretaries, 16 August 1842, *WMMS*, reel 2, Mp2107; Benjamin Hurst to General Secretaries, 8 July 1843, *WMMS*, reel 2, Mp2107, NLA.
38  Günther, journal, 2 February 1838, *WVP*.

pouring a steady and increasing stream of comparative purity into the stagnant pool of Australian society'.[39] Chief protector GA Robinson even went so far as to tell the 1845 Select Committee on the Condition of the Aborigines, that Indigenous people's circumstances were improving in Port Phillip, partly because of the increase in free migrants and 'respectable proprietors'.[40] (Robinson's wish to maintain his own beleaguered protectorate was relevant here, but his reasoning is illustrative nonetheless.) Such remarks can seem startling, given philanthropists' awareness of the devastating impact of dispossession. They did not discuss immigration very often, so it can be difficult to judge, but these occasional statements of support do follow a certain logic of encouraging the growth of an empire structured around an Evangelical middle class and strengthened and justified by missionary work.

These issues would become more glaring in British publications, which expressed stronger, more articulate support for free migration to Australia. The *Evangelical Magazine* (1835–36) looked forward to the settlement of South Australia by a young population of equal gender demographic and agricultural interests, hoping this would provide a fresh start for British artisans and rural labourers – 'our peasants, once so distinguished for a spirit of manly independence.' The greater church influence and 'kind and Christian procedure' assumed to accompany this would, they believed, improve Indigenous people's circumstances.[41] Similarly, an 1841 article in the Aborigines Protection Society journal, by an auxiliary of the British and Foreign Society for the Protection of the Aborigines, blamed convicts for the destruction of the Tasmanian Indigenous peoples, but concluded that future problems could best be avoided by providing moral training for emigrants before they left Britain.[42]

Church of England journals particularly praised respectable emigration to Australia around the middle of the century (a time when the first Aboriginal missions and protectorates were collapsing). *The Colonial Church Chronicle* for 1848–50 mentioned Indigenous Australians only rarely and without much optimism. More attention was given to further colonisation, and the hope of seeing *'our noble England spread her roots*, and multiply her branches, till she shall have covered all the isles of the East.' The journal argued that free emigration could solve New South Wales's labour shortage and spare Britain the expense of supporting able-bodied paupers. Respectable rural labourers could be attracted with promises of becoming land-owners themselves, as 'fresh tracts of fertile

---

39  James Dredge to [unnamed correspondent], 28 November 1838, *WMMS*, reel 1, Mp2107, NLA.
40  GA Robinson, Report to the Select Committee on the Condition of the Aborigines, 1845, in Frauenfelder (ed) 1997: 51.
41  *Evangelical Magazine and Missionary Chronicle*, vol XIII, December 1835: 503; *Evangelical Magazine and Missionary Chronicle*, vol XIV, February 1836: 51–52.
42  APS, *Extracts from the Papers and Proceedings of the Aborigines' Protection Society*, vol II–III, April 1841: 91.

land are continually being discovered'. The fate of the people already living there was not mentioned.⁴³ This location of violence and sin on the margins of colonial society, amongst early criminal arrivals now being displaced, enabled Aboriginal dispossession (or at least, its worst excesses) to appear anomalous, not intrinsic to settler-colonialism.

## 'Men, and Englishmen, and ministers of Christ': complexities of mission and nation

During this era, Christian missions and imperial nationalism had become powerfully, if problematically, linked. As noted earlier, missionaries were amongst the empire's fiercest critics, but they could also be outriders of empire, helping form spheres of British influence. Anna Johnston depicts missionary work and writing as central to the imagining and legitimising of British colonialism, while Susan Thorne has argued that the half-century between 1795–1845 saw middle class Dissenters move from the margins of British politics and society to the centre – 'The missionary project helped to associate the Dissenting middle classes with the nation and the nation, in turn, with evangelical middle classes, in the eyes of British society and of the world at large.'⁴⁴ At the same time, the mission project could address fear and guilt on a national scale; Elizabeth Elbourne sees the 1835–37 Select Committee on Aborigines (British Settlements) as directly concerned with relationships between nation and God.⁴⁵ All of this affected how philanthropic advocates came to understand morality and destruction within colonialism.

Some missionary publications made clear that their work was understood within an imperial framework. At a London Missionary Society valedictory service in 1837, speakers expressed thanks for the support received from all classes of 'British society' and from 'the Parliament of England ... the public of England ... the Colonial Secretary of England'. South Australia, with its promise of respectable settlers and Aboriginal protectors, was praised as a burgeoning colony 'of which a Queen of England need not be ashamed'. Missionaries were reminded to do their duty as 'men, and Englishmen, and ministers of Christ'.⁴⁶ At the LMS's 1839 annual meeting, the chair, Sir Culling Eardly Smith, spoke of the refuge of faith amidst political woes. He added, however, 'Not that man by becoming a Christian parts company with his patriotism – his patriotism becomes enlightened, sanctified, and increased.'⁴⁷ However, the strongest

---

43   CMS, *The Colonial Church Chronicle, and Missionary Journal*, vol II, July 1848: 3–6. See also, CMS, *The Colonial Church Chronicle, and Missionary Journal*, vol III, July 1849 – June 1850: 49–50, 278, 292–295, 425–426.
44   Johnston 2003a: 3, 13; Thorne 1999: 52.
45   Elbourne 2003.
46   LMS, *The Missionary Magazine and Chronicle*, vol 1, no xviii, November 1837: 285.
47   LMS, *The Missionary Magazine and Chronicle*, vol 1, no xxxvii, June 1839: 83.

imperial nationalist sentiments were promoted by Church of England bodies. The CMS *Church Missionary Intelligencer* (1850) contrasted Britain's Christian crusade with the failures of other European empires: degeneracy, apathy, Catholicism. The article concluded 'the living, earnest, expansive Christian, who has a heart big enough to embrace the whole world, is the only true patriot'. An accompanying article argued that England's internal stability was a sign of their special duty to evangelise: 'If our own age is the era for missions, no less plainly is our own country the messenger-people to the whole earth. The Heathen cry, and they cry to us – to Englishmen of the nineteenth century.'[48]

Yet, perhaps curiously, nationality as a topic did not receive much explicit attention in philanthropic writings from the Australian colonies. The emergence of Australian settler identities during this period (generally coexisting with British loyalties) has been traced by historians like Alan Atkinson, Richard White, Neville Meaney and Ben Wellings.[49] However, if missionaries and protectors witnessed such developments they made no reference to them, and their papers contained few overt discussions of British or English nationalities either. Britishness may have been crucial in relation to governance and subjecthood, but it was largely obscured in the realms of identity and society.

There might well have been strategic reasons for a certain vanishing of Britishness, given the mixed cultural backgrounds of missionaries themselves. Paul Jenkins, for example, has noted that by 1824 over a third of the missionaries sent overseas by the Church Missionary Society were from other European countries, mostly German-speaking regions.[50] This was apparent in the Australian colonies; the CMS station at Wellington Valley, for instance, employed JCS Handt, originally a Prussian Lutheran, and James Günther, who was from Würtemburg, educated at the Basel Mission Institute. Meanwhile, in South Australia, Lutheran missionaries operated in Adelaide, Port Lincoln and Encounter Bay, and the Moreton Bay station was run by missionaries trained within the Bohemian church and organised by Johannes Gossner. Their German backgrounds, while distinguishing them socially, do not seem to have provoked much discussion or criticism, aside from occasional mutterings by the acerbic William Watson about the CMS favouring his 'German Lutheran' colleagues at Wellington Valley.[51] In a missionary climate reliant on labourers from across Europe, it could be useful to encourage a certain downplaying of nationality within overarching Protestant civilisation.

---

48  CMS, *The Church Missionary Intelligencer*, vol I, no 3, 1849 (volume published 1850): 51–52; CMS, *The Church Missionary Intelligencer*, vol I, no 4, 1849 (volume published 1850): 77.
49  Atkinson 1988: 10–15; Meaney 2001: 81, 83; Wellings 2004: 149; White 1981: 52–56.
50  Jenkins 2000: 43–50.
51  William Watson to William Jowett, 12 September 1842, *WVP*. See also Bridges 1978: 454–455; Johannes Gossner to W Beecham, 27 January 1837, *MMS*, reel 9, AJCP M126, SLV; Le Couteur 1998: 141, 143.

At the same time, Britishness could be imagined in terms of an expansive, imperial subjecthood, associated so closely with 'civilisation' itself that there was little need to differentiate between the two. By the late 1840s, writers for the Aborigines Protection Society and the Church Missionary Society were reminiscing (albeit with some ambivalence) about the glory of the Roman empire and its lessons for Britain. Highlighted was the Roman policy of sharing civilisation and incorporating colonised peoples as loyal subjects.[52] Thus, in missionary writings, Britishness was associated most powerfully with what Krishan Kumar has called 'state-bearing' peoples, who embraced an imperial or 'missionary' nationalism, subsuming their identity in their 'two empires': Great Britain at home and the colonies abroad.[53] Within such imperial and state-based nationalism, philanthropists could demand that colonised peoples be recognised as British subjects, while still insisting that 'civilisation' (and the full social inclusion that went with it) would have to be taught and worked towards.

Visions of expansive Britishness could be both potent and problematic. This was hinted at when Lake Macquarie missionary LE Threlkeld turned Britannic people into subjects of cultural critique. During the late 1820s, Threlkeld urged the London Missionary Society not to underestimate Indigenous Australians' capacity for Christian progress, reminding them that the English themselves were descended from bloodthirsty, primitive pagans. People who remembered the British resistance to Roman occupation admiringly might, he said, have felt a similar respect for Aboriginal resistance, had it only been militarily stronger. Again, in 1838, he encouraged the New South Wales government not to despair of Aboriginal prospects; after all, the Romans had once thought the Britons too savage to improve – 'Such was the character of our forefathers, the White Aborigines, given by her darker colored conquerors.'[54] In his 1850 publication, *A Key to the Structure of the Aboriginal Language*, Threlkeld told his readers once more that the nudity and traditional dancing of the Awabakal people were probably similar to the customs of ancient British tribes.[55] Related imagery was used by protector William Thomas, when he first arrived in Port Phillip. He reflected in his journal on his early meetings with Kulin peoples:

> As they descended the hill with their spears, &c, I have gazed upon them and thought of what materials our forefathers were. Oh that God

---

52  Aborigines Protection Society (APS), *Annual Report*, 3 May 1848: 16, APS, Transactions, reel 1; CMS, *The Church Missionary Intelligencer: A Monthly Journal of Missionary Information*, vol I, no 3, 1849: 51–52.
53  Kumar 2003: xi, 31–37, 179, 186, 193.
54  LE Threlkeld, London Missionary Society, Mission to the Aborigines, New South Wales: Circular, 8 October 1828, London Missionary Society Records (*LMS*), AJCP M73, SLV; LE Threlkeld to E Deas Thomson, Annual Report, 31 December 1838, in Gunson (ed) 1974 vol 1: 149.
55  LE Threlkeld, 'A Key to the Structure of the Aboriginal Language', reproduced in LE Threlkeld 1892, *An Australian Language As Spoken by the Awabakal, the People of Awaba or Lake Macquarie*: 88–89.

who called our ancestors from their wild state would look down on these and make us who are sent for the purpose of civilizing them the honoured instruments.[56]

Such comments presented a challenge to colonial racism and a call to universal humanity, and they may have destabilised somewhat the 'normal' order of imperial dominance. (Duncan Bell, for example, has argued that references to ancient Rome in Victorian discourse were marked by anxiety as much as by identification, with strong awareness of Rome's decline and fall.)[57] However, philanthropists' emphasis on the power of civilisation to elevate barbarians served to highlight, not minimise, the alleged differences between Indigenous people and British imperialists. The emphasis was less on challenging binaries of 'savagery' and 'civilisation' and more on emphasising the possibility of moving between them. Moreover, another contrast was also reinforced: between visible, ethnic 'Others' and rational, civilised observers, as represented by Threlkeld and Thomas. Here, civilisation – which the British were shown to have attained – was associated with an authoritative invisibility, a power to look and define.

The possibilities and limitations of inclusive Britishness were also suggested in formal missionary publications, where comparisons were made between colonised peoples and 'inferior' whites. A striking example occurred in the Aborigines' Protection Society's journal *Colonial Intelligencer* (1849–50), which contrasted the advance of the North American Seneca people in farming, building houses, educating their children and giving up alcohol, with the supposed filth and laziness of Irish peasants, whose poverty was blamed on their own savagery. At the same time, mention was made of the achievements of Irish intellectuals; if this race could produce superior specimens, surely indigenous races could do likewise. The same edition highlighted the violent ambitions and degraded habits of other European nations, who had abandoned true Protestantism, as well as the supposedly contemptible state of the urban poor.

> Which would appear the most hopeless task – to endeavour to educate and refine the Indian and the New Zealander, or to induce those dissolute inhabitants of the crowded courts of our large towns to abandon their habits of idleness, filth, and immorality, for those of the respectable and rising mechanic?[58]

Such claims promoted imperial missionary work by combining a message of universal human potential with the strategic use of tropes of Irish and working-

---

56 William Thomas, January to March 1839 journal, in Cannon (ed) 1983, *Historical Records of Victoria: Aborigines and Protectors, 1838–1839 (HRV)*, vol 2B: 438.
57 Bell 2007: 207–230.
58 APS, *The Colonial Intelligencer, or Aborigines' Friend*, vol II, 1849–50: 131; APS, *Transactions*, reel 3. Also: 70, 133.

class hopelessness and Continental degeneracy. On one level, the journal did minimise racial difference, but challenges to inequality were limited here. The assumed superiority of dominant British classes went unquestioned, and the suggestions of racial equality focused deliberately on Indians and Maori, as supposedly higher races.

The ongoing notion of hierarchies of civilisation was apparent in records from the Australian colonies, when philanthropists tried to educate Indigenous people about other colonised nations, allegedly further advanced in Christianity. Maori were held up as a particular example. Protector William Thomas mentioned the 'New Zealand Blacks' in his sermons to Kulin peoples in Port Phillip, and Maori were also discussed at Wellington Valley. Watson and Günther were glad that some Wiradjuri men had met Maori people in Sydney, hoping these more 'advanced' natives would serve as role models. In their sermons, they described how Maori prayed and learned to read.[59] This indicates how missionary 'knowledge' was not merely broadcast from a central British metropole, but rather passed around the empire, mingling with local needs. In 1838, for instance, missionary James Günther went out cutting bark with a group of young men from Wellington Valley and read aloud to them from *Campbell's Travels in the South of Africa*. He especially pointed to 'the Blacks of that country being much better than themselves, more attentive to the missionaries etc etc and exhorted them by their example.'[60]

## 'Black fellow won't believe you': vision, struggle and legitimacy

Debates over class, gender and nationality pointed to a discursive contest over who would have the power to envisage and define the colonial future. Within such debates, Indigenous people's own views on nationality were mentioned only occasionally. The London Missionary Society published with relish speeches made at Exeter Hall by African converts, who spoke of their eagerness to become British subjects and 'children of England'. These speeches – no doubt strategic or edited performances of Christian civilisation – helped create precisely the image Evangelical philanthropists sought, one which defined them as 'real' Britons, in contrast to thuggish, racist colonists. It particularly bolstered missionary aims to reshape colonialism in the Cape colony. The 'Caffre Chief Tzatzoe' commented 'Many Englishmen in the colonies are bad, but I will hardly believe that these Englishmen belong to you. You are a different race of men – they are South Africans – they are not Englishmen.'[61]

---

59  See, William Thomas, 7 July 1844, *WTP*, ML MSS 214, reel 3, State Library of NSW; Watson, journal, 29 December 1833, 26 April 1834, 9 January 1835, *WVP*.
60  Günther, journal, 17 August 1838, *WVP*.
61  LMS, *The Missionary Magazine and Chronicle*, no IV, September 1836: 56.

However, Indigenous Australians' opinions on Britishness do not seem to have been eagerly sought or recorded. On one rare occasion in 1834 when Britishness was discussed, the emphasis was on the visible ethnicity of other nations, in relation to the imperial state. A young Wiradjuri girl, Geanil, had asked missionary William Watson about the backgrounds of settlers in Wellington Valley.

> Geanil: Who is that white master, Mr Watson, is he an Englishman?
>
> Mr W: No.
>
> Geanil: O. He is an Irishman then?
>
> Mr W: No. He is a Scotchman. He comes from another country, but is also belongs to my King.
>
> Geanil: All about master belong to your King, King William.[62]

When this dialogue was reproduced in the CMS *Missionary Register* it was altered slightly. 'White master' became 'Gentleman', the neighbour became a 'Scotch Gentleman', the question of Scottish sovereignty was raised by Geanil, and Geanil's last remark became 'all white masters belong to your King'.[63] These alterations may have been innocuous, intended to make the conversation flow better, but the result was a slightly greater impression of settler respectability and Wiradjuri interest in the reach of empire.

Elsewhere in missionaries' records, there are traces of how their representations of different national groups could be reinterpreted, utilised or challenged by Indigenous people. Wiradjuri people, for instance, used understandings of the 'superior' Maori to strengthen their own demands and point out missionary weaknesses. When requesting guns for hunting, the young men reminded Günther: 'New Zealand from Black fellows got guns'. Günther's response emphasised the superiority of Evangelical civilisation, while also suggesting unease at the spread of imperialism in unruly, secular forms:

> Yes … I will tell you what they say: 'We were very glad when English men came, & brought us guns & brought us shooting; but we were still more glad when you, Missionaries came & taught us to read'.[64]

---

62   Watson, journal, 2 September 1834, *WVP*.
63   CMS, *Missionary Register*, September 1836: 427.
64   Günther, journal, 28 June 1838, *WVP*.

Such explanations were not necessarily accepted. The young man Jemmy Buckley laughed at Günther's lectures about how lazy and ungrateful Aborigines were compared to the New Zealanders, retorting 'Very well, go to New Zealand; there are the good Natives!'[65]

The visibility of Britishness to Indigenous people could be a point of some concern to missionaries, when they found themselves unable to control how it appeared. This was hinted at in 1840, when young Daungwurrung men questioned Port Phillip protector James Dredge about his origins. His account of their conversation about England was marked by a mixture of vibrant imagery and fear that the Christian nature of his mission would be obscured by the material details of civilisation.

> When I informed them of the great distance [from England], that we were 5 moons without seeing anything but water, that we were sent on purpose to take care of them, they were amazed, as they were also at hearing about the English people, ships, soldiers &c. *Poor things*, I wish I could describe to them the great things their God and Saviour hath done to redeem them.[66]

However, philanthropists soon came to fear that worse images of British civilisation were developing, thanks to the behaviour of other colonists, whose sins undermined Evangelical authority. From their first arrival at Wellington Valley, William Watson and JCS Handt found themselves engaged in contests over the nature of colonial power, marked by intertwining of race and class, the ever-present threat of violence and loss, and the question of whose vision of the future was dominant and legitimate. Local settlers and stockmen – whom Watson called 'agents of Satan' – had told Wiradjuri people to stay away from the mission, warning that their children would be kidnapped and sent to gaol in Sydney, while the men would have to work in the fields, yoked like bullocks. These accusations were repeated again years later. When a young woman, Warrahbin, chose to live at the mission instead of with neighbouring white men, her husband, Narrang Jackey, was told that the missionaries would send all the women away to prison, then transport them to another country. Such claims emerged again when Watson, urging Wiradjuri to compare themselves to 'higher' nations, spoke of his longing to take people to New Zealand to meet the Maori. However, he believed – and they concurred – that they would think he was kidnapping them.[67] Similar concerns were also voiced in Melbourne, when Indigenous women hesitated to send their children to William Thomas's protectorate school, as white men had told them the children would be abducted

---

65   Günther, journal, 15 March 1838, *WVP*.
66   Dredge, 27 January 1840, *JDD*, MS11625, MSM534, SLV.
67   Handt, journal, 30 September, 1832, *WVP*; Watson, journal, 30 September 1832, 8 October 1833, 9 January 1835, *WVP*; William Watson, 1832 Report, *WVP*.

onto ships and sent away to Sydney.⁶⁸ Philanthropists were angry at being misrepresented, their authority challenged, but their offence may have also been related to the discourse in which they found themselves implicated. The colonists involved may have been thinking of many things, including African slavery, the earlier removal of Indigenous children to the Parramatta school, and the transportation of 'savage' peoples to Britain for public display. Yet, they were also threatening Indigenous people with what had been, essentially, their own convict experience – an experience missionaries found distasteful and antithetical to their plans for Aboriginal advancement. Ironically, over subsequent decades, as former convicts began to prosper and redefine themselves positively as 'native born', their threats would indeed come to shape Indigenous life: incarceration, forced labour, child removal, exile from home. These elements would be alternately opposed and supported by protectors and missionaries.

In imagining future roles for Indigenous people as labourers, philanthropists voiced concerns about the current structure of colonial society, including the penal system and Indigenous people's own capacity to view and interpret the class structure. As Henry Reynolds has observed, philanthropists (at least in the south-east) longed to reshape Aboriginal Australians as respectable workers, whilst at the same time separating them from the actual white working classes.⁶⁹ In 1841, for instance, Port Phillip protector James Dredge complained of Indigenous people associating with prisoners and learning their bad behaviour. He attributed this not to Indigenous naivety, but rather to their acute awareness of class distinction; they took liberties with prisoners, he said, that they would not have done elsewhere.⁷⁰ Philanthropists worried especially that the convict system, where the labourers lacked freedom or respectability, would make labouring life unappealing to Indigenous people. Quaker missionary writers James Backhouse and George Walker commented on their 1832 visit to Flinders Island that the people there appreciated gifts of European clothing but resented any offer of convict-style garments.⁷¹ Missionary CG Tiechelmann noted that Indigenous people in South Australia valued their independence and would only work for Europeans if they could relate to them as kinsmen; being an employee was considered degrading.⁷² Meanwhile, at Wellington Valley in 1836, Watson was annoyed when a man called Kabbarrin refused to wear a jacket Watson had bought him, saying it made him look like 'new chum', a newly assigned servant.⁷³ Such exchanges could signify rejection not only of labouring roles but also of the dynamic of charitable benevolence and gratitude which

---

68   Thomas, 27 January 1846, *WTP*, ML MSS 214, reel 3, State Library of NSW.
69   Reynolds 1983: 129–130.
70   James Dredge to Jabez Bunting, 10 May 1841, *MMS*, reel 55, AJCP M172, SLV.
71   Walker 1898: 9.
72   CG Tiechelmann 1841, *The Aborigines of South Australia*: 6.
73   Watson, journal, 19 June 1836, *WVP*.

missionaries hoped to establish. Günther's journal recorded a similar incident in 1838, when a group of Wiradjuri men went out to cut wood in the rain, wearing coarse gabardine frocks which the missionaries had lent them. These resembled convict clothing, and the young man Jemmy (Goongeen) joked 'Here they are, all Government men'. Günther realised he was making a point to the missionaries, 'for they do not like at all, to wear the dress of prisoners & often call out with great stress, "We are free men!"'[74]

Once again, philanthropists' concerns touched on issues of higher class status, as well as lower. Handt recorded an incident in 1835, when he visited a camp and tried to talk to people about God. His efforts were rejected, particularly by three men who wore brass name plates and said that they were gentlemen. Handt wrote 'I took occasion from this to talk to them of the pride of the human heart, and of that Great Being, who loves one as well as the other, and with whom there is no respect of persons.'[75] Protector GA Robinson was similarly perturbed to meet some influential men on Mr Docker's station near the Murray, who accepted rations as their due but refused to undertake manual work, telling Robinson they were gentlemen, and 'white gentlemen did not work only poor fellow.' Robinson, himself an upwardly-mobile working class man, blamed colonists for encouraging such ideas, grumbling in his diary that drinking, smoking, swearing and debts were the main signs of a colonial gentleman.[76]

At stake here were issues of colonial authority and identity. In their sinful behaviour, colonists were seen by missionaries as making whiteness hyper-visible and deeply problematic (in contrast to the philanthropists' own whiteness, which was normalised and in many ways obscured). Günther, for instance, found it hard to respond when Wiradjuri men replied to missionary reprimands about sexual depravity by asking 'Why don't you talk that way to White fellas?'[77] His colleague Watson recorded a similar argument with a man called Frederick in 1837. Frederick dismissed Watson's lectures on sin and swearing by saying:

> Black fellow won't believe you ... White fellow too swear when he wants Black woman and she won't go with him, he too say never mind parson and swears again, and says bad things of you, I cannot tell you what he says but I dare say you know.[78]

Here, colonists' behaviour was especially unwelcome because it drew attention to the contested, vulnerable nature of philanthropists' authority. Port Phillip

---

74  Watson, journal, 26 March 1838, *WVP*.
75  Handt, journal, 19 July 1835, *WVP*.
76  GA Robinson 1998, *Journals: Port Phillip Aboriginal Protectorate*, Clark (ed) vol 2: 75.
77  Günther, journal, 14 March 1838, *WVP*.
78  Watson, journal, 8 January 1837, *WVP*.

protectors James Dredge, William Thomas and GA Robinson all complained of white men mocking them in front of Indigenous people. Robinson was particularly irked when working class men, hanging around an Indigenous camp near Melbourne, reminded people loudly of his controversial actions in Tasmania, where he had persuaded many Indigenous survivors to withdraw from the mainland to government stations in Bass Strait. These men taunted him 'Are you going to drive the poor creatures away here Mr Robinson as you did in Van Diemen's Land?'[79]

The frustration and anger philanthropists felt here can be understood partly in terms of arguments by contemporary scholars of 'whiteness' about the need for white power to be rendered implicit and impartial. Dyer, for example, argues that the invisibility of whiteness is both an expression and mechanism of power, demonstrating the positioning of whiteness as 'real' humanity: 'Whites must be seen to be white, yet whiteness as race resides in invisible properties and whiteness as power is maintained by being unseen.'[80] Aileen Moreton-Robinson has emphasised the particular importance of this 'invisible regime of power' to Australian life.[81] It can be a challenge, though, to relate such ideas to the early colonies, where racial difference was powerfully and violently enforced but not always articulated in sophisticated ways. Liz Reed has considered how protector William Thomas's accounts of isolation and danger served to construct his own image as Aboriginal 'expert', protecting whiteness from inferior Europeans; this argument is a valuable one, but I would question to what extent 'whiteness' as a trope is appropriate to this era.[82] The broader questions raised about the stability and visibility of colonial power are certainly relevant, though. In such accounts, philanthropists revealed points of weakness and frustration in their own authority, but they also worked to reinforce common Evangelical concerns about class and colonialism; in their papers, anxiety and affirmation co-existed. Imperial authority may have been unstable, but it was also well worth fighting over.

The images philanthropists produced of themselves often emphasised their isolation, struggle and vulnerability in the face of massive immorality. Watson, for example, used his journal to lament his loneliness and feeling of being unappreciated. He wrote in 1836 of:

> Having left behind our beloved native land ... to wander, solitary and forsaken ... to be hated by many, loved by none ... to dwell where Satan

---

79 Dredge, 17 December 1839, *JDD*, MS11625, MSM534, SLV; Robinson 1998, *Journals: Port Phillip Aboriginal Protectorate*, Clark (ed) vol 1: 27; William Thomas to CJ La Trobe, 13 April 1840, f67–71, *WTP*, ML MSS 214, reel 4, State Library of NSW.
80 Dyer 1997: 45, see also 1–4, 12–13, 18–20, 35, 45, 52–53.
81 Moreton-Robinson 2004: 75–76, 79.
82 Reed 2004: 88–89, 94, 98.

has his seat — to see in every human face an enemy to our God and his cause ... to labour amongst the very lowest heathens in the world, and to have impediments to our usefulness thrown in our way at every step by men of our own country — bearing the same hallowed name as ourselves.[83]

This image of the philanthropist as outsider has re-appeared, at times, in Australian Aboriginal historiography. Reynolds, for instance, has depicted humanitarians as lonesome figures, considered traitors by their white neighbours, their work bringing the colonial venture into question: 'The Aboriginal cause often did attract outsiders, eccentrics, obsessive personalities ... They came to hate their own society for its unfeeling brutality. Resulting isolation fed further embitterment.'[84] Some other historians have questioned this; Kociumbas, for example, warns that the romanticising of rebels in Australian story-telling (including, ironically, convict history), has carried over into contemporary representations of missionary humanitarians — 'constituted as stirring heroes of this period, courageous campaigners for justice and Aboriginal land rights ... virtually latter-day Ned Kellys, fearless rebels who dared to defy the colonial *status quo*.'[85] While this point has some validity, I would argue that the historiography surrounding Australian missions has been more complex than this. I would also stress that such images of vain-glorious humanitarians are not merely a product of recent scholarship, but can be traced in many ways back to philanthropists' own writings. It is a challenge for historians to examine such matters without obscuring the very real destruction and dispossession that philanthropists were witnessing. Here, it can be valuable to consider further the place of grief, loss and religious struggle in philanthropists' lives. It is also important to encourage ongoing examination of Australia's place within international religious debates surrounding British imperialism. The sense of victimisation philanthropists articulated in the Australian colonies fit into wider Evangelical discourse, but it must also have been influenced by their own relatively minor place within missionary and philanthropic cultures, where, once again, Australian Indigenous issues tended to be relegated to the boundaries.

The troubled tone taken by many philanthropists was genuinely felt, but this was also a productive anxiety, a source of definition and debate. The records of Australia's first missions and protectorates have often been valued for their quasi-anthropological descriptions of Indigenous cultures and languages, but their passionate views about their own society could be, in some ways, more revealing. Their writings bring to light images of a degenerate colonial society,

---

83    Watson, journal, 31 December 1836, *WVP*.
84    Reynolds 1998: xiv, also 11–12.
85    Kociumbas 2001: 35–36.

where whiteness was both vaguely defined and vitally influential, intertwined with disputes over class and power. Philanthropists' attempts to implement Evangelical leadership – where Britishness was equated with civilisation but also strategically obscured, and where efforts to incorporate native peoples as British subjects were significant but partial – point to the complex relationship between empire, nation and the civilising mission. Within this, philanthropists may well have wished to render their authority natural and invisible, but they were also required to demonstrate British civilisation to Indigenous viewers, counter the behaviour of other colonists, and respond to Indigenous critiques of this. These mixed demands on philanthropists led to a mingled sense of weakness and a drive for authority. This helps explain the sense of thwarted longing expressed by James Günther, who wished to make his mission 'a city on a hill, in this dreary wilderness, among a savage tribe, and in the midst of a perverse generation of professing Christians'.[86]

---

86  Günther, journal, 23 April 1838, *WVP*.

# 'Our country all gone': rights, charity and the loss of land

> Within these boundaries of their *own country*, as they proudly speak, they feel a degree of security and pleasure which they can find nowhere else – here their forefathers lived and roamed and hunted, and here also their ashes rest. And this is the scene of their fondest and earliest recollections ... with every nook they are familiar, they know just where their favourite roots are most abundant, the haunts of the Kangaroo, Emu and Opossum – in short, it is their home.[1]

So wrote Port Phillip assistant protector James Dredge in June 1842, describing in his diary the material, personal and historical attachment to country he saw amongst the Daungwurrung people of northern Victoria. Dredge's spell with the Port Phillip protectorate had been brief, passionate and ultimately disappointing. Arriving in New South Wales in 1838, in time to witness the public furore over the trials of the Myall Creek murderers, he had few illusions about the impact of colonialism on Indigenous peoples. By the time of writing, he had left his station in the Goulburn River district after an acrimonious resignation from the protectorate, and was continuing to lobby on Aboriginal policy from Melbourne, where he ran a china shop and applied for work as a missionary. In his journals and letters, issues of traditional land ownership and its destruction emerge as fundamental. In 1840 he explained to a missionary colleague 'each Tribe has its own district the extent and boundaries of which are well known to themselves, and they speak of their country to a stranger with emotions of pride.'[2] Indigenous territories were, he said, 'amongst themselves well understood and sacredly recognised from one generation to another.'[3] He had been disturbed, upon his arrival in Melbourne, to observe the precarious situation of people camped 'on that part of the territory of their fathers' about to be turned into city streets.[4] At the same time, however, Dredge described Daungwurrung as 'wandering savages' and usually refused to travel with them. He urged that reserves be established for each community on lands acceptable to them, but also advocated use of (unspecified) 'restraints' to stop them leaving

---

1  James Dredge, 6 June 1842, James Dredge, Diaries, Notebook and Letterbooks, ?1817–1845 [hereafter *JDD*], MS11625, MSM534, State Library of Victoria (SLV).
2  James Dredge to Rev D Harding, 12 September 1840, *JDD*, MS11625, MSM534, SLV.
3  Dredge, 6 June 1842, *JDD*, MS11625, MSM534, SLV.
4  James Dredge to Jabez Bunting, 20 April 1839, in Methodist Missionary Society, Records [hereafter *MMS*], reel 55, AJCP 172, SLV.

their designated country.⁵ His records bring the reader up against some of the conflicts and complexities that developed when philanthropists encountered Indigenous land ownership and dispossession.

The writings of these missionaries and protectors, as well as broader philanthropic publications produced in Britain at the time, offer insights into particular ways of thinking about land in early colonial Australia, which ultimately waned or failed. These included an acknowledgement of Indigenous entitlements to land, a prioritising of free agriculture over pastoralism with convict labour, and an attachment to imperial authority and the Crown's ability to control and distribute land. Through these accounts emerge alternative, largely unrealised visions of Australian colonisation. Considering debates over Indigenous land during the first half of the 19th century also forces the reader to look more closely at the intellectual lineage of white support for land rights. This includes the troubled relationship between rights and charity, the mixed place of Aboriginal voices within these discussions, the ways that Indigenous 'compensation' was tied to Christian agricultural instruction – funded through the very proceeds of dispossession itself – and the way philanthropists' discourse on land changed between their personal and political writings and more generalised publications. Through an emphasis on local records, this chapter contributes to an ongoing conversation about how entitlements to land were understood.

## 'Country belonging to me': land ownership and dispossession

The loss of Indigenous land and resources through the rapid spread of colonialism emerged as an urgent issue in philanthropic records. While much of this 'settlement' occurred beyond legal boundaries, it was not strongly opposed by government. In South Australia, for example, the *South Australia Colonisation Act*, 1834 proclaiming British control over the region declared all the land 'waste and unoccupied'. Governor Bourke and Lord Glenelg responded to the invasion of Port Phillip by passing an Act in Council in 1836, the practical outcome of which was to recognise and accept the unavoidable spread of the pastoralist economy. Meanwhile, the British government, while expressing concern about Indigenous dispossession and making certain attempts to guarantee ongoing access to land, nonetheless enabled and encouraged colonial expansion. The *Second Imperial Waste Lands Act* of 1846, for instance, followed by 1847 Orders in Council in New South Wales, allocated the longest leases to squatters occupying land that was classified as unsettled, in order to further

---

5   Dredge to Harding, 12 September 1840, *JDD*; James Dredge to Jabez Bunting, 10 May 1841, Wesleyan Methodist Missionary Society, Archive: Australasia 1812–1889 [hereafter *WMMS*], reel 2, Mp2107 (Record ID: 133095), National Library of Australia (NLA); James Dredge to Dr Thomson, 14 September 1840, *JDD*, MS11625, MSM534, SLV.

facilitate pastoralism.[6] The mixed intentions of imperial government, and their often close but troubled connections to philanthropic movements, led to some uneasy exchanges on land issues. This was encapsulated rather neatly in 1842, when Lord Stanley told Gipps of the recent Act to regulate the sale of waste lands in Australia. He reiterated that up to 15 per cent of the gross proceeds of land sales should be used for Indigenous protection and civilisation, and added that this process should stay under Crown control, suggesting a certain mistrust of colonial authorities. However, another item Stanley wished to keep under Crown control was also notable: expenditure on roads, bridges and other infrastructure designed to make land contemplated for sale more easily accessible.[7] When philanthropists came to write about land issues, they did so with mingled loyalty and mistrust towards the colonial project.

Philanthropists' personal papers and correspondence are particularly valuable because they provide some of the strongest statements of Indigenous land ownership and dispossession from this era – statements which emerged (however partially) from conversations and relationships with Indigenous people themselves. Writing from Newcastle, LE Threlkeld informed London Missionary Society treasurer GA Hankey as early as 1825 that 'every tribe has its district the boundaries of which must not be passed without permission from the tribe to which it belongs'.[8] Rev George King, writing from Fremantle, reported with interest to the United Society for the Propagation of the Gospel that the local people possessed great expertise and intimate knowledge about the landscape, plants and animal life.[9] Missionaries Francis Tuckfield and Joseph Orton were surprised at how carefully and intricately the country around Geelong was divided according to kinship systems. Tuckfield informed the Wesleyan Methodist Missionary Society in 1840 that 'There does not seem to be a single spot of this continent wholly unoccupied – "wherever human beings can exist there human beings are already to be found"'.[10] Similarly, in 1841 Woiwurrung guides showed protector William Thomas the boundaries of their country in Port Phillip and explained why the borders had been placed where they were.[11] Chief protector GA Robinson also recalled a man's statement

---

6   Cannon and Jones (eds) 1981, *Historical Records of Victoria (HRV)*: vol 1, Beginnings of Permanent Government: 24–25; Waterhouse 2005: 22.
7   Lord Stanley to Sir George Gipps, 15 September 1842, *Historical Records of Australia (HRA)*, 1924, series 1, vol xxii, April 1842 – June 1843: 281.
8   LE Threlkeld to GA Hankey, 29 Aug 1825, London Missionary Society, Records, AJCP M73, SLV.
9   Rev George King to Rev Ernest Hawkins, 11 June 1847, United Society for the Propagation of the Gospel, Records [*USPG*], AJCP M1222, SLV.
10  Francis Tuckfield to General Secretaries, 30 September 1840, *WMMS*, reel 2, Mp2107. Also, Joseph Orton to General Secretaries, 18 July 1839, *WMMS*, reel 1, Mp2107; Francis Tuckfield to General Secretaries, 30 October 1841, *WMMS*, reel 2, Mp2107, NLA.
11  William Thomas to GA Robinson, Journal of the Proceedings during the months of June, July & August 1841, Public Records Office of Victoria (PROV), VA 512 *Chief Protector of Aborigines*, VPRS4410, unit 3, 1841/70 (reel 2).

of land ownership: 'when Tung.bor.roong spoke of Borembeep and the other localities of his own nativity, he always added "that's my country belonging to me!! That's my country belonging to me!!"'[12]

Within these sources, the seizure of Indigenous land was recognised and lamented for its destructive effects. In 1841, when Robinson asked a family he met on the Glenelg river where they came from, 'they beat the ground and vociferated, Deen! Deen! (here! here!), and then, in a dejected tone, bewailed the loss of their country.'[13] Another man, Yaw-en-nil-lum, whom Robinson met at Tarrone, pointed to the squatters' enclosed land and said that white men had stolen it.[14] Even by the end of the protectorate, Robinson was still urging superintendent CJ La Trobe that 'Aboriginal natives have a right to a reasonable share in the soil of their Fatherland and ought not to be driven from their haunts and homes at the caprice of any person.'[15] Protector ES Parker found it difficult to respond to repeated Indigenous complaints about the loss of their country. He claimed they were being 'beaten back by the "white man's foot" ... excluded, perforce, from lands which they unquestionably regard as their own ... classified with and treated as wild dogs.'[16] Meanwhile, Joseph Orton, infuriated by settlers' complaints about Aboriginal sheep theft, retorted 'what else can be expected from savages who are conscious of being intruded upon their natural rights violated – and their only means of subsistence destroyed ... and they thus violently and unjustly deprived of their own soil?'[17] His colleague, Francis Tuckfield, complained to the WMMS in 1840 that Indigenous people in western Victoria were being rapidly dispossessed by squatters and government, losing the lands they had lived on from 'time immemorial'. He noted that people from the districts around Geelong often asked him when they would get their own mission. They did not seem very interested in Christianity, but instead lamented 'Our country all gone.'[18]

The clearest examples of Indigenous people during this period attempting to engage directly with government policy on land rights came from around

---

12   GA Robinson 1998, *Journals: Port Phillip Aboriginal Protectorate, 1 October 1840 – 31 August 1841*, Clark (ed) vol 2: 318.
13   GA Robinson 2001, 'A Report of an Expedition to the Aboriginal Tribes of the Western Interior during the months of March, April, May, June, July and August, 1841', *The Papers of George Augustus Robinson, Chief Protector, Port Phillip Aboriginal Protectorate*, Clark (ed) vol 4: 23.
14   GA Robinson 2001, 'A Report of an Expedition to the Aboriginal Tribes of the Western Interior during the months of March, April, May, June, July and August, 1841', *The Papers of George Augustus Robinson, Chief Protector, Port Phillip Aboriginal Protectorate*, Clark (ed), vol 4: 19.
15   GA Robinson to CJ La Trobe, 1 January 1849, PROV VPRS2895, unit 1, 1849/1 (reel 3).
16   ES Parker to GA Robinson, 1 April 1840, in Cannon (ed) 1983, *HRV*, vol 2B: 413. Also, ES Parker to GA Robinson, 1 December 1843, PROV VPRS12 unit 4, 1843/16 (reel 3).
17   Joseph Orton, 24 May 1839, see also 23 May 1839 and 31 May 1839, in Joseph Orton, Journal 1832–1839 and 1840–1841, ML ref A1714–1715, CY reel 1119, State Library of NSW.
18   Francis Tuckfield to General Secretaries, 30 September 1840, *WMMS*, reel 2, Mp2107, NLA. Also, Francis Tuckfield to the General Secretaries, WMMS, 31 June 1840, in Francis Tuckfield, Journal, 1837–1842 [hereafter *FTJ*], MS11341, Box 655, SLV.

Melbourne, and were recorded in the papers of protector William Thomas. In 1843, Woiwurrung leader Billibellary, who had greeted John Batman in 1835 and made repeated efforts to negotiate with the new order, told Thomas that his people were too miserable to survive as they were, but 'if Yarra black fellows had a country on the Yarra that they would stop on it and cultivate the ground.'[19] Even the people who drank and begged around Melbourne in the 1840s told Thomas 'give us all land in our own country and we live like Whites.'[20] Another offer was made by the Gunnai of Gippsland in 1849, who lobbied Thomas unsuccessfully for land on the River Tanner where they could obtain food and medicine, promising to send their children to school there. To a certain extent, this may have been framed by knowledge of imperial policy, or at least of Thomas's interpretation of it. According to Diane Barwick, Thomas told Woiwurrung and Boonwurrung people in 1849 of 'Earl Grey's humane despatch' promising them reserves, and assured them that they would soon have a country. The limitations to this would become clear over the years as various attempts to secure Victorian reserves failed, and this was hinted at early on, when a senior Boonwurrung man, Benbow, tried to lobby superintendent La Trobe on the subject, but was turned away.[21] Ten years later, a Kulin delegation visited Thomas (by then the sole Guardian of Aborigines) requesting land at the junction of the Acheron and Little Rivers. After years of complaining that Indigenous people were lazy, Thomas was surprised by their enthusiasm to work this site. He told the Commissioner of Lands and Surveys that the failures of previous 'civilising' projects may well have stemmed from selecting land where people did not want to live.[22]

## 'A plain and sacred right'? Dispossession and entitlement

Local philanthropists' journals, correspondence and reports to government and missionary societies tended to acknowledge fairly clearly traditional land ownership and the injustice of dispossession. Such sources have been drawn upon, most notably by Henry Reynolds, to demonstrate humanitarian awareness of land issues during this period, thus working to denaturalise Aboriginal dispossession and strengthen the historical basis of more recent native title

---

19  William Thomas to GA Robinson, 1 December 1843, PROV VPRS4410 unit 3, 1843/78 (reel 2).
20  William Thomas to GA Robinson, 1 December 1843, PROV VPRS4410 unit 3, 1843/78 (reel 2).
21  Barwick 1998: 34–35.
22  William Thomas to Commissioner of Lands and Surveys 20 July 1859, in Massola 1975: 8. For other references to missionaries claiming missions should be built on land acceptable to Indigenous people, see James Dredge 1845, *Brief Notices on the Aborigines of New South Wales*: 40; William Thomas petition to Sir George Gipps, undated, placed after entry for 28 January 1844, in William Thomas, Papers, 1834–1868 [hereafter *WTP*], ML MSS 214, reel 3, State Library of NSW; Francis Tuckfield to General Secretary, 1 January 1844, *WMMS*, reel 2, Mp2107, NLA.

struggles.²³ However, while I accept that philanthropists were witnessing and concerned about Indigenous land ownership and loss, I would suggest that their advocacy was complicated by other factors.

Issues of readership and voice, for instance, warrant further consideration. The above statements of ownership and loss did contribute to official and administrative discourses about Aboriginal policy, as well as more in-house missionary understandings. However, Australian philanthropists also published some more mainstream works, aimed at a wider audience, which showed a somewhat different approach. Of the publications and statements for the public record released by the protectors Parker, Dredge and Robinson, references were made to Indigenous communities having lost the areas of land that were their economic bases, leaving them in severe poverty. Meanwhile, missionaries Joseph Orton and William Watson mentioned the need for missions to be built on secure land, free from European corruption.²⁴ However, with the possible exception of Dredge (who had left the protectorate by then), none of these writers spoke strongly in this public context of traditional rights or the injustice of dispossession. Greater attention was paid to anthropological descriptions of Indigenous societies and to the need to save the 'remnant'. (LE Threlkeld's publications, in particular, rarely emphasised land issues.²⁵) Reasons for this probably varied. Threlkeld and Parker were publishing later in their careers, at a time when Indigenous access to land in their neighbourhoods had already been largely destroyed, while Dredge had also seen his former protectorate decline and was losing hope for the future. Meanwhile, Robinson, speaking in 1845, may have been more concerned with defending his role as chief protector than with dwelling on the broader implications of loss of country. When writing for the general public or broader political audiences, local philanthropists were more likely to portray Indigenous societies as interesting and needing charitable help, rather than dispossessed and needing acknowledgement and autonomy.

In publications by British philanthropic bodies, the distances between local experiences and strategic arguments became even more apparent. Their discussions of Australian land rights were comparatively brief and rare, in contrast to their focus on the more powerful Maori, First Nations or Pacific islanders. Still, within this limited discourse, various Australian messages were

---

23   See particularly, Reynolds 1992[1987]; Reynolds 1998.
24   Dredge 1845, *Brief Notices on the Aborigines*: 14–15; ES Parker 1846, *The Aborigines of Australia*: 14, 29–30; Joseph Orton 1836, *The Aborigines of Australia*: 9; ES Parker 1967, 'The Aborigines of Australia, 10 May 1854', in Morrison (ed): 12–13, 27; GA Robinson, Evidence to the Select Committee on the Condition of the Aborigines, 1845, in Frauenfelder (ed) 1997: 52; William Watson, examined before the Executive Council, 28 May 1839, in *British Parliamentary Papers (BPP): Papers Relating to Australia, 1844*, Colonies: Australia, vol 8, 1969: 47.
25   For instance, LE Threlkeld 1892, *An Australian Languageas Spoken by the Awabakal, the People of Awaba or Lake Macquarie*, Fraser (ed); LE Threlkeld, 'Reminiscences 1825–1826', in Gunson (ed) 1974 vol 1: 43–71; LE Threlkeld 1832, *Specimens of a Dialect, of the Aborigines of New South Wales*.

conveyed. In 1830–31, the Church Missionary Society approached, somewhat tentatively, the subject of Indigenous land rights in New South Wales. They observed that Australian colonisation had succeeded at the expense of 'the original inhabitants and proprietors of the soil', and applauded the government's decision to fund a mission, defining this as compensation.

> The Revenues of the Crown in New Holland are derived from the culture of lands of which the ancient proprietors have been deprived forcibly and without compensation. The small sum subtracted from those Revenues for the benefit of that injured race is due to them, in the strictest sense, as a debt of justice.[26]

Such ideas were expanded upon several years later, by the Select Committee on Aborigines (British Settlements). Church of England Archdeacon William Broughton testified to the Committee in 1835. Broughton had supported Threlkeld's work and the establishment of Wellington Valley, but now doubted the likelihood of Aboriginal Christianity. He observed that Indigenous people had refused to stay on farming land selected by Governor Macquarie, but added:

> they have a notion among themselves of certain portions of the country belonging to their own particular tribe; they have frequently said to me that such a part was their property, but that is all assigned now to Europeans ... They have a conception of our having excluded them from what was their original property.[27]

He also read out an extract (possibly from Rev Robert Cartwright of the Parramatta Native School) lamenting that European occupation had been so harmful, when it should have elevated Indigenous people – 'as in the occupation of their soil we are partakers of their worldly things, so in justice should they be of our spiritual'.[28] During his interview with the Select Committee, Dandeson Coates of the CMS also mentioned that Indigenous people had lost much of the land 'they were previously in the habit of traversing and partially occupying' and that any rights they may have had had been ignored.[29] Meanwhile, New Zealand missionary Rev William Yate acknowledged that Indigenous communities laid claim to areas of land, but also asserted they had never used it correctly. Yate concluded that they should be 'recompensed' for their loss by being gathered together and taught to become Christian farmers.[30]

---

26  Church Missionary Society, *Missionary Register*, 1831: 118–119. Also, Johnstone 1925: 165–166.
27  Archdeacon Broughton to the Select Committee, *BPP: Report from the Select Committee on Aborigines (British Settlements)*, vol 1, 1836: 16–17, 19.
28  Archdeacon Broughton to the Select Committee, *BPP: Report from the Select Committee on Aborigines (British Settlements)*, vol 1, 1836: 15.
29  Dandeson Coates to the Select Committee, *BPP: Report from the Select Committee on Aborigines (British Settlements)*, vol 1, 1836: 491.
30  Rev W Yate to the Select Committee, *BPP: Report from the Select Committee on Aborigines (British Settlements)*, vol 1, 1836: 202–203.

The Committee's 1837 conclusions were mixed. They expressed concern that the 1834 Act declaring the formal colonisation of South Australia had not mentioned Indigenous land claims. They recommended that funds be allocated 'judiciously' for missionaries and protectors and that 'necessary' land be set aside for Indigenous people to live on. This was only fair, given that all the territory had recently been 'the undisputed property of the Aborigines'. More generally, the Committee argued 'It might be presumed that the native inhabitants of any land have an incontrovertible right to their soil: a plain and sacred right'; it was disturbing that native peoples' lands worldwide were sold routinely, without any funds put aside to help them. Protection of colonised people was, they said, perfectly affordable given the profits from the lands seized, and besides, humane protection ultimately made for more successful colonial governance.[31]

In the following decade, other philanthropic publications mentioned Aboriginal land ownership and loss occasionally. The CMS's *Missionary Register* included complaints from Wellington Valley and Buntingdale that loss of land was harming Indigenous people, encouraging a degrading dependence on colonists.[32] The WMMS's New South Wales auxiliary made some stronger statements in their annual reports during the early 1840s, where the updates from Buntingdale often mentioned the impact of dispossession. Joseph Orton made some particularly frank remarks in 1840, stating that the greatest obstacle to missionary success was not Indigenous nomadism but the government's rapid disposal of their lands.[33] Such statements were striking, but they were also rare, within a wider philanthropic discourse which allocated relatively little space to Australia.

Publications by the Aborigines Protection Society also made several references to Australian Indigenous land use. Some articles were impassioned; their annual report from 1840 included an argument (possibly informed by James Dredge) that the Port Phillip protectorate and its 'civilising' efforts were inherently ineffective as long as dispossession continued unchecked – 'The land is wholly and unreservedly the settler's – the native is wholly and unreservedly dispossessed – acreless, helpless.'[34] Several articles from the late 1840s also observed that Aboriginal land had been 'gratuitously invaded' with no reserves created and no thought for their wellbeing, leading to poverty and violence.[35]

---

31  BPP: *Report from the Select Committee on Aborigines (British Settlements)*, vol 2, 1837: 4–5, 12, 15, 83.
32  Church Missionary Society (CMS), *Missionary Register*, August 1839: 386–387; CMS, *Missionary Register*, May 1843: 238.
33  WMMS, 1840, *Report of the Wesleyan Methodist Missionary Society for the year ending April 1840*: 31. Also, WMMS, 1842, *Report of the Wesleyan Methodist Missionary Society for the year ending April 1842*: 45; WMMS, 1843, *Report of the Wesleyan Methodist Missionary Society for the year ending April 1843*: 40–41.
34  Aborigines Protection Society, Third Annual Report, 23 June 1840, Exeter Hall, in Aborigines Protection Society (APS), Transactions, c.1839–1909, MIC/o6550, reel 1 (Records the property of Anti-Slavery International): 33, also 32–34.
35  *Colonial Intelligencer, including APS Annual Report*, 3 May 1848: 28–29; Aborigines Protection Society, *Colonial Intelligencer, or Aborigines' Friend*, vol II, 1849–50, London: 398–399, 408 (in APS, Transactions, reel 3); *Twelfth Annual Report of Aborigines' Protection Society*, May 1849, in APS, Transactions, reel 1: 9–10.

Fig 3. British missionary publications were even more dismissive of pre-colonial life than were their Australian counterparts, as this juxtaposition of Indigenous people and native animals suggests.

'An Australian Group', Wesleyan Methodist Missionary Society, *Wesleyan Juvenile Offering*, February 1853, Wesleyan Mission House, London. Mitchell Library, State Library of New South Wales, 266.705/W.

These British publications shared certain general beliefs. There was an acknowledgement of Indigenous rights to land on grounds of original habitation and ownership, and some articulation of the fact that people's land had been seized against their will, with highly destructive results. Some writers also remarked that massive, unregulated dispossession of native peoples could undermine Christian philanthropy itself. However, there were some notable differences to the comments made by local missionaries and protectors. In local records, Indigenous voices and opinions emerged passionately and assertively, even when the records themselves were incomplete or disrespectful. However, such voices were rarely heard at all in the Select Committee's reports or the philanthropic journals, where Indigenous agency was downplayed. Furthermore, British publications, however concerned about dispossession, rarely wavered in their support for British imperialism in its ideal forms. Philanthropists in the Australian colonies were empire-builders too, of course, but their immediate experiences of Indigenous dispossession made for a different discourse – more personal and conversational, and rather less confident of the ultimate benefits of colonialism.

## 'The fruits and results of Industry': morality and land use

When protectors GA Robinson and ES Parker were travelling around Port Phillip in 1840, a squatter, Mr Hutton, told them 'it was never intended that a few miserable savages were to have this fine country.'[36] Rationales for colonialism often relied on the notion that Indigenous Australians had no legal or moral claim over their land, as they had (supposedly) never used it productively. The idea that nomadic life and communal land use were signs of backward savagery that could be justifiably supplanted by progressive civilisation was present in European thought at least as far back as Enlightenment philosophers like John Locke. Such theories placed commercial enterprise at the end of a scale of civilisation beginning at hunting, then progressing through pastoralism and agriculture. Each stage of socio-economic change was believed to be reflected in more sophisticated systems of government, law and culture. The cultivation of the soil and the private enclosure of land were primary factors legitimising ownership and denoting civilisation.[37] As Bruce Buchan has explored, the doctrine of 'natural law' allowed for the claim that all human beings, including indigenous peoples, had a certain entitlement to enjoy nature's bounty (water, animals, and so forth) but that this was considered different and inferior to commercial land use.[38] By the early 19th century, such theories had become

---

36   GA Robinson 1998, *Journals: Port Phillip Protectorate, 1 January 1839 – 30 September 1840*, Clark (ed): 139.
37   Arneil 1996: 61–62, 109–110; Butcher 1994: 374; Meek 1976: 1–2, 12–13, 16–17, 22; Symcox 1972: 233, 238–242.
38   Buchan 2001: 146; Buchan 2007: 389–390.

implicated in the privatising of land in Britain (including the often violent enclosure of the commons) and the worldwide expansion of empire. As Jean O'Brien points out in her work on North America, the denial of native land ownership and the creation of the 'wandering Indian' figure also helped authenticate white settlers' ties to this newly colonised land – 'the English, who as colonists were rootless people by definition, displaced their own dislocation onto Indians.'[39]

While philanthropists were distressed and angered by Indigenous dispossession, they had a complex relationship to such theories of progress and legitimacy – as indeed, did the broader colonial society developing in Australia. Richard Waterhouse, Henry Reynolds and Heather Goodall have observed that early colonists arrived from a Britain mid-way between traditional village life and modern industrial capitalism. The rapid growth of Australian pastoralism existed in tension with a long-standing perception of pastoralism as rather anti-social and culturally inferior to agriculture.[40] Such concerns shaped colonial politics in various ways. The 1830s and 40s saw efforts to make land distribution more systematic – the abolition of the New South Wales grants system in 1831, the introduction of land auctions, then of flat costs per acre and annual license fees – but also the continued unlawful occupation of land by squatters. Waterhouse notes 'The initial occupation of the island was not under British law but rather in defiance of colonial authority.'[41] Notions of squatters and graziers as less than civilised – a small population, isolated from church and state, taking up large areas of land and making few intensive improvements – combined with apprehension at squatters' growing power. With their political factions and demands for cheaper land and greater security of tenure, as well as their support for the convict system and indentured Asian labour, it is unsurprising that pastoralists attracted hostility, notably from urban professionals and newer migrants seeking their own land. Peter Cochrane has observed 'It was the question of questions. Who shall control the land? – the Crown in trust for the empire, or the men on the spot who gave the so-called waste lands their value?'[42] Yet historians of 19th century politics and land use have not always expanded this question to consider the people who originally controlled the land and continued to value it.

The models of land occupation developing in the colonies must have seemed problematic to philanthropic observers, who were concerned about Indigenous dispossession, convict labour and the relative weakness of small-scale agriculture. Jean and John Comaroff have observed how missionaries in the Cape colony

---

39  O'Brien 1999: 212
40  Goodall 1996: 39–42; Reynolds 1992[1987]: 73–74; Waterhouse 2005: 23–24, 98–102.
41  Waterhouse 2005: 20–22.
42  Cochrane 2006: 71, also 75, 452. See also, Hirst 1988: 21; Irving 2006: 17, 128, 136; McKenna 1996: 33–35; Thompson 2006: 176–177; Waterhouse 2005: 24–25, 86, 94–97.

promoted agriculture for Africans partly in contrast to the alleged savagery of both the Boers (with their pastoralist systems) and the indigenous traditions of cattle herding.[43] The idealised notion of tilling the soil was important to how missionary societies imagined colonialism in general. Church of England societies particularly urged that migrants to the Australian colonies realise the benefits of small land-holdings and agricultural villages. The *Colonial Church Chronicle* (1847–48) urged: 'what is required is an *agricultural* colony, where gentry, yeomanry, and peasantry may be established with old English habits and old English church principles.'[44] The fact that such progress would depend upon further Indigenous dispossession was not addressed, and serves as another reminder of the qualified nature of Evangelical support for Aboriginal rights.

In the Australian colonies, philanthropists accepted that Indigenous forms of land tenure existed. However, this did not equal a validation of pre-colonial land use, or a willingness to negotiate equally with Indigenous people. Rather, they saw people's future in their country as linked intimately to the adoption of agriculture. When the Watsons set off for Wellington Valley in 1831, they were told by the Church Missionary Society that their duties would include encouraging the 'beating of the sword into the ploughshare, and the spear into a pruning hook'.[45] In 1840, Francis Tuckfield was pleased to tell the Wesleyan Methodist Missionary Society that people were working in the vegetable garden at Buntingdale mission. He looked forward eagerly 'to the period when the wanderer of Australia shall become a cultivator of his own soil'.[46] Similarly, protector Thomas stated in 1843 that he hoped to see Aboriginal farms established in every district, surrounded by respectable European farmers, so the protectors could 'permanently settle the Aborigines on their own country … surrounded with the fruits and results of Industry.'[47] This keen attachment to agricultural ideals (never realised completely in practice) was significant to how the first philanthropists understood Indigenous rights to land.

Agriculture held strong symbolic appeal for Evangelical philanthropists. Pleased by the sight of people at his Narre Narre Warren station attending Sunday service in neat European clothing, protector Thomas expressed hope for the station's future: 'to see the Sable sons of Australia coming from one direction

---

43   Comaroff and Comaroff 1997 vol 2: 122–124.
44   CMS, *Colonial Church Chronicle and Missionary Journal*, vol 1, July 1847 – June 1848, 1848: 465. See also, CMS, *Church Missionary Intelligencer, A Monthly Journal of Missionary Information*, vol III, 1852: 4; CMS, *Colonial Church Chronicle, and Missionary Journal*, vol II, June 1848 – June 1849, 1849: 2–6; Colonial Church Society (CCS), *Colonial Church Record*, vol 1, no 3, October 1838: 36–45.
45   T Woodrooffe and D Coates to Mr and Mrs Watson, 7 October 1831, in *British Parliamentary Papers (BPP): Correspondence and Other Papers Relating to Aboriginal Tribes in British Possessions*, 1834: 152.
46   Francis Tuckfield to General Secretaries, WMMS, 31 June 1840, *FTJ*, MS11341, Box 655, SLV.
47   William Thomas to GA Robinson, 1 December 1843, Journal of Proceedings, September 1843 – December 1843, PROV VPRS4410 unit 3, 1843/78 (reel 2). Also, William Thomas to GA Robinson, 9 July 1840, *WTP*, ML MSS 214, reel 4, State Library of NSW.

& another at the tolling of the Bell ... like the Pathways in a village church.'[48] Similarly, Tuckfield, optimistically describing the growth of Buntingdale in 1841, commented 'our station at present has the appearance of a bustling village.'[49] Jean and John Comaroff, in their study of missions amongst the Tswana people at this time, have noted the irony that Britain's own rural economy was highly precarious during the early 19th century, making missionaries' wish for small-scale colonial farms both paradoxical and understandable. If the rural ideal was becoming unattainable in Britain, some Britons could focus their hopes instead on the 'open vistas' of the new colonies.[50]

Moreover, the process of farming itself was associated with moral improvement, linked to individual initiative, regular labour, rational subjugation of the natural world, and the accumulation and valuing of property. William Thomas, for instance, expressed faith in the transformative power of agriculture; when people at his station planted potatoes, he trusted that 'when they behold the first fruit of their own labor spring out of the earth a radical change will take place among them.'[51] This spilled over to affect philanthropic language in general. In his study of missionaries in New Guinea in the 19th century, Richard Eves has observed how the discourse of agriculture – 'cultivation', 'harvest' and so on – was powerful here, portraying missionary work as a shaping of immature natural resources, guiding them to fruition.[52] This was apparent in the papers of Methodist missionary John Smithies of Western Australia, who in 1845 described his religious instruction of young Indigenous people: 'It is now our sowing time among them; the seed we scatter day by day is the incorruptible seed of the kingdom.'[53] Later, in 1849, when reporting the tragic deaths of several of Smithies' students, the WMMS's *Missionary Register* described how they had 'early blossomed, early ripened, and as early sickened and died'.[54] As the Comaroffs have also observed, 'the Christians were from a world in which cultivation and salvation were explicitly linked – and joined together, more often than not, in a tangled mesh of horticultural imagery, much of it biblical in origin.'[55]

These moral understandings of land use help explain philanthropists' distaste at Indigenous people's travelling around their country, journeys in which missionaries and protectors rarely participated. While travelling and living off the land were important spiritual experiences for Indigenous societies, philanthropists' records show little understanding of this. Instead, Indigenous

---

48  Thomas, 28 March 1841, *WTP*, ML MSS 214, reel 2, State Library of NSW.
49  Francis Tuckfield to General Secretaries, 30 October 1841, *WMMS*, reel 2, Mp2107, NLA.
50  Comaroff 1989: 667–668; Comaroff and Comaroff vol 2 1997: 132–133.
51  William Thomas to GA Robinson, 6 October 1840, PROV VPRS11 unit 7, 1840/335 (reel 1).
52  Eves 1996: 99.
53  WMMS, *Report of the WMMS for the year ending April 1845*, April 1845: 32–33.
54  CMS, *Missionary Register*, May 1849: 218–219.
55  Comaroff and Comaroff 1997 vol 2: 121–122.

people were described disapprovingly as 'wanderers', 'vagrants', 'fickle' and 'feckless'. George Langhorne, head of the short-lived Melbourne mission of the late 1830s, concluded that they must be forced to remain in one place; 'their wandering and unsettled habits are so diametrically opposed to civilized life'.[56] The Indigenous practice of spreading tasks throughout the day, not distinguishing strongly between work and leisure time, was hard to reconcile with understandings of labour becoming dominant in industrial Europe.[57] The Wellington Valley missionaries accused Wiradjuri people of 'remarkable aversion to labour' and 'wild, volatile & wandering habits'.[58] During Bible classes, James Günther took care to emphasise the text 'In the sweat of thy brow thou shalt earn thy bread', remarking tersely 'they require a lesson on that point often and daily'.[59] Philanthropists acknowledged Indigenous rights to land on grounds of prior ownership, use and attachment, but believed that it was through agricultural labour that a new sense of material property rights (so crucial to British citizenship) would be created, and connections to land itself would be transformed, modernised and further legitimised. This points to a problem in associating early 19th century sources with contemporary understandings of native title. While governance around land rights from the late 20th century onwards has been predicated on notions of 'traditional' land use, these early philanthropic accounts portrayed people's rights to land as being strengthened by their movement *away* from such traditions.

Not that agricultural systems were fully implemented at the time, since mission farms faced numerous obstacles and were not always sustainable. In this context, philanthropists tolerated traditional activities, if they could be administered and assessed for monetary value. The Port Phillip protectors in the 1830s and 1840s accepted and even encouraged hunting and handicrafts when the products were sold or traded for rations, and attempted to set standard prices for skins, nets, baskets, mats and other items. Here, they aimed to stop colonists from cheating Indigenous people, but also hoped to impart a consistent sense of these items' new material worth.[60]

Further ambiguity existed concerning private property. Despite the idealisation of the independent peasant, dividing mission land into individual allotments

---

56  George Langhorne to CJ La Trobe, 15 October 1839, in Cannon (ed) 1983, *HRV*, vol 2B: 508.
57  Broome1994: 203–207.
58  William Watson to Dandeson Coates, 31 December 1832: 2, in Carey and Roberts (eds) 2002, *The Wellington Valley Project: Letters and Journals Relating to the Church Missionary Society Mission to Wellington Valley, NSW, 1830–42, A Critical Electronic Edition* [hereafter *WVP*]: <http://www.newcastle.edu.au/wvp/>; William Porter to Dandeson Coates, 22 February 1841, *WVP*.
59  James Günther, Journal, 5 March 1839: 4, *WVP*.
60  For example, Arkley 2000: 7; Blaskett 1979: 220; O'Connor 1991: 10; GA Robinson to CW Sievwright, ES Parker and William Le Souef, 21 August 1840, PROV VPRS10 unit 2, 1840/815 (reel 1); Thomas, 26 October 1839, 12 July 1840, 26 July 1840, *WTP*, ML MSS 214, reel 1, State Library of NSW; William Thomas to GA Robinson, 11 September 1841, PROV VPRS11 unit 8, 1841/392 (reel 2); LE Threlkeld to George Burder, 25 April 1825, in Gunson (ed) 1974 vol 2: 183.

for Indigenous farmers was suggested only occasionally. When the Parramatta institution, Threlkeld's mission at Reid's Mistake, and George Langhorne's Melbourne mission were initiated (in 1819, 1825 and 1836 respectively) there were brief, initial discussions of dividing the land, but little came of this.[61] During the 1850s, protector ES Parker boasted of several young men whom he had known for years successfully cultivating their own plots of land, and the Buntingdale missionaries mentioned one man who wanted his own house and garden on the mission.[62] However, these examples were short-lived and rare. The scarcity of such discussions can be attributed partly to practical obstacles: Indigenous people's continued attachment to communal life, as well as the problems of securing mission land. Group farming enterprises, with some ongoing hunting and gathering, may have also seemed explicable and tolerable in light of the old system of commons land in Britain, where large expanses of uncultivated or temporarily cultivated land were used by communities for grazing, farming, hunting and gathering natural produce – a system, ironically, being eradicated in Britain at this time.[63] It is also possible, though, that considerations of private property were implicitly discouraged by philanthropists' belief that Indigenous Australians were unusually degraded, needing paternalistic supervision. This points to a broader tension in missionaries' aims to recreate Indigenous people both as privatised individuals and institutionalised subjects.

Perhaps the most complex connections between economics, morality and rights to land occurred in relation to urban districts. In protector Thomas's papers, we can trace an Indigenous sense of historical entitlement to Melbourne. Thomas wrote to chief protector GA Robinson in 1839 that people had refused official orders to leave the city, saying 'Plenty white man sit down, Black fellow no sulky, Plenty black fellows sit down & white man sulky, no good that. Long time ago before white man come Goldburn [sic] Black fellow sit down here.'[64] He explained to superintendent La Trobe in 1840 his failure to remove a gathering of 300 people from the banks of the Yarra, by asserting that Melbourne had been a pre-colonial meeting place for different groups to talk, settle grievances and avenge deaths.[65] People camping nearby were angered by Thomas's reprimand that they were damaging land and resources owned by colonists: 'I again tell

---

61  Announcement by Sir Thomas Brisbane, forwarded to Earl Bathurst, 8 February 1825, in *BPP: Papers Relating to Australia, 1830–36*, Colonies: Australia, vol 4, 1970: 160, also: 162; Rev Robert Cartwright to Governor Macquarie, 6 December 1819, in *BPP: Papers Relating to Australia, 1830–36*, vol 4: 156; Rev Robert Cartwright to Governor Macquarie, 18 January 1820, in *BPP: Papers Relating to Australia, 1830–36*, vol 4: 158; Christie 1979: 83.
62  Lewis 1987: 19; Morrison 2002b: 236–237, 241–242; Parker 1967, 'The Aborigines of Australia, 10 May 1854', Morrison (ed): 23; Tuckfield, 9 May 1841, 11 May 1841, *FTJ*, MS11341, Box 655, SLV; Francis Tuckfield to General Secretaries, 30 October 1841, *WMMS*, reel 2, Mp2107, NLA.
63  De Moor et al 2002: 15–27; Mingay 1997: 4–5, 8, 126–130, 138; Neeson 1993: 28–33.
64  William Thomas to GA Robinson, 29 December 1839, *WTP*, ML MSS 214, reel 7, f61, State Library of NSW.
65  William Thomas to CJ La Trobe, 13 April 1840, *WTP*, ML MSS 214, reel 4, f67–71, State Library of NSW.

them they make Willums [shelters] on white man's ground, and cut down Trees & cut off Bark, make white man sulky – they say no white man's ground, black man's.'[66] Thomas also noted in his diary in 1841 'The Blacks this morning very dissatisfied & talk much about no good white man, take away country, no good bush, all white man sit down ... Black fellows come to Melbourne & white man sulky no good that.'[67] Such statements of traditional ownership were as clear as those articulated in other districts. However, this did not lead to protectorate support for Indigenous access to Melbourne. Thomas continued (sometimes reluctantly) to move people on from districts where settlement was intensifying, and called for the use of vagrancy laws and employment registers to restrict their movements and access to cities.[68] Similarly, Buntingdale missionary Tuckfield, who protested dispossession and stressed the need for reserves acceptable to Indigenous people, nonetheless added that force might be advisable to keep them out of towns and in their (designated) native regions.[69]

Thus, historical ownership of country was not enough to convince philanthropists of the legitimacy of Indigenous people's presence there. Economics and morality were also important. Mission and protectorate accounts complained frequently about the begging, alcohol, violence and illicit sex associated with cities. The issue was highlighted in the evidence to the Select Committee, with Archdeacon Broughton and New Zealand missionary William Yate complaining that Indigenous people in Sydney lived 'an idle vagrant life'; 'they go about the streets begging their bread, and begging for clothing and rum.'[70] Methodist missionary Joseph Orton described people living around the settlements as 'pilfering – starving – obtrusive mendicants', 'a tax upon the [white] inhabitants'.[71] Meanwhile, Thomas struggled to keep people away from Melbourne, claiming they picked up lessons in pauperism there. He lamented 'Their visits to the settlement has much corrupted them [sic], encouraged indolence & profligacy, and is one of the most formidable barriers against their moral improvement'. He referred to Melbourne resentfully as 'that den of indolence'.[72]

---

66  William Thomas, 15 September 1840, *WTP*, ML MSS 214, reel 1, State Library of NSW.
67  William Thomas, 17 September 1841, *WTP*, ML MSS 214, reel 2, State Library of NSW.
68  For example, William Thomas, 25 July 1844, 3 December 1846, *WTP*, ML MSS 214, reel 3, State Library of NSW; William Thomas to GA Robinson, Journal of the Proceedings during the months of June, July & August 1841, PROV VPRS4410 unit 3, 1841/70 (reel 2); William Thomas to GA Robinson, 1 December 1843, PROV VPRS4410 unit 3, 1843/78 (reel 2).
69  Francis Tuckfield, Report on the Wesleyan Missionary Society's Mission to the Aborigines, August 1843, *WMMS*, reel 2, Mp2107, NLA.
70  Archdeacon Broughton, evidence, 3 August 1835, in *BPP: Report from the Select Committee on Aborigines (British Settlements)*, vol 1, 1836: 14; Rev William Yate, evidence, 13 February 1836, in *BPP: Report from the Select Committee on Aborigines (British Settlements)*, vol 1, 1836: 203.
71  Joseph Orton to General Secretaries, 13 May 1839, *WMMS*, reel 1, Mp2107, NLA; Joseph Orton to General Secretaries, 18 July 1839, in Joseph Orton, Letterbooks 1822–1842, ML ref A1717–A1720, State Library of NSW.
72  William Thomas to GA Robinson, 17 November 1840, PROV VPRS4410 unit 3, 1840/67 (reel 2); William Thomas, 23 July 1841, *WTP*, ML MSS 214, reel 2; William Thomas to GA Robinson, 24 May 1842, PROV

When philanthropists did tolerate or facilitate Indigenous presence in cities, this was not justified on grounds of pre-colonial rights to land, or personal freedoms. Rather, it occurred when city visits were linked to moral improvement. James Dredge, for instance, was touched when people from the Goulburn River visited his house in Melbourne in order to greet his family and ask him to return to their country.[73] Thomas tolerated some Indigenous visits to Melbourne when they were selling handicrafts and behaving politely, or when he could take them to view the courthouse and gaol.[74] He also described feeling reluctant to force Kulin groups away from Melbourne, since he believed they had protected Europeans from violence from other Indigenous peoples in the early months of colonisation, an occurrence of which they indignantly reminded him.[75]

However, the clearest illustration of how people could be rendered 'deserving' of access to urban space was apparent in Perth in the 1840s, where Indigenous presence was permissible but regulated. This was explained not in terms of rights to country, but on the grounds that they were useful labourers who might become more 'civilised' through city life. Thus, protector Charles Symmons reported to the Governor in 1840 that Indigenous people made valuable servants and that he did not want to ban them from Perth, but rather preferred to discipline and supervise their presence there, removing their weapons and expelling offenders from the city as punishment. Symmons and fellow protector Peter Barrow also hoped that the attractions of cities would help them gain control over Indigenous children. Symmons was particularly supportive of the Methodist mission school in Perth, which by 1840 was requiring children to work for settlers.[76] Here, the demand for cheap labour was clearly influential. Meanwhile, Adelaide seems to have fallen somewhere between the two approaches, with the residence of two or three hundred Indigenous people near the city apparently accepted by the protectorate, who hoped to train them as labourers, but where concerns about 'vagrancy' also led to attempts to confine people to their Parklands location.[77]

---

VPRS4410 unit 3, 1842/71 (reel 2); William Thomas to GA Robinson, Journal of Proceedings, 1 December 1842 – 1 March 1843, PROV VPRS4410 unit 3, (reel 2); William Thomas, 8 April 1845, *WTP*, ML MSS 214, reel 3, State Library of NSW.
73   James Dredge, 10 Oct 1840, also 12 August 1841, *JDD*, MS11625, MSM534, SLV.
74   William Thomas to CJ La Trobe, 1 August 1846, f51–52, *WTP*, reel 8, State Library of NSW; William Thomas to GA Robinson, Quarterly Report, 1 December 1846 – 28 February 1847, PROV VPRS4410 unit 4, 1847/93 (reel 2).
75   William Thomas to GA Robinson, 14 September 1840, PROV VPRS11 unit 7, 1840/327 (reel 1); William Thomas to GA Robinson, 1 March 1841, PROV VPRS4410 unit 3, 1841/68 (reel 2).
76   Peter Barrow, Annual Report, 31 March 1841, *BPP: Papers Relating to Australia, 1844*, vol 8: 391; Charles Symmons to Colonial Secretary, report on the Wesleyan Missionary School in Perth, September 1840, and Charles Symmons to Colonial Secretary, 31 December 1840, in *BPP: Papers Relating to Australia, 1844*, Colonies: Australia, vol 8: 387–389. See also, Hetherington 1992: 48–52.
77   Matthew Moorhouse to Colonial Secretary, 12 April 1847, State Records of South Australia (SRSA), GRG24/6/1847/440.

Here, a certain irony is apparent: those philanthropists (mostly in the south-east) who voiced the strongest support for Indigenous land rights, appear to have been the most opposed to Indigenous presence in cities. This tells us something about how land and the right to live on it were being conceptualised. At this time in Britain, there was little acknowledgement that people dependent on the state for their survival should be able to choose where they lived. State support for the poor had long been accompanied by settlement regulations and vagrancy laws allowing for the arrest and transfer of people, sometimes thousands every year. The surveillance and policing of poverty – and the flexible category of 'vagrancy' – gained particular political currency from the 1830s onwards, often with strong involvement by philanthropic bodies.[78] Australian comparisons should not be oversimplified, but we can trace a certain belief that charities and the state were entitled to control the movements of people they supported. Relevant too was the vague but powerful association between homelessness and criminality contained in the figure of the 'vagrant', a status Indigenous people were often considered to occupy. In a way, it seems curious that Aboriginal people's right to occupy urban space should be so contested, given the supposedly public nature of the city. However, as Don Mitchell has argued, from the late 18th century legitimate presence in city space became increasingly linked to individualism, respectability and property ownership – 'To be public means having access to private space to retreat to (so that publicness can remain voluntary)'.[79] Penelope Edmonds, for instance, has observed of 19th century Melbourne how privatisation and commercialisation of space worked to deny the authenticity of the Indigenous presence, once so vivid in the town.[80] Thus, while philanthropists might acknowledge traditional claims over areas of rural land, any extension of such rights to urban space depended crucially on whether or not Indigenous people were believed to occupy a legitimate place in the city's labouring and economic life. While not diminishing philanthropists' broader support for Indigenous access to country, this complicates any clear distinction between rights and charitable control.

## Complex heritage, contemporary questions

In scholarly debates about the use of land in Australia, there is continuing interest in the distinctions between rights acknowledged and favours granted. Henry Reynolds, for instance, has pointed out how British authorities guaranteed Aboriginal reserves on grounds of prior occupation, and how colonists persisted in misinterpreting this, dismissing these reserves as mere

---

78  Crowther 1981: 247–251; Englander 1998: 2–5, 33; Ribton-Turner 1887[1972]: 217–238, 244–250, 253–259; Rose 1988: 4–5, 17–18, 22.
79  Mitchell 2003: 132, also 131–136.
80  Edmonds 2006: 171–195.

kind gestures that could be withdrawn.[81] While I would not necessarily dispute this particular contrast, I am uneasy with drawing too strong a division between rights and benevolence in the early 19th century. As Reynolds himself has observed, philanthropists saw Indigenous people as entitled only to minority portions of their ancestral country, on grounds that colonisation would put it to more productive use.[82] Missionary Benjamin Hurst, for example, urged superintendent La Trobe in 1841 to support the principle recommended by the Secretary of State for the Colonies, Lord John Russell, of reserving land for each 'tribe' at a cost of 15 per cent of the land revenue. Hurst pleaded 'They are the original proprietors of the soil, and have therefore a strong claim upon the consideration of Government when it is disposing of waste lands.'[83] Such statements asserted Indigenous rights to land, but did not challenge the notion that these entitlements were diminished in a context of imperial advancement. The equivocal nature of philanthropy was also hinted at by the Aborigines Protection Society in the same year, when their delegates lobbied Russell about the proposed colonisation of Western Australia. They urged him to extinguish native title over Crown lands and replace it with a secure portion of land 'adequate to supply the means of their peaceful existence'.[84] The frequent philanthropic assertion that Aboriginal missions should be paid for out of the land fund was also interesting; it forced an acknowledgement of colonial Australia's debt to its dispossessed people, whilst also implying that only a 'small sum' was necessary to repay Indigenous people for their loss. Land and compensation, moreover, were linked to compliance with paternalistic projects. Aborigines Protection Society publications, for example, usually called for Indigenous Australians to receive 'adequate compensation' through greater missionary efforts, funded from a 'due portion' of the profits of land sales.[85] This would have ominous implications for Indigenous people's access to land when missionary work failed and ceased.

The close association between missionary work and Indigenous wellbeing may not have been accepted by everyone, but few alternative suggestions were made. When, during the 1840s, imperial enthusiasm for philanthropic projects waned, promises of support for Aboriginal welfare continued, but the resulting policy statements were often quite vague. In 1840, for instance, Lord John Russell recommended to Governor Gipps that 15 per cent of the yearly produce of land sales should be used for Indigenous improvement.

---

81  Reynolds 1992[1987]: 169–171.
82  Reynolds 1992[1987]: 172.
83  Benjamin Hurst to CJ La Trobe, 22 July 1841, *MMS*, reel 4, AJCP M121, SLV.
84  APS 1841, *Extracts from the Papers and Proceedings of the Aborigines' Protection Society*, vol II, no III, April 1841: 87–88.
85  For instance, APS, Second Annual Report, 21 May 1839, Exeter Hall: 14, 24 (in APS, Transactions, reel 1); APS, Third Annual Report, 23 June 1840, Exeter Hall: 35–36; *Twelfth Annual Report of Aborigines' Protection Society*, May 1849 (in APS, Transactions, reel 1): 9–10.

He sidestepped Wellington Valley missionaries' requests for more support, though, telling Gipps that HM government could not easily advise from such a distance.[86] In the same year, Lord Stanley agreed with Gipps that the various civilising projects seemed to have failed, and gave permission to discontinue funding. Stanley commented:

> I have great doubts as to the wisdom or propriety of continuing the missions ... I fear that to do so would be to delude ourselves with the mere idea of doing something, which would be injurious to the Natives as interfering with other and more advantageous arrangements, and unjust to the Colony, as continuing an unnecessary and pointless expenditure.[87]

As Reynolds has noted, this was an odd juxtaposition of waning humanitarianism and continued commitment to aiding Indigenous welfare through land sales.[88] It might suggest a wish to separate Indigenous wellbeing from missionary work, but alternative policies were thin on the ground; the 'advantageous arrangements' alluded to by Stanley went unspecified. Earl Grey's writings provide some ambiguous suggestions here. His famous instruction to Governor Fitzroy in 1848 that pastoral leases did not incur exclusive rights to uncultivated land – Indigenous people could continue travelling and living off the land – implied a greater than usual recognition of ongoing traditional life. However, Grey also considered establishing reserves for farming, schools and other 'civilising' institutions. These suggestions were pursued to some degree; at least 40 small reserves were created in New South Wales, following 1848 instructions by the Commissioners for Crown Lands. But Grey's suggestions for more intensive 'civilising' projects prompted less action. In 1849, Fitzroy told him that previous efforts to improve Indigenous people had proven useless. An enclosure from the Executive Council assented to Grey's claim that Indigenous people were entitled to live off 'unimproved' Crown land, but their main suggestion was for small reserves far from European settlement. It is questionable how sustainable this system was expected to be, given that missionaries had attempted something similar already, only to find that their locations did not stay 'remote' for long. The function of such reserves had been re-imagined; the Council wanted them to stay under direct control of the Commissioners of Crown Lands, who would keep notes on how friendly and useful Indigenous people were towards Europeans. Any repeat of the earlier, more intensive philanthropic system was not mentioned.

---

86  Lord John Russell to Sir George Gipps, 5 August 1840, *HRA* 1924, series 1, vol xx, February 1839 – September 1840: 735; Lord John Russell to Sir George Gipps, 25 August 1840, *HRA* 1924, series 1, vol xx: 776.
87  Lord Stanley to Sir George Gipps, 20 December 1842, *HRA* 1924, series 1, vol xxii, April 1842 – June 1843: 437–439.
88  Reynolds 1998: 57.

While Grey responded by stressing again the urgency of pursuing 'the best arrangements which can be made for their protection and civilization', his intentions would be largely unrealised.[89]

Given the strong but complex place of Indigenous land ownership in the records of early philanthropists, and the ongoing controversies over contemporary land rights, questions of how to interpret this material remain pertinent. A certain tension has developed between approaches like that of Henry Reynolds, who (while acknowledging humanitarian shortcomings) has used philanthropic sources to trace a heritage of support for Indigenous entitlements to land, and other arguments, like that of Bain Attwood, that the history of land campaigns should be seen more in terms of change and shifting discussions of Aboriginality.[90] Meanwhile, Tim Rowse, Claire McLisky and Hannah Robert have argued that the 'humanitarians' of the 1830s and 1840s should be understood more in terms of charity and paternalism, expressing discomfort with reading their records within a rights discourse at all.[91]

Certainly, these early philanthropic records are a valuable source of Indigenous commentary on land ownership and loss. Comments by philanthropists (especially local ones) are also important, helping to denaturalise and make visible a dispossession that was obscured and excused elsewhere. However, in some ways the most useful function of these records is to historicise the problems in reading land 'rights' as absolute, indivisible and equal. Philanthropists' acceptance of Britain's seizure of large areas of Indigenous country, and their belief that the meaning and legitimacy of land ownership were bound up with economics and Christian morality, made their support for land rights equivocal.

Consideration of early debates also draws our attention to some shortcomings of contemporary political discourse, where the 'special' rights of minority groups (for example to Indigenous land) are often portrayed as existing in tension and contrast to the 'normal', 'civil' rights of citizens. This perceived disparity of rights – highlighted, for example, in Nicolas Peterson and Will Sanders' anthology, *Citizenship and Indigenous Australians*[92] – has often been structured around the question of whether liberal democracies, premised on equality, can accommodate minority rights and identities. However, such notions can be destabilised when we look more closely at these early colonial records, where the relationship between 'civil' and 'Aboriginal' rights was

---

89   Governor CA Fitz Roy to Earl Grey, 12 November 1849, *BPP: Papers Relating to Australia, 1850*, vol 12, 1969: 59–61; Earl Grey to Gov Fitz Roy, 30 August 1850, *BPP: Papers Relating to Australia, 1851–52*, Colonies: Australia, vol 13, 1969: 47.
90   Attwood 2003: xi, xiv; Reynolds 1998: xi–xvii, 36–37, 59–60.
91   McLisky 2005: 61–63; Robert 2002: 9–14, 19; Rowse 2000: 33–36.
92   For example, Peterson and Sanders 1998: 1–4, 27–28.

more complex. For one thing, philanthropists associated Indigenous people's 'special' entitlement to reserves with projects aiming to transform them into loyal British subjects. Philanthropists also showed a certain awareness that loss of land was connected powerfully to the loss of other essential qualities, like health, safety and political recognition; 'Indigenous' rights were not quarantined from other issues. The reader's attention is also drawn to white settlers' demands for property rights and political influence. Their enjoyment of these 'normal' rights of citizens rested fundamentally on the invisibility and destruction of Indigenous people's rights to land and indeed survival.

# Deserving poverty? Rationing and philanthropy

Church Missionary Society representative JCS Handt of Wellington Valley was a sensitive, easily downcast man. A Prussian Lutheran and former tailor struggling to reinvent himself as a clergyman, he lived in frequent conflict with his Anglican colleague, William Watson, and quickly realised that Aboriginal affairs would not provide an easy route to advancement. In particular, he worried about being unappreciated by the Wiradjuri people he lived amongst, who relied on mission rations of food, clothing, blankets and tools. One day, in October 1833, he recorded speaking to a man who had been away travelling. Handt pointed out how thin the man had become, hoping this would demonstrate the value of staying at the mission and obtaining food through agricultural labour. Instead, to Handt's frustration, the man took this as a reminder of missionary bounty, replying that 'I ought to take him into the room and give him plenty to eat, then he would get fat again.'[1] The following year, Handt recorded another incident, which he found even more disturbing, when a group of people left the mission in a 'clandestine manner'. They took with them the blankets they had received, which were supposed to be conditional upon mission residence.

> They ... made their escape by plunging into [the] river, and swimming to the other side, like persons pursued by their enemies. These are very discouraging circumstances, and try the feelings. The more we endeavour to do them good, the more they seem to withdraw. They do not appear to care for anything but for food.[2]

Handt's troubled anecdotes point to the significance of rationing systems to the first missions and protectorates. Indigenous people, while obtaining sustenance from other colonial and traditional sources, were nonetheless becoming dependent on charitable supplies as their dispossession worsened. Thus, the early 19th century witnessed the first attempts at large-scale Indigenous relief, and the accompanying arguments about what Aboriginal people were entitled to and what they had lost. Rationing systems were never simple or unconditional. Rather, as Tim Rowse has observed, rationing was connected to a range of relationships and ideologies – 'an issuing of goods for a more complex and ill-defined return.'[3] British understandings of pauperism and 'deserving'

---

1  JCS Handt, Journal, 4 October 1833, in Carey and Roberts (eds) 2002, *The Wellington Valley Project: Letters and Journals Relating to the Church Missionary Society Mission to Wellington Valley, NSW, 1830–42, A Critical Electronic Edition* [hereafter *WVP*]: <http://www.newcastle.edu.au>. For more on Handt, see Le Couteur 1998: 141–144.
2  Handt, journal, 2 March 1834, *WVP*.
3  Rowse 1998b: 20.

poverty were transferred to the colonies with mixed results; Indigenous relief was conceptualised both as a group entitlement, based on their status as a dispossessed people, and as an individual reward for compliance with 'civilising' regimes. Rationing was, in other words, less an unconditional right and more an intrinsic element of becoming subjects of empire.

At the same time, the place of rationing in daily interactions between philanthropists and Indigenous people was complex, connected to both philanthropic agendas and personal relationships. Philanthropists often claimed that Indigenous people were greedy for possessions but also careless of them; a desire for property and an ability to regulate such desires through labour, charity and the nuclear family were vital elements of missionary and protectorate projects. Moreover, rationing, while clearly an example of state intervention, also emerged in philanthropic records as a deeply personal and local experience. It functioned not only to attract and control people, but also to draw both Indigenous people and philanthropists into shifting relationships of closeness, gratitude, conflict and obligation.

## 'A sort of compensation': Indigenous entitlement to support

When colonial sources acknowledged Indigenous dispossession, the main area highlighted was the destruction of traditional food sources. (Indeed, Bruce Buchan argues that many Europeans believed 'nature's bounty' was the only entitlement Indigenous people possessed.[4]) Distribution of food and clothing played a broad part in colonial governance, dating back at least as far as the Sydney native feasts from 1814. Governor Macquarie used these annual gatherings to demonstrate paternalistic good will, solicit children for the Parramatta institution, and urge Indigenous groups to elect 'chiefs', in the hopes that they would embrace a hierarchical system of government more comprehensible to colonists. The feast system was phased out by Governor Bourke in the mid 1830s and replaced by an annual blanket distribution throughout New South Wales by magistrates, Crown Land Commissioners and some settlers, who were urged to compile Aboriginal records for their districts. Bourke hoped this would encourage Indigenous people to become labourers, and urged that distribution should reflect charity and work ethics by favouring the sickly and the industrious.[5] On the volatile frontiers of central and western Australia, rationing was also considered a useful way of reducing violence and easing the rural labour shortage by encouraging Indigenous people into pastoral jobs.[6] Thus, when examining philanthropic rationing regimes, we are

---

4  Buchan 2001: 146; Buchan 2007: 388–389.
5  Brook and Kohen 1991: 65–66, 72, 90–102; Reece 1974: 20, 125, 209–210.
6  Rowse 1998b: 17.

reminded again of philanthropists' connections to the state, with its (limited) systems of administration and surveillance. However, philanthropists' own use of rationing warrants special attention. Their particular views on dispossession and state responsibility, and their relationships with Indigenous people, make their place within histories of welfare systems especially vivid, characterised by intensive efforts to change people's behaviour.

The earliest advice protectors and missionaries received about gift-giving and rationing was conflicted. Any notion of universal human entitlement to state support was absent; what emerged instead was an intriguing mixture of ideas about colonial dispossession and the deserving poor. The claim that colonisation made Indigenous people impoverished by destroying their food sources was emphasised by Archdeacon Broughton's evidence to the Select Committee on Aborigines (British Settlements), Church Missionary Society secretary Dandeson Coates' advice to Lord Glenelg, and articles in the CMS's *Missionary Register*.[7] Some sense of colonial responsibility was present; Rev William Yate, for example, told the Select Committee that the government had a duty to 'recompense' Indigenous Australians for the loss of their lands, by gathering them together and 'for some time supplying them with food, leading them to habits of industry; to cultivate their own land, that they may supply themselves with food'.[8]

Tim Rowse, considering later sources from northern Australia, has argued that rationing regimes, while raising various moral issues about settler-Aboriginal relationships, avoided and obscured 'the ultimate moral question of land ownership'.[9] However, this was not necessarily the case during this earlier period. Anne O'Brien, in a rare study of initial ideas about rationing and pauperism, suggests that compensation for dispossession was an idea relevant to rationing programs in the early 19th century.[10] I would add that local missionaries and protectors, perhaps because of their closeness to the issue, tended to state more strongly and explicitly than their counterparts in Britain that Indigenous people were entitled to rationing because of their loss of land. The Port Phillip Methodists were particularly passionate on the subject. Protector James Dredge, angry at having insufficient food to deter Daungwurrung people from travelling and theft, wrote angrily in his diary 'Shame upon the Government who can permit such a state of things in reference to the blacks, by the sale of whose lands they

---

7   Archdeacon Broughton, evidence, 3 August 1835, in *British Parliamentary Papers (BPP): Report from the Select Committee on Aborigines (British Settlements) together with minutes of evidence, appendix and index*, Anthropology: Aborigines, vol 1, 1836: 17–18; Church Missionary Society (CMS), *Missionary Register*, August 1839: 387; CMS, *Missionary Register*, May 1843: 238; Dandeson Coates to Lord Glenelg, 31 October 1838, in *BPP: Papers Relating to Australia, 1844*, Colonies: Australia, vol 8, 1969: 29.
8   Rev William Yate, evidence, 13 February 1836, in *BPP: Report from the Select Committee on Aborigines (British Settlements)*, vol 1, 1836: 203.
9   Rowse 1998a: 98–99, 119.
10  O'Brien 2008: 150–166.

are aggrandising themselves'. When colonists shot at Daungwurrung people who were trying to steal wheat, Dredge blamed the government for sending insufficient supplies.[11] Meanwhile, Benjamin Hurst and Francis Tuckfield of the Buntingdale mission and their Wesleyan Methodist Missionary Society correspondent Joseph Orton commented many times in their private papers and missionary society letters that dispossession drove Indigenous people to begging and crime. Tuckfield told the WMMS in 1840 that people had suffered 'a serious loss' from the invasion of their lands by settlers, sheep and cattle, 'without an equivalent being rendered. There [sic] territory is not only invaded, but their game is driven back ... valuable roots eaten by the white man's sheep'. Their fear of violence if they moved into foreign country, combined with their supposedly 'savage' disposition, pushed them, he said, towards crime: 'In such circumstances what can be expected but that the savage at once hungry and indolent will beg, and if he fails in that he will steal, and if the liberties he sees fit to take are resented, he will seek his revenge.'[12] Sheep theft, which may have also had symbolic and spiritual meanings for Indigenous people,[13] was assumed by the missionaries to be a pragmatic response to poverty, a rough equivalent to the loss sustained. Orton wrote in his diary:

> If a European kills a kangaroo or by some means drives them quite off the ground nothing is thought about it ... If a native spears a sheep for use, which has destroyed his food & deprived him of his natural means of subsistence, he is stigmatized as a nuisance – summarily punished by shooting ... or sent to Sydney to be tried for his life ... poor fellows though no one would teach them to steal sheep, as it is called, who can blame them?[14]

Thus, Indigenous entitlement to support was claimed on grounds of their particular status as dispossessed and unwilling subjects of empire. As Tuckfield told the WMMS in 1840:

> There can be no question but that the Aborigines of any country have a right to food and certain articles of clothing from the soil left them by

---

11  James Dredge, 26 February 1840, 2 June 1840, James Dredge, Diaries, Notebook and Letterbooks, ?1817–1845 [hereafter *JDD*], MS11625, MSM534, State Library of Victoria (SLV).

12  Francis Tuckfield to General Secretaries, 30 September 1840, Wesleyan Methodist Missionary Society, Archive: Australasia 1812–1889 [hereafter *WMMS*], Mp2107 (Record ID: 133095), National Library of Australia (NLA). Also, Benjamin Hurst to CJ La Trobe, 7 May 1840, in Cannon (ed) 1982, *Historical Records of Victoria (HRV): The Aborigines of Port Phillip, 1835–1839*, vol 2A: 148–149; Francis Tuckfield to the WMMS General Secretaries, 31 June 1840, Francis Tuckfield, Journal, 1837–1842 [hereafter *FTJ*], MS11341, Box 655, SLV.

13  For discussion of this, see Kenny 2007.

14  Joseph Orton, 23 May 1839, Joseph Orton, Journal 1832–1839 and 1840–1841 [hereafter *JOJ*], ML ref A1714–1715, CY reel 1119, State Library of NSW.

their forefathers and if Government occupy their ground and thereby deprive them of their accustomed means of subsistence government is bound in justice to provide for them.[15]

However, this did not mean philanthropists saw the state's obligations as one-sided or unconditional. On the contrary, philanthropists, both in Britain and the colonies, emphasised how rationing should be contingent on – and constitutive of – participation in mission life. People's entitlement to sustenance, like their entitlement to land, must be mediated through their participation in charitable projects.

Here, the implications for policy could be imprecise. The advice of the Select Committee's 1837 report was rather vague, concluding that the Protectors of Aborigines should make 'occasional presents' to gain people's confidence, but should also focus on devising appropriate labour for them.[16] The relationship between these conciliatory and conditional aspects of rationing led to ongoing confusion. Instructions to the Port Phillip and South Australian protectors (drafted 1837–38) stated that they would be responsible for any distribution of rations and clothing, but that they must also encourage agriculture and church attendance, which, in practice required food and gifts.[17] This tension became more explicit in the instructions to the Western Australian protectors, drawn up by Governor Hutt in 1840. These stated that Indigenous people were unfamiliar with hard work, and must be encouraged gradually 'to perform occasional services for hire and reward'. Presents were appropriate to reward the deserving or to gain people's confidence, but 'gratuitous charity' was unacceptable. The protectors were reminded sternly 'A savage is always a beggar, and neither he, nor any other man, will work if bread can be procured by mere asking and importunity.'[18] The initial instructions to the Buntingdale missionaries also mentioned the benefits and dangers of dependence. Wesleyan Methodist Missionary Society organiser Joseph Orton reminded them that they must feed the local people, to prevent them becoming 'vagrant mendicants' throughout the countryside, but at the same time they must try to use food as a reward for work, to discourage idleness.[19] Thus, while colonialism was acknowledged to destroy traditional foods, and while their replacement with a rationing system

---

15  Francis Tuckfield to General Secretaries, 30 September 1840, Methodist Missionary Society, Records [hereafter *MMS*], AJCP M126, SLV.
16  *BPP: Report from the Select Committee on Aborigines (British Settlements)*, vol 2, 1837: 83.
17  Sir George Arthur, Memorandum to applicants, in Sir George Arthur to Lord Glenelg, 15 December 1837, in Cannon (ed) 1982, *HRV*, vol 2A: 33; Lord Glenelg to Sir George Gipps, 31 January 1838, Cannon (ed) 1983, *HRV*, vol 2B: 374–375.
18  Instructions to the Protectors of the Aborigines in Western Australia, in Governor John Hutt to the Marquis of Normanby, 11 February 1840, in *BPP: Papers Relating to Australia, 1844*, Colonies: Australia, vol 8, 1969: 372.
19  Joseph Orton to Benjamin Hurst, 8 January 1839, in Joseph Orton, Letterbooks 1822–1842, ML ref A1717–A1720, State Library of NSW.

was accepted, this was not framed in terms of Indigenous people's unconditional entitlements. Rather, food distribution was associated with conciliatory gestures and the need to encourage Indigenous labour; in other words, with drawing people into systems of colonial benevolence and authority. This mix of beliefs was clear when protector ES Parker described his difficulties in answering complaints of dispossession from Djadjawurrung and Djabwurrung people. He framed rationing in terms of compensation, whilst hinting that he knew it was not wholly adequate, but also stressed that it was dependent on cooperation with protectorate regimes. These, in turn, functioned through personal relationships, with Parker believing himself uniquely qualified to supervise his district.

> [T]hey have been informed in answer to their repeated complaints of the loss of their country, that the government gave them provisions and clothing and furnished them with protection, as a sort of compensation; and that the continuance of these advantages was dependent on their good behaviour. They are peculiarly susceptible to any breach of faith.[20]

Thus, rationing, like land, was understood to be rooted in Indigenous people's specific status as a colonised group who must be both conciliated and institutionalised – in a sense, Indigenous people had a 'right' to be recipients of charity. It was no coincidence that this was an era of change for welfare policies in Britain, where the 1834 Poor Law reforms ushered in a more regulated system of relief, emphasising individual initiative and responsibility but also greater observation and control over the poor and stronger distinctions between the working poor and dependent 'paupers'. Felix Driver has observed a central irony here: the new enthusiasm for free market labour and lessening the dependence of the poor involved the extension of state power and moral discipline, made most explicit in the spectre of the workhouse – 'the janus-face of modern liberalism.' Driver argues that these reforms did not confirm the right of paupers to relief, but rather the duty of the state of relieve the poor under certain circumstances, a duty understood in terms of expediency and governance.[21] Explicit analogies with Australia are problematic; in some ways Aboriginal welfare was clearly 'different', complicated by their status as a distinct colonised group with particular entitlements. Nonetheless, there was a relevant distinction between the state's (or the philanthropist's) responsibility to provide relief, and people's right to demand it. Moreover, on missions and protectorate stations the regulating of relief and the importance of ideas about deserving poverty would become clear.

---

20  ES Parker to GA Robinson, 1 December 1843, Public Records Office of Victoria (PROV), VA512 *Chief Protector of Aborigines*, VPRS12 unit 4, 1843/16 (reel 3).
21  Driver 1993: 18–19.

## 'The bread that perisheth': property and work ethics

In practice, rationing was shaped by ideology, practical circumstances and personal negotiations. Particularly relevant was the tension between using rations as a friendly gift and making them conditional on labour. Missionaries and protectors were conscious of the need to persuade Indigenous people to stay near them, at a time when people remained fairly mobile and could obtain food from other sources considered immoral by the philanthropists. Protector Parker, for instance, asserted 'I cannot persuade the younger females to resist the importunities of the white man, while I am unable to offer a counter-inducement in the shape of food, clothing or shelter.'[22] The use of food and clothes to attract people also merged with traditions of spreading the Gospel. Wellington Valley missionary James Günther remarked on the common practice of rewarding church attendance with food: 'we must use these inducements, giving them the bread that perisheth, if we want an opportunity of administering to them the unperishable lifegiving bread from heaven.'[23] This was also apparent within the Port Phillip protectorate. Chief protector GA Robinson announced in 1841 that additional rations should be set aside to reward people for attending church services at the protectors' homesteads, while protector William Thomas concluded 'no preacher will succeed with the Bible without the loaf'.[24]

Supplying people en masse was inherently problematic, though. Missions and protectorate stations risked unpleasant publicity if they were seen as having degenerated into rations depots, failing to demand Indigenous labour or distinguish between the deserving and undeserving. Magistrate Henry Fysche Gisbourne, embroiled in disputes with the Wellington Valley missionaries, told the New South Wales Executive Council in 1839 that Wellington Valley had failed, asserting that Wiradjuri people were lazy and stayed there only for food.[25] Rev Richard Taylor seconded this claim regretfully to the Church Missionary Society, who were re-evaluating their support for the mission. Stating that Wiradjuri people were not embracing mission life, Taylor mused 'I feel convinced that the general idea entertained of the missionaries is, that they are stationed amongst them by Government only to distribute provisions.'[26] Similarly, when Colonial Secretary E Deas Thomson questioned CW Sievwright's suitability for his protectorate job, one accusation voiced was that Sievwright was issuing

---

22  ES Parker to GA Robinson, 1 April 1840, in Cannon (ed) 1983, *HRV*, vol 2B: 695.
23  James Günther, journal, 15 August 1837, *WVP*.
24  GA Robinson to CW Sievwright, 9 January 1841, in Lakic and Wrench (eds) 1994: 33; William Thomas, 14 June 1846, William Thomas, Papers, 1834–1868 [hereafter *WTP*], ML MSS 214, reel 3, State Library of NSW.
25  Henry Fysche Gisbourne, evidence to Executive Council, 17 April 1840, in *BPP: Papers Relating to Australia, 1844*, vol 8: 41–42.
26  Rev Richard Taylor to Rev William Cowper, 6 February 1839, in *BPP: Papers Relating to Australia, 1844*, vol 8: 46.

rations indiscriminately.²⁷ Regardless of the accuracy of these claims, they point to a trap inherent in the philanthropist's role: they risked being dismissed as useless if Indigenous people did not settle with them, or accused of profligate generosity if they did.

Underwriting this was a colonial trope that Indigenous people were both greedy and lazy. While such slurs were a standard part of the racist discourse of dispossession, they took on different, specific meanings for philanthropists. Greed and sloth were assumed to be essentially linked, as greed was understood as a desire for profit without equivalent effort. This made feeding people a fraught process. The Wellington Valley missionaries bemoaned Wiradjuri people's 'irregular, beastly and immoderate habits' – 'Food is their only inducement to do anything' – concluding 'Poor piteous creatures they seem to have no thought but that of eating.'²⁸ Although the missionaries themselves had started the practice of rewarding religious participation with food, they were disturbed when people began to demand this payment blatantly, interrupting religious discussions with food requests. They lamented that Wiradjuri were 'as indifferent as stones' to Christian teaching but 'cunning enough as regards their stomach'.²⁹ Other philanthropists also expressed fear of voracious Aboriginal appetites. Orton described people eating like 'beasts of prey', while Parker imagined sheep thieves 'luxuriating in all the waste of savage and uncontrolled appetite, with their mangled and half-roasted prey'.³⁰ Such concerns, from Wellington Valley and Moreton Bay, were repeated by the CMS in *Missionary Register* (1839), which noted that people demanded generous helpings of food from the missionaries, whilst appearing indifferent to everything else.³¹

This did not mean that desire for commodities was automatically considered negative. On the contrary, philanthropic writers expressed equal (and related) concern that Indigenous people might not care *enough* about material things. Some religious commentators cited this as a reason for pessimism about the Aboriginal future. Archdeacon Broughton, for example, warned the Select Committee that Indigenous people's alleged lack of property sense made them hard to civilise, as they could not be bribed; 'they do not desire anything that I have, if they have enough food.'³² Similarly, JCS Handt gave a pessimistic assessment of his work at Moreton Bay in 1838, reproduced in the *Missionary*

---

27  E Deas Thomson to CJ La Trobe, 25 February 1842, PROV VPRS10 unit 4, 1842/491 (reel 1).
28  Günther, journal, 28 August 1837, 19 December 1837, *WVP*; Handt, journal, 15 June 1833, 4 October 1833, *WVP*; William Watson, journal, 7 September 1834, *WVP*.
29  Günther, journal, 23 December 1837, *WVP*; Handt, journal, 24 August 1833, *WVP*; Watson, journal, 17 November 1836, *WVP*.
30  Orton, 20 May 1839, *JOJ*, ML ref A1714–1715, CY reel 1119, State Library of NSW; ES Parker 1846, *The Aborigines of Australia*: 8.
31  CMS, *Missionary Register*, August 1839: 387, 389.
32  Archdeacon Broughton, evidence, 3 Aug 1835, *BPP: Report from the Select Committee on Aborigines (British Settlements)*, vol 1, 1836: 18.

*Register*, complaining that people did not value the clothing he gave them because they sold some of the clothes and used the others to make headbands. (In fact, this might suggest the clothes were indeed valued, in a different way, but this was not Handt's perspective.[33])

Thus, the assertion that Indigenous people were both greedy for material things and careless about them became a vital, if paradoxical, element of policy-making. In a report to Robinson in 1842, Thomas described how he lectured people crossly:

> that the Blacks would take the example of the Whites in eating what they eat, in being clothed with their clothing, talk as they talk, and yet would not build house to live in like the white man and have of their own without asking others, put seed in the ground etc [sic].[34]

Philanthropists may have associated this alleged greed and carelessness with traditional life, but they were more concerned about its new colonial manifestations. As the impacts of dispossession and Indigenous social breakdown worsened, many people were living partly off the proceeds of begging, crime and sex with white men. One of the many reasons why this distressed philanthropists was because it seemed to represent greed and gain for no labour. Watson, for instance, was outraged that some Wiradjuri men were 'well supplied with food' for lending female relatives to white men, while Thomas complained that beggars in Melbourne were 'pamper'd not merely beyond the wants of man but far exceeding what the public would credit or imagine'.[35]

Rationing was designed to prevent this, and yet fears of mendicancy often surfaced in discussions of rationing itself. This was a particular concern for the Port Phillip protectorate, under pressure to justify their spending. Robinson reprimanded Thomas in 1841 for allowing able-bodied people who had not yet 'settled' at his station to access food supplies, warning that they were still 'wanderers without any sort of control'.[36] He assured superintendent La Trobe in 1849 that he deplored a handout system; it had 'a tendency to lower them rather than to elevate them'.[37] Even James Dredge, usually sympathetic to Indigenous claims, was irritated when people asked him constantly for food, and called them 'sable mendicants'.[38] As Tim Rowse has observed, the concept of pauperism

---

33  CMS, *Missionary Register*, August 1839: 390; JCS Handt to William Cowper, Annual Report of the Church Missionary Society Mission at Moreton Bay, 1838, Sir William Dixson, *Documents relating to Aboriginal Australians, 1816–1853*, Dixson Library, ADD 80–82: CY reel 3743, State Library of NSW.
34  William Thomas to GA Robinson, 24 May 1842, PROV VPRS4410 unit 3, 1842/71 (reel 2).
35  William Thomas to CJ La Trobe, 1 October 1844, PROV VPRS10 unit 6, 1844/1761 (reel 1); William Thomas to GA Robinson, Report of Proceedings 1 March to 1 June 1843, PROV VPRS4410 unit 3, 1843/76 (reel 2); Watson, journal, 27 August 1833, *WVP*.
36  GA Robinson to CJ La Trobe, 15 December 1841, VPRS10 unit 3 (reel 1).
37  GA Robinson to CJ La Trobe, 23 December 1839, in Cannon (ed) 1983, *HRV*, vol 2B: 487.
38  Dredge, 12 October 1839, *JDD*, MS11625, MSM534, SLV.

(being finessed in British discourse at this time) was both fundamental and problematic to Australian colonialism. The first philanthropic records certainly highlight Indigenous dependence and the horror it excited, but it is also clear, as Rowse notes, that efforts to separate dependent paupers and the working poor, conceptually and physically, did not always apply. Instead, Indigenous people were portrayed as inherently suspect, both passive and devious in their greed.[39] This blurring between poor and pauper was unsurprising, given the use of material goods to attract residents, the fact that Indigenous dependence on charitable aid was so widespread, and the nature of the rationing system itself, where rewards for labourers were distributed in much the same way as the items doled out to the needy and reluctantly ceded to the demanding. Neither the rations nor the people themselves could be clearly divided.

Such difficulties did not make philanthropists any less passionate on the subject. They still hoped to inculcate a sense of the value of material property earned through honest work. Robinson articulated this with particular enthusiasm, assuring La Trobe at the start of the protectorate that Indigenous people 'should be taught to know their wants, should feel their necessities; a desire for civilized comforts and for the possession of property should be created.'[40] When attempting to justify the protectorate's operation to the 1845 New South Wales Select Committee on the Condition of the Aborigines, Robinson assured them that blankets and clothing were only supplied to the needy and the hard workers; 'the effect has been very beneficial ... calculated to lead to industrious habits, and to the knowledge of the value of the property'.[41] Three years later, he was still hoping (largely in vain) to reward hard workers with sheep, property and land, believing this would encourage them to stop travelling and develop a sense of 'rights and interests to watch over and property to protect'.[42] Robinson's unusually strong statements about material property might be traced to his weaker grasp of the inadequacy of resources, of which his assistants frequently complained. It is also possible that, being less passionately Evangelical than some of his colleagues, he was drawn more to a 'civilisation first' approach. However, Evangelical philanthropy did not exclude the benefits of consumption. On the contrary, Jean and John Comaroff, in their discussion of mission work amongst the Tswana, argue that material desires were seen as a potentially elevating force, if combined with rationality, self-control and regular labour; 'saving the savage meant teaching the savage to save'.[43]

---

39   Rowse 1998b: 20, 25–26, 32–33, also 40–41.
40   GA Robinson to CJ La Trobe, 23 December 1839, in Cannon (ed) 1983, *HRV*, vol 2B: 488.
41   GA Robinson, Evidence to the Select Committee on the condition of the Aborigines, 1845, in Frauefelder (ed) 1997: 52.
42   GA Robinson 2001, 1848 Annual Report, in *The Papers of George Augustus Robinson, Chief Protector, Port Phillip Aboriginal Protectorate*, Clark (ed) vol 4: 150.
43   Comaroff and Comaroff 1997 vol 2: 166–167, 191–194, 219.

Thus, supplying rations was connected to encouraging work ethics. Parker and Thomas stressed in their reports that they tried to make food and blankets for the able-bodied conditional upon labour or trading of traditional handicrafts.[44] Watson, similarly, wished to make meals contingent on regular work. This became clear in one diary entry from 1836, when a young man called George, who had been 'wandering about all the day', asked Watson for his supper.

> I told him that I could not give food to natives who neither attended to instruction nor worked. He said 'Black fellow not that way when born you know, he not work, he not learn.' I told him that, wild natives lived on opossum &c and if he wanted to live as a wild native he must look out for Wild natives food [sic]. That if he wished to have his wants supplied here, he must either attend School, or work.[45]

Even children (generally recognised in charitable discourse as vulnerable and entitled to sustenance) had their rations used to control their behaviour, with meals and clothes provided as incentives for schooling. Thomas, for example, promised extra clothes to children who were attentive in class.[46] South Australian protector Matthew Moorhouse arranged for flour to be given as a reward for school attendance in Encounter Bay, while Indigenous parents in Adelaide who sent their children to school were prioritised in the annual blanket distribution.[47] More ominously, some philanthropists connected rations to punishments; in 1837, George Langhorne claimed that children could come and go from his Melbourne mission freely, but those who left without permission would lose a meal that day.[48]

Philanthropists believed work should be not only hard but also regular and differentiated from leisure time. Langhorne's original plans for his Melbourne mission in 1837 aimed to divide time, labour and meals in a fashion reminiscent of British workhouses, stating that the adult residents must work at least four hours daily in return for three regular meals, and would be supplied with clothing (marked to prevent theft). He added that 'Black occasional comers' should be remunerated 'on a regular scale, according to the space of time employed, or the nature of the work done', and suggested 1/2lb of bread for two hours' work, plus 1/4lb of meat for four hours.[49] Robinson also expressed

---

44   For example, ES Parker, Quarterly Journal, 1 June – 31 August 1842, PROV VPRS4410 unit 2, 1842/62 (reel 2); William Thomas to GA Robinson, 3 December 1840, PROV VPRS11 unit 7, 1840/351 (reel 1); William Thomas to GA Robinson, 11 September 1841, PROV VPRS11 unit 8, 1841/392 (reel 2).
45   Watson, journal, 19 Dec 1836, *WVP*.
46   Thomas, 22 February 1842, *WTP*, ML MSS 214, reel 2, State Library of NSW.
47   Matthew Moorhouse to Colonial Secretary, 13 December 1842, *Protector of Aborigines, Letterbook, 1840–1857*, State Records of South Australia (SRSA), GRG52/7, unit 1; Matthew Moorhouse to Colonial Secretary, 20 March 1846, SRSA, GRG24/6, Colonial Secretary's Office, Correspondence files, no 300 of 1846.
48   George Langhorne to Colonial Secretary, 14 August 1837, in Cannon (ed) 1982, *HRV*, vol 2A: 173.
49   GM Langhorne to Colonial Secretary, 14 August 1837, Cannon (ed) 1982, *HRV*, vol 2A: 174.

initial hopes that 'savages' newly introduced to labour would work between 6–8 hours a day, in contrast to the 10 hours he thought appropriate for Europeans.[50] It is doubtful this was ever really enforced in practice. Ideals of mechanisation, regulation and observation, derived from the industrial revolution, did not sit easily with traditional Indigenous economies, which were seasonal and variable, and tended to emphasise obtaining food on a collectivist basis for minimal effort.[51] Nor, indeed, did they have much to do with rural life. However, the wish to divide the day regularly according to work, meals, leisure and prayer did not wholly vanish, and it remained particularly apparent in attempts to institutionalise the children.

## 'Like a swarm of bees': rationing and the family

The use of rationing to encourage a sense of private property was linked, in turn, to notions of the family unit and the individual self. Accumulation of property and pride in personal labour were dear to philanthropists, who linked these things to the stability and respectability of the home. However, on Aboriginal missions and protectorate stations, Evangelical ideals about autonomous individuals saving and valuing their property within the bourgeois nuclear family came into tension with Indigenous views on family obligations, and with missionaries' own institutional practices.

Philanthropists came to believe that a key obstacle to success lay in Indigenous people's own understandings of the family. To missionaries' frustration, people on their stations did not necessarily draw a clear distinction between workers and non-workers, and instead distributed food according to complex networks of kin obligation.[52] Thus, philanthropists complained about 'idlers' expecting to share workers' rations. Günther wrote in frustration:

> whenever we give our Natives meat, they will be sure to take it to the camp ... Some idle fellows these who we do not feel justified to feed or another who for bad behaviour ought to be punished with receiving nothing will come & either by entreaties or by threatenings obtain part of the portion of those who have deserved it. Nay the poor fellow (who is deserving) loses some time the whole of his meat.[53]

The young man Jemmy Buckley, who had visited the mission since its commencement, gave this as a reason for refusing to perform farm labour, telling

---

50  GA Robinson to CJ La Trobe, 23 December 1839, Cannon (ed) 1983, *HRV*, vol 2B: 487.
51  Broome 2001: 56, 70.
52  McGrath 1987: 124–125.
53  Günther, journal, 19 December 1837, *WVP*.

Watson 'What shall I do with it? directly Black fellow know I got wheat they come up and eat it all up at once, and then I shall have to go into the Bush like another Black fellow.'[54]

Thus, philanthropists' use of rationing could aim to dismantle what they considered to be unruly or immoral family structures. This was especially evident with regard to young people, on whom philanthropists focused most of their energies, believing them to be more open to Christian influences than the adults. Protector Thomas, for example, once threatened to withhold rations from the camp if the adults took the children out of school.[55] However, the most extreme and troubling instances took place at Wellington Valley, where Watson often described 'purchasing' children for blankets, tea, shirts, tobacco and necklaces. Some adults took the gifts and left their young relatives for short periods, retrieving them soon afterwards, much to the missionaries' vexation.[56] At other times, aggressive confrontations occurred. In March 1835, Watson described a 'trying week', when a woman called Nelly tried to remove her daughter, Eliza, from the mission. (A year before, Eliza had left the station with her relatives and been forced back by Watson.) Watson believed Nelly had been frightened by rumours circulating of grave spiritual danger to Wiradjuri girls living with white people, and he refused to let Eliza go.

> The Mother wept aloud and scolded on the outside of the kitchen, and the girl wept in the kitchen. Being anxious to go I gave the old woman as much Wheat and Beef as she could carry, as also Tobacco and Pipes but all would not do. My feelings almost overcame my Judgment in this affecting scene, and indeed nothing but the licentiousness to which I knew the girl would be exposed prevented me from letting her go.[57]

Given that Nelly was ill and dependent on mission aid, she may have felt unable to press the subject. Watson stated that she eventually left the mission with a man called Old Bobagul, 'having received a Cake, a Blanket, and a Neck handkerchief'.[58]

As such scenes show, the exchange of goods for temporary child custody occurred in a climate of inequality, sometimes heightened by missionary bullying. Nonetheless, the dynamic was not a simple one. Philanthropists may have resented and tried to undermine communal obligation, but they also became implicated in it. Historians such as Ann McGrath and Richard Broome have observed Indigenous people's efforts to draw settlers into systems

---

54  Watson, journal, 7 July 1836, *WVP*.
55  Thomas, 20 August 1841, *WTP*, ML MSS 214, reel 2, State Library of NSW.
56  Watson, journal, 21 February 1834, 26–27 February 1837, 18 October 1834, 6 March 1835, *WVP*.
57  Watson, journal, 28 March 1835, *WVP*.
58  Watson, journal, 28 March 1835, *WVP*. Also, Watson, journal, 25 October 1834, 31 January 1835, 1 August 1835, *WVP*.

of reciprocity, stretching beyond individuals to their extended families. Most examples of this explored by historians have focused on issues of work or sex, but it seems likely that contact with young people was also a relevant area of rationing obligations on the first missions and protectorate stations.[59] Here, Broome's work on the later Coranderrk station in Victoria is helpful. Arguing against the belief that rations simply oppressed people and created one-sided dependence, he suggests instead that European dynamics of paternalism could be incorporated into Indigenous understandings of asymmetrical mentoring and kinship. Broome points to assertive statements by mission residents that colonial authorities had a duty to care for them, partly in payment for the loss of their land.[60] Similar dynamics – not always comfortable or peaceable – can be detected in earlier philanthropic projects. Ironically, in order to gain access to young people, philanthropists were obliged to satisfy Indigenous demands for material rewards, exchanges which philanthropists associated with begging, laziness and greed, but which Indigenous people may have understood in terms of kinship obligations.

Thus, some people who left children with the missionaries or protectors were confident and even aggressive in their material demands. This was evident at Thomas's station and especially at Wellington Valley. Thomas complained in 1844 that children were refusing to attend school, and that the older men pointed out 'too much get em bread Melbourne, no hungry no school.'[61] One man threatened to remove his child from school after Thomas refused him a new blanket, and Thomas fumed that some adults told him 'Give my piccaninny black money and then school.'[62] While Thomas experienced this as ungrateful begging, the people involved may have believed themselves entitled to demand resources from the protector, who was so eager to live with their young people, in their country. Thomas stated 'they consider they are rendering you a great service [by sending their children to school] & that you are under great obligation for teaching their offspring.'[63] Some Wellington Valley examples were even more emphatic. In 1836, Watson described one man, Ngarrang Bartharai, whose daughter, Fanny, was staying at Wellington Valley:

> He thinks that because we have a child belonging to him, that we must give him every thing he desires. Not only would he have us supply his own wants; but he brings up other natives saying, they are 'his brothers'... This time, I have given to Bartharai, a Razor, a Pocket Knife, a Blanket, Wheat – Beef – Tobacco &c &c.[64]

---

59   Broome 2001: 57; McGrath 1987: 124–125, 141.
60   Broome 2006: 42.3–42.4, 43.10.
61   Thomas, 26 January 1844, *WTP*, ML MSS 214, reel 3, State Library of NSW.
62   William Thomas to GA Robinson, 31 November 1844, PROV VPRS4410 unit 3, 1844/82 (reel 2); Thomas, 13 August 1846, *WTP*, ML MSS 214, reel 3, State Library of NSW.
63   Thomas, 19 November 1846, *WTP*, ML MSS 214, reel 3, State Library of NSW.
64   Watson, journal, 18 October 1836, *WVP*.

On another occasion, Watson wrote:

> The natives came up this morning like a swarm of Bees, demanding Beef – Wheat – Tobacco and Pipes. One native whose little girl is living with us said, 'I have many Black fellows belonging to me, you must give me for all.'[65]

Such disputes highlight an irony in early philanthropic work: philanthropists' efforts to weaken the ties of extended Indigenous families, and to impart Evangelical British ideals of labour to the young people, required them to enter into the very relationships of obligation and kinship which they wished to undermine.

Indigenous views on obligation were by no means simple, though, and arguments over food distribution can be hard to interpret from philanthropic records, where the scenarios could seem garbled, impatient or confused. Aside from child custody, the other issue to emerge powerfully in connection to rationing was Indigenous control over traditional lands. Angry scenes could ensue when philanthropists supplied rations to people from foreign districts. When a large group of 'wild Natives' travelled to Wellington Valley, one of the older Wiradjuri men was offended when Watson said he would welcome the visitors. The man commented 'Hy Hy, but them wild fellows, they ask you give blanket, give flour, pipes, tobacco'. He interrogated Watson 'will you give it them?' When Watson replied that he might, the man was 'very far from being pleased'.[66] Watson may not have taken this issue entirely seriously, but missionaries at the more volatile Buntingdale station soon learned to. In 1841, Hurst recommended to La Trobe that separate missions be established for each 'tribe' in Port Phillip, in an effort to recognise (and probably to reshape and cement) divisions between groups. He agreed that food and clothes should be used as an incentive to attract people, but added that missionaries should not give gifts to foreign 'tribes'; the associated risks were too great.[67] Such examples demonstrate philanthropists' use of rationing to exercise personal and cultural power, but at the same time they make clear the limits of this power in a context of Indigenous mobility, local compromises and unequal mutuality.

By involving themselves in community networks via rationing, philanthropists also found their own families implicated. The boundaries philanthropists constructed between their private world and the 'savage' outdoors were both vital and permeable, and disputes over food supply made this apparent. Here, missionary women's domesticity was linked to the wider spheres of government policy and Indigenous kinship. Accounts from Wellington Valley place Ann

---

65  Watson, journal, 14 February 1837, *WVP*.
66  Watson, journal, 1 September 1834, *WVP*.
67  Benjamin Hurst to CJ La Trobe, 22 July 1841, *MMS*, reel 4, AJCP M121, SLV.

Watson at the centre of several fierce arguments with Wiradjuri men over food and blankets. On one occasion in 1833, when a group of men demanded blankets from the missionaries, Watson was afraid that one man might attack Mrs Watson because she had refused him a new blanket after he gave his old one away.[68] A similar scene occurred a year later, when Watson described a rationing session characterised by a tense mix of domestic closeness, obligation and hostility. Mrs Watson had set aside milk for Narrang Jackey (whose young wife lived at the mission sometimes), not noticing that another person had taken it.

> Shortly afterwards Jackey came up and asked for milk. Mrs W said I gave it to you. He went out of the hut in a rage, threw down his pannikin with the greatest violence, summoned his two yeeners [women] and went away, and although Mrs W went out after him to give him milk he would not have it. With a hut full of Natives pressing closely to her on all sides it is no wonder she made a mistake, especially knowing that Jackey would very readily come again and again for his share of provisions.[69]

Thomas's diaries provide similar accounts of Mrs Thomas supplying people with food, sometimes independently of her husband, negotiating this with difficulty when rations were insufficient. When some men, who chopped wood for Mrs Thomas, instructed her to cook plenty of cabbage for their dinner, Thomas remarked 'poor things they consider their friends had nought to do but cook for them'.[70] On another occasion, a fight broke out on Thomas's station when a woman he called 'Kurbro's lubra' hit the schoolteacher's wife, Mrs Wilson, with her digging stick because Mrs Wilson had refused to give her water.[71] Ironically, it was the Evangelical ideal of women's nurturing role, as well as the uneasy reciprocity that developed between Indigenous people and missionary households, that implicated the domestic Evangelical world in a rationing process that was both administrative and passionately ideological.

## 'Still they are dissatisfied': the problem of gratitude

Such encounters remind us that early philanthropists' views on poverty and rationing were developing in small, face-to-face environments, where missionaries sought to maintain what Bain Attwood has termed 'distant intimacy' with Indigenous people.[72] In this context, rationing systems brought to the fore philanthropists' wish to structure relationships according to

---

68   Watson, journal, 24 August 1833, *WVP*.
69   Watson, 5 December 1834, *WVP*. Also, 24 August 1835.
70   Thomas, 31 December 1846, *WTP*, ML MSS 214, reel 3. See also Thomas journal, undated fragment, 1839, *WTP*, reel 3, f18; Thomas, Journal, 30 June 1840, *WTP*, ML MSS 214, reel 1, State Library of NSW.
71   Thomas, 31 March 1841, *WTP*, ML MSS 214, reel 2, State Library of NSW.
72   Attwood 1989: 28.

gratitude and paternalism, and the varied ways this related to the Indigenous wish to prioritise relationships of kinship and traditional exchange. Evangelical advocates saw gratitude as fundamental to the success of the charitable encounter. It (theoretically) affirmed the philanthropist's benevolent authority and demonstrated the willing compliance of the recipient. The frequent colonial claim that Indigenous people were incapable of gratitude was, therefore, especially disturbing. This was hinted at in Broughton and Yate's testimony to the Select Committee, where they disagreed over whether Indigenous people were too mercenary and 'volatile' to feel grateful for acts of kindness.[73]

Indeed, Evangelical attitudes towards sustenance as a whole were shaped by ideas of thankfulness and submission to a higher power. Protector Thomas, when scolding people for not embracing farming life, told them that 'their very actions was a disgrace to them – that if white men only for one season was as indifferent as them, & God should not send rain that half the families of the earth should perish.'[74] This suggests a belief that nourishment and basic comforts were not so much universal entitlements as boons derived from higher benevolence. Such generosity must not be taken for granted. Watson employed a similar logic in 1834, when a wet spell endangered the mission's wheat crop. When people asked him 'What for God let water come up all over wheat?' he explained that 'we had an opportunity of seeing how soon God could destroy everything and leave us without anything to eat.'[75]

Such ideas about benevolence and gratitude suggest, again, that while philanthropists and the state had a duty to supply goods to the needy, Indigenous people did not have the right to demand them. As O'Brien puts it, 'To most evangelicals, it was anathema to treat kindness as a right.'[76] This became problematic, however, when it clashed with Indigenous assumptions that missionaries were obliged to share their belongings, because of their access to goods, residence in Indigenous country and partial incorporation into local networks. Misunderstandings and disputes followed. Philanthropists' journals and some of their publications complained about Indigenous ingratitude; here, Evangelical ideology mingled with personal offence and hurt. South Australia's first protector, Bromley, recorded lengthy disputes with Kaurna people over their hated oatmeal rations. The elders scolded him for not providing bread and biscuits instead, while parents taught their children to nag him for better supplies. They were, he said, 'clamorous and troublesome' – 'these things

---

73   Archdeacon Broughton, evidence, 3 August 1835, *BPP: Report from the Select Committee on Aborigines (British Settlements)*, vol 1, 1836: 19; Rev William Yate, evidence, 13 February 1836, *BPP: Report from the Select Committee on Aborigines (British Settlements)*, vol 1, 1836: 202.
74   William Thomas to GA Robinson, 24 May 1842, PROV VPRS4410 unit 3, 1842/71 (reel 2).
75   Watson, journal, 27 August 1834, *WVP*.
76   O'Brien 2008: 163.

are extremely discouraging to a person of acute feelings'.[77] Publications by CG Tiechelmann of South Australia and Peter Nique of Moreton Bay in 1841 highlighted similar claims that Indigenous people were dictatorial, treating their new missionaries like servants. Nique, in particular, gave a disgruntled account of his travels in the barely-colonised country of Toorbal, amongst people who were often aggressive or disdainful towards Europeans.

> They are exceedingly indolent, and would readily accept of it [sic] if we made ourselves their slaves, to fetch wood and water for them. As soon as we had got some water for ourselves, they wanted to drink it ... They would not even rise to fetch an oyster or anything beyond their reach, but wanted us to hand it to them.[78]

Meanwhile, protector Thomas, whose relationships with Kulin nations in Port Phillip were more intimate and enduring, nonetheless became angry when he felt unappreciated. He lamented that he must tolerate people's material demands, lest they go begging elsewhere. When one man borrowed his horse without asking, Thomas burst out angrily in his journal 'these are unbearable people, it is useless scolding or coaxing them while they can get their wants supplied by begging.'[79]

Complaints were loudest, however, at Wellington Valley. In one incident in 1838, Jemmy Buckley became angry when Günther refused to give him a cake, and said 'You stupid fellow ... you never give me anything.' Günther remarked 'It is grievous to observe the ingratitude, even of the best of them.'[80] His colleague, Watson, was irate when another man, Kabbarin, ordered him away from the camp, declaring that Watson had not fed him adequately: 'I do not want you here you did not give me good meat this morning it was all bone. I chucked it away it was dog's meat.'[81] The most distressed member of the mission house, though, was the gloomy and easily discouraged JCS Handt, who mused frequently over Wiradjuri people's apparent indifference to his charitable gestures. On one occasion in 1835, he approached the local camp and was dismayed when several boys left immediately. He wrote mournfully in his journal:

> Thus they shun us and our house, as though they had been ill treated, when quite the contrary has always been the case. They have had their regular meals, and as much as they could eat at each, without any

---

77 Protector Bromley to Colonial Secretary, 26 June 1837, SRSA GRG24/1, Colonial Secretary's Office, Letters and other communications received, no 206 of 1837; Protector Bromley to Governor Stirling, 29 June 1837, SRSA GRG24/1/1837/210.
78 P Nique, 'Aborigines: Diary of Messrs Nique and Hartenstein of the German Mission to the Aborigines', in *Colonial Observer*, vol 1, no 4–5, 1841. Also, CG Tiechelmann 1841, *Aborigines of South Australia*: 11.
79 Thomas, 28 December 1845, *WTP*, ML MSS 214, reel 3, State Library of NSW.
80 Günther, journal, 17 January 1838, *WVP*.
81 Watson, journal, 29 December 1835, *WVP*.

trouble and labour of their own, as we are often afraid to ask them to do anything, lest they should be offended and go away ... but still they are dissatisfied.[82]

Such comments indicate more than simple irritation; they suggest a sense of painful rebuff when a paternalist dynamic was (apparently) refused. Without this, philanthropists found their work hard to conceptualise at all.

Philanthropists' sense of a mission frustrated did not derive from their belief in Indigenous ingratitude alone, however. It was also suggestive of their fear of being unable to sustain an authoritative, providing role in an atmosphere of colonial discontent and limited resources. Supply shortages, for which they often blamed the government, were especially discouraging. This was apparent at Wellington Valley in 1833, during a heated dispute over government-issue blankets (referred to earlier). A group of Wiradjuri men demanded the blankets, reminding Watson that supplies were sent by the Governor and should not be his to control. Watson relented and distributed some of them, whilst telling the men they had not behaved well enough to deserve them. Later, however, he complained in his diary (in comments presumably meant for the Church Missionary Society) that he was forced to restrict access because supplies were inadequate – here, his 'civilising' lectures merged with practical constraints.[83] His colleague, James Günther, lamented in 1839 that they still did not have enough food to entice people to stay at the mission. Their agriculturalist, William Porter, told Governor Gipps during his 1840 visit that he deeply regretted being unable to pay people wages or reward them properly. (Gipps, instead of supporting regular remuneration, suggested small gifts for the well-behaved.[84]) More overt statements of the inadequacy of state support came from Port Phillip protectors James Dredge and ES Parker. Dredge complained in 1839 that he did not have enough supplies to employ people regularly.[85] A decade later, Parker was pleased to report that his station's residents had begun to work hard in agricultural jobs, but complained he could not reward them properly. He told Robinson that he was reduced to purchasing gifts for the labourers himself and begging donations from neighbours – a statement which emphasised both his paternalistic generosity and his compromised professional status. Parker argued that his workers should receive a 'full equivalent' in food, clothes and (interestingly) money: 'The mere "name of wages" said one of the young men on a recent occasion, "made his heart very glad".'[86]

---

82   Handt, journal, 26 November 1835, *WVP*.
83   Watson, journal, 24 Aug 1833, *WVP*.
84   Sir George Gipps, Memorandum respecting Wellington Valley, in Sir George Gipps to Lord John Russell, 5 April 1841, in *BPP: Papers Relating to Australia, 1844*, vol 8: 68; Günther, journal, 31 March 1839, *WVP*.
85   Dredge, 6 September 1839, *JDD*, MS11625, MSM534, SLV.
86   ES Parker to GA Robinson, 16 January 1849, PROV VPRS4410 unit 2, 1849/64 (reel 2).

Philanthropists' disappointment take quite personal forms. Protector Thomas, for instance, was depressed during a journey he made around Melbourne in July 1839, without servants or supplies. Camped by the Yarra amongst Kulin peoples, he was forced to accept the kindness of Woiwurrung man Billy Lonsdale, who brought him bread and tea and tutted sympathetically at what he saw as the Governor's meanness. Thomas mused that he would never before have contemplated eating and sleeping in such savage circumstances.[87] Similarly, when James Dredge left the protectorate, the explanation to Daungwurrung people he recorded in his journal was 'that I could not bear to see all my black fellows "hungry" and nothing to give them – that I had sent for more a long time since – but that no letter had come back – and therefore I should go away.'[88] Here, Dredge was simplifying his numerous reasons for leaving, but his comments are interesting nonetheless. They indicate the importance to Aboriginal policy of personal connections, of benevolence and gratitude – what might be called the pleasures of philanthropy.

The distribution of food and other provisions to Indigenous people provides valuable insights into a number of the elements that distinguished philanthropists' efforts at governance in the first half of the 19th century: the centrality of local relationships, the necessity for negotiation, and the philanthropists' vexed position as agents of imperial policy and critics of dispossession. Perhaps most striking, however, is the way it illuminates the conditional and unequal mutuality of philanthropic governance. Any concept of universal, unequivocal rights (even to the basic necessities of life) was largely absent. What appeared instead was a sense of Aboriginal welfare emerging from a complex, contradictory set of obligations – between conqueror and colonised, givers and receivers of charity, clergymen and their congregations, and members of turbulent but close-knit communities. These dynamics, while in many ways particular to the early 19th century colonies, nonetheless provided a foundation for policies and controversies that have proved long-lasting.

---

87   Thomas, July 1839 abstract, *WTP*, ML MSS 214, reel 1, State Library of NSW.
88   Dredge, 12 March 1840, *JDD*, MS11625, MSM534, SLV.

# Keeping body and soul together: creating material 'civilisation'

At his Goulburn River station in September 1839, Port Phillip protector James Dredge recorded a day's events which demonstrated, he believed, the importance of the physical self to Christian civilisation. His wife, Sarah, gave a dress to a Daungwurrung woman (whose name went unrecorded) in return for a woven basket, a scene Dredge described thus: 'A stranger can scarcely imagine the pleasure this poor creature felt, and the gratitude she manifested in being clothed like a "white lubra" – and throwing aside her filthy rags.' To the protectors, trading Indigenous goods for European ones seemed morally preferable to one-sided 'pauperism'. At the same time, from the Dredges' viewpoint, charitable dynamics still structured this encounter: the transition from alleged 'filth' and inadequate clothing to cleanliness and decency, and the enactment of a specifically feminine benevolence and gratitude. It was quite a day for physical change, as Dredge then showed the woman her reflection in his mirror. She and another friend were amused and fascinated by the mirror, presenting food to their reflections. Dredge, who also spent the day brooding over his past year in Port Phillip, feeling unhappy and useless as a philanthropist, concluded 'What a mercy or mercies it is that *my lot* was not cast amongst "the rude barbarian" Tribes of this land.' The place of the mirror in this story is intriguing, reminiscent of the accounts – discussed at length by Jean Comaroff – of South African missionaries presenting people with mirrors. (Dredge, in fact, knew he was contributing to existing discourse, commenting that 'savage' people's surprise at mirrors was something 'I have often read of'.[1]) Mirrors were intended not only to impress people with European innovation, but also to encourage introspection and enlightenment.[2] Ideas about cleanliness, clothing and privacy were important to the first philanthropists in the Australian colonies, as they made paradoxical plans to reshape Indigenous people both as autonomous individuals and objects of institutional conformity.

The association of native peoples within imperial discourse with the physical, natural world, and the claim that they were less intellectual or spiritual than their colonisers, scarcely needs reiteration. It is worth noting, however, that this association had particular significance for Evangelical philanthropists, who, while insisting on the equal value of all human souls, nonetheless located 'heathens' firmly within the earthly sphere. At Wellington Valley, in 1839, James Günther described talking to a Wiradjuri man, Cochrane, about the phrase in

---

1 James Dredge, 24 September 1839, James Dredge, Diaries, Notebook and Letterbooks, ?1817–1845 [hereafter *JDD*], MS11625, MSM534, State Library of Victoria (SLV).
2 Comaroff 1991: 8–10.

Romans 8:1 'There is therefore now no condemnation to them which are in Jesus Christ, who walk not after the flesh, but after the Spirit.' Cochrane, who pleased Günther by learning to read but also aggravated him by continuing to participate in young men's ceremonies, asked 'Do I walk after the flesh?' Günther, pleased that the question had arisen, sternly confirmed that he did.[3] Meanwhile, Methodist missionaries Francis Tuckfield and John Smithies and protector ES Parker all claimed that their attempts to preach in local Indigenous languages were hindered by the supposed deficiency of these languages, which contained a wealth of terms for the natural world but 'no sacrifices, no prayers: no fears or hopes with reference to another state'.[4] South Australian missionary, CG Tiechelmann, went further, informing his readers in 1841 that Indigenous people were mired in the world of the flesh, unable to understand Christian philosophy, and lacking the convert's necessary humility:

> From the visible world they derive their existence, from the visible world they expect good and evil, and the whole creation again they believe to have under their control. Therefore, we cannot expect to find morality or any idea of final and individual responsibility amongst them.[5]

However, this attitude did not indicate a lack of Evangelical concern with the material world. A powerful paradox of 19th century missionary work was the coexistence of belief in a mind-body split and a determination to see civilisation lived and displayed physically. Here, a religious wish for spiritual transformation to be made visible mingled with the growing 19th century emphasis on 'disciplinary technologies'; the urge, as explored by Foucault, to civilise though observation and introspection. For some philanthropists, bodily issues were included explicitly in their job descriptions. LE Threlkeld, for instance, was instructed in 1825 to teach the people of Lake Macquarie about decency and cleanliness, while the covering of nudity was one of the duties of the West Australian and South Australian protectors.[6] Missionaries, as Jean Comaroff has noted,

---

3    James Günther, journal, 19 December 1839, in Carey and Roberts (eds) 2002, *The Wellington Valley Project: Letters and Journals Relating to the Church Missionary Society Mission to Wellington Valley, NSW, 1830–42, A Critical Electronic Edition* [hereafter *WVP*]: <http://www.newcastle.edu.au>

4    John Smithies to General Secretaries, 26 October 1844, Wesleyan Methodist Missionary Society, Archive: Australasia 1812–1889 [hereafter *WMMS*], reel 2, f84–85, Mp2107 (Record ID: 133095), National Library of Australia (NLA). Also, ES Parker 1967, 'The Aborigines of Australia', 10 May 1854, in Morrison (ed): 19–20; ES Parker to GA Robinson, 16 January 1849, Public Records Office of Victoria (PROV) VA512 *Chief Protector of Aborigines*, VPRS4410 unit 2, 1849/64 (reel 2); Francis Tuckfield to General Secretaries, 30 September 1840, *WMMS*, reel 2, NLA.

5    Christian Gottlieb Tiechelmann 1841, *Aborigines of South Australia: Illustrative and Explanatory Notes of the Manners, Customs, Habits and Superstitions of the Natives of South Australia*: 10–11, also 8–10.

6    Instructions to the Protectors of the Aborigines of Western Australia, in Lord Stanley to Governor Grey, 14 November 1843, in *British Parliamentary Papers (BPP): Papers Relating to Australia, 1844*, Colonies: Australia, vol 8, 1969: 372; Matthew Moorhouse to Colonial Secretary, 14 March 1842, State Records of South

knew instinctively what students of culture have only recently discovered: that the fundamental axioms of being are vested in routine mundanities ... profound 'inner' transformations could be achieved by working on the humble 'outer' terrain of the body, dress, or subsistence production.[7]

Or, as James Günther remarked irritably about Wiradjuri people who resisted his teachings, 'all want not merely preaching to them, occasionally, in the bush, they want instructing & training up like children'.[8]

Several historians of Aboriginal Australia have developed an interest in material regimes of observation and control, particularly in accounts of the stolen generations by scholars like Anna Haebich, and in works on institutional cultures by Bain Attwood, Jane Lydon and Anna Cole. Missionary ideas of bodily civilisation in other colonies have also been explored in the works of Patricia Grimshaw, Jean and John Comaroff and Richard Eves, amongst others. The Australian colonies in the 1830s and 40s offer important additions to this area of enquiry. The exceptionally derogatory views expressed about Indigenous bodies, and the particular obsession with gaining control over children within the philanthropists' own domestic space – at a time when missionaries and protectors had comparatively little coercive power – made for unique yet formative regimes. The important, if contradictory, efforts to recreate colonised peoples as both individual subjects and institutional communities also deserve further examination.

## Fine figures and the idea of dirt

Physical depictions of Indigenous Australians by philanthropists (published and unpublished) were mixed. They showed some limited understanding of the cultural meanings of paint, jewellery and body modification for people travelling into foreign country or taking part in ceremonies.[9] Indigenous beliefs that the human body was permeable to the outside world, vulnerable to intrusion by sorcery, were also evident (albeit in partial, unsympathetic ways) in descriptions of Aboriginal responses to illness.[10] Philanthropists' physical

---

Australia (SRSA), GRG24/6, Colonial Secretary's Office, Correspondence files, no 39 of 1842; Daniel Tyerman and George Bennett to LE Threlkeld, 24 February 1825, London Missionary Society, Records [hereafter *LMS*], AJCP M73, SLV.
7   Comaroff 1991: 11. Also, Comaroff and Comaroff 1991 vol 1: 193.
8   James Günther to Dandeson Coates, 12 February 1839, *WVP*.
9   For example, Parker 1967, 'The Aborigines of Australia': 22; GA Robinson 1998, *Journals: Port Phillip Aboriginal Protectorate*, Clark (ed) vol 1: 26; Robinson 1998, *Journals*, Clark (ed) vol 2: 181, 215; Francis Tuckfield, 14 December 1839, Francis Tuckfield, Journal, 1837–1842 [hereafter *FTJ*], MS11341, Box 655, SLV; LE Threlkeld, 'Memoranda', in Gunson (ed) 1974 vol 1: 98.
10  For example, ES Parker, Quarterly Journal: July 1841, PROV VPRS4410 unit 2, (reel 2); ES Parker, Quarterly Journal: 1 September – 30 November 1841, PROV VPRS4410 unit 2, 1841/59 (reel 2); Robinson

descriptions of Indigenous men could even be quite appreciative; the men were described as 'remarkably erect in their carriage with very fine and broad chests', 'a fine, stout, athletic race ... well proportioned and finely limbed', 'fine open countenances', 'muscular forms, fine models for the sculpture.'[11] However, such remarks were limited. No such admiration was expressed for Indigenous women, whose physical descriptions mirrored the broader image of them promoted by missionaries: as degraded and helpless, in need of Christian aid and supervision. Furthermore, missionaries also made numerous more general claims that Indigenous people's bodies – which in fact displayed a wide range of coverings, decorations and modifications – were 'naked' and 'dirty'.

The missionary trope of Indigenous 'filth' took a number of forms, all concerned with the need for cultural control and British bourgeois notions of privacy. One assertion was that the Indigenous use of body paint and oil was offensive. Günther, for example, disdainfully described Wiradjuri men who used fish-fat and oil on their hair and bodies as 'dirty fellows'.[12] Painting or decorating the skin was a centuries-old taboo in Judeo-Christian societies, with connotations of sexual depravity, but such comments can also be understood according to Mary Douglas's argument that the concept of 'dirt' is used to denote objects that appear in the wrong place, offending social order.[13] As Anne McClintock has observed, such concerns were on the rise during this period; 'In Victorian culture, the iconography of dirt became deeply integrated in the policing and transgression of social boundaries.'[14] Missionaries, of course, had some awareness that bodily decorations were not dirty within Indigenous societies, where they held an array of cultural meanings, but this did not lessen their own sense of disorder – rather the contrary. The oiled or painted native body showed allegiance to social and spiritual systems alien to the philanthropists, and suggested fundamentally different understandings of the self. As the Comaroffs note, during the 19th

---

1998, *Journals*, Clark (ed) vol 1: 40; William Thomas, March abstract 1839, 4 October 1839, 19–20 November 1839, William Thomas, Papers, 1834–1868 [hereafter *WTP*], ML MSS 214, reel 1, State Library of NSW; LE Threlkeld 1892, *An Australian Language As Spoken by the Awabakal, the People of Awaba or Lake Macquarie*, Fraser (ed): 48; Francis Tuckfield to General Secretaries, 30 October 1841, *WMMS*, reel 2, Mp2107, NLA; Tuckfield, 14 December 1839, *FTJ*, MS11341, Box 655, SLV; Francis Tuckfield, Report on the Wesleyan Missionary Society's Mission to the Aborigines, August 1843, *WMMS*, reel 2, Mp2107, NLA; William Watson, journal, 12 May 1833, *WVP*.

11   James Dredge to Jabez Bunting, 20 April 1839, in Cannon (ed) 1983, *Historical Records of Victoria (HRV): Aborigines and Protectors*, vol 2B: 433; Joseph Orton 1836, *The Aborigines of Australia*: 7; Parker 1967, 'The Aborigines of Australia': 9; Robinson 1998, *Journals*, Clark (ed) vol 1: 132; Robinson 1998, *Journals*, Clark (ed) vol 4: 205; GA Robinson 2001, 'Brief report of an expedition to the Aboriginal tribes of the interior over more than two thousand miles of country during the five months commencing March to August 1846', in Clark (ed) vol 4: 67; GA Robinson 2001, 'A Report of an Expedition to the Aboriginal Tribes of the Western Interior during the months of March, April, May, June, July and August, 1841', in Clark (ed) vol 4: 18; LE Threlkeld, 'Reminiscences 1825–1826', in Gunson (ed) 1974 vol 1: 46.
12   Günther, journal, 25 and 29 September 1837, *WVP*.
13   Douglas 1966: 2, 4, 35–36.
14   McClintock 1995: 153.

century the image of the 'greasy' native became a common imperial trope. It represented a particular threat to the Evangelical sense of a modern, civilised self: individual, private and self-controlled.

> It [ochre, fat or the vague term 'grease'] suggested stickiness, a body that refused to separate itself from the world ... Little could have been further from the contained, inward-turning person of the Protestant ideal, a self 'discreet' because 'discrete'.[15]

Here, it is useful to consider Norbert Elias's argument that the emergence of modern Western society and the individual self involved an advance in the threshold of embarrassment and shame, and a growing sense of oneself as separate from and observed by others.[16] Concepts of civility and manners were crucial here, and this was another area in which philanthropists saw Indigenous Australians as disorderly. Several missionaries were particularly disturbed by people's table manners. Threlkeld described kangaroo meat being 'torn off and eaten, whilst the blood streams down the arm of the hunter whether Male or Female in a most disgusting manner'; openly handling meat and blood demonstrated too great a closeness to one's food and to its violent origins.[17] William Watson, even more pointedly, commented that the sight of 'these poor creatures half or entirely naked lying on the ground, pulling to pieces an opossum with their hands and teeth, covered with filth and dirt' would be enough to make anyone wonder 'can these dry bones live?' While Watson concluded that they could, his profound physical disgust indicates the importance of manners and management of appetites to Christian temperance and individualism.[18]

Ideas about physical integrity were also associated with disease. Watson, in particular, complained of the 'loathsome condition and dirty habits' of sick people at Wellington Valley, calling them 'filthy and corrupt in their bodies'.[19] Here, the moral stigma of venereal disease lay close to the surface, as Watson commented 'I am often sick while I am dressing the wounds of their emaciated bodies, and my heart is frequently overwhelmed within me when I think of their diseased souls'.[20]

Notions of 'dirt' were also linked closely to concerns about scarcity of European clothing. Günther commented disapprovingly on '[t]he dirty fellows – it must be remembered that they were quite naked', while Threlkeld would not invite Awabakal people into his house 'in consequence of their filthy habits and

---

15  Comaroff and Comaroff 1997 vol 2: 224–227.
16  Elias 1978: 47, 63, 68–82.
17  Threlkeld, 'Reminiscences, 1825–1826', in Gunson (ed) 1974 vol 1: 46.
18  Watson, journal, 30 June 1833, *WVP*.
19  Watson, journal, 28 February 1833, 30 June 1833, *WVP*.
20  Watson, journal, 6 Oct 1833, *WVP*.

disgusting appearance, being often in a state of nudity.'[21] Indigenous Australians' relative lack of concern about physical exposure had long troubled European travellers, not only because of its supposed immodesty, but also because it appeared to contradict the Biblical claim that Adam and Eve's transgression had made humans naturally ashamed of nakedness. To Evangelicals, this could only be interpreted in terms of grave degradation. Threlkeld told the London Missionary Society in 1825 of the drinking and violence he had observed in the townships, adding as further proof of depravity 'though English friends may start at the idea of naked females parading, it is so common in this Colony, that it is scarcely noticed, although exhibited in the midst of towns and streets'.[22] While Threlkeld believed that Britons had once lived similarly – 'our mothers in a state of nudity danced before the mystic grove besmeared with pipe clay' – this was not intended to dignify nudity or paint, but rather to stress the changes brought about by Christianity.[23] LMS representatives themselves had been appalled to see people in Sydney 'in a state of absolute and shameless nudity', while James Günther's first glimpse of partially clothed Wiradjuri people at Wellington Valley made him reflect that they were 'more like beasts than rational beings.'[24]

So strong was the assumed connection between clothing and civilisation that when Indigenous people took off their European clothing this could be interpreted as a scornful rejection of philanthropic work. This could be assumed even when the people in question had long-lasting connections to missionaries. In 1833, Watson was disappointed when Warrahbin, a girl who had previously chosen to stay at Wellington Valley to avoid white men, left with her husband. She took off the clothes Mrs Watson had given her and put on her blanket, and Watson contrasted her 'wild and savage appearance' with 'that modesty of demeanour which characterised her when, dressed like an English female, she resided with us.'[25] The missionaries were similarly downcast when the young man Jemmy (Gungin) – who also retained ongoing relationships with the missionaries – left for a ceremonial battle; he 'threw off his clothes and followed the rest, naked, into the bush.'[26]

Rather less concern was expressed about traditional forms of body modification (apart from self-harming as an expression of mourning, discussed elsewhere). Where disputes did occur, they were linked to the fragility of missionary

---

21  Günther, journal, 29 September 1837, *WVP*; LE Threlkeld, Second Half Yearly Report of the Aboriginal Mission Supported by the London Missionary Society, 21 June 1826, *LMS*, AJCP M73, SLV.
22  LE Threlkeld to LMS, December 1825, in Gunson (ed) 1974 vol 1: 193. See also Strong 1986: 180; Williams 1981: 41.
23  Threlkeld, 'Correspondence', in Gunson (ed) 1974 vol 2: 205.
24  James Günther to Dandeson Coates, 1 September 1837, *WVP*; Daniel Tyerman and George Bennett, quoted in Gunson, 'Introduction', in Gunson (ed) 1974 vol 1: 14.
25  Watson, journal, 14 September 1833, 2 October 1833, *WVP*.
26  Günther, journal, 15 August 1837, *WVP*; Watson, journal, 14 September 1833, *WVP*.

authority. This became evident at Wellington Valley in 1835, in controversies over nose-piercing. Hilary M Carey and David A Roberts have described the growth of a Wiradjuri belief at this time that the powerful deity Baiame would destroy all Europeans because they had seduced his wife, or would kill Wiradjuri who lived with Europeans or lent their female relatives to them, or would harm people who did not pierce their noses and attend the Waganna ceremony. Carey and Roberts identify this as part of a revivalist movement focused partly on concerns about sexual relationships between Indigenous women and white men. They suggest that nose-piercing, possibly less significant before colonisation, grew in importance as Europeans tried to eradicate it and may have symbolised wider battles for control over women's bodies.[27] While the missionaries may have been mystified by the spiritual nature of this revival, they were well aware of the bodily contests involved. Watson complained of girls being removed from the mission by their relatives and worrying about not wearing bones through their noses; 'we frequently detect them feeling the cartilage of the nose or probably endeavouring to make a hole through it ... We find it necessary to tell them plainly that they shall never go into the Bush.'[28]

## Soap and salvation: making Christian bodies

Philanthropists initiated numerous daily routines designed to clothe and clean the Indigenous body. Particular emphasis was placed on washing and dressing for the Sabbath. Port Phillip protector William Thomas handed out a piece of soap to each family to encourage them to prepare for Sunday, and was so pleased when people attended church washed, shaved and wearing European clothes that he scarcely minded when they took them off afterwards.[29] In Perth, John Smithies reported happily that children attended school and chapel fully clothed, and Günther took melancholy pleasure in noting that people attended the funeral of a young girl, Nanny (Geanil), 'all decently dressed'.[30] Published accounts from Wellington Valley placed particular emphasis on the hopeful symbolism of people attending church dressed appropriately; for instance, two publications in 1834 described a man called Bogin, who beat his wife when he arrived at the mission but shortly afterwards accepted new clothes from the missionaries and promised to attend church and live like a white man.[31] Here, clothes helped to symbolise what philanthropists believed was a contrast between heathen male savagery towards women and the peaceable enlightenment of Christianity.

---

27   Carey and Roberts 2002: 821–823, 832–838, 843; Watson, journal, 1 April 1835, *WVP*.
28   Watson, journal, 19 December 1835, *WVP*.
29   Thomas, 15 November 1840, 22 November 1840, 31 January 1841, *WTP*, ML MSS 214, reel 2; Thomas, 15 April 1846, 17 May 1846, 16 August 1846, 5 October 1846, *WTP*, ML MSS 214, reel 3, State Library of NSW.
30   Günther, journal, 28 July 1839, *WVP*; John Smithies to General Secretaries, 8 October 1840, *WMMS*, reel 2, Mp2107, NLA.
31   Church Missionary Society (CMS), *Church Missionary Paper: for the use of weekly and monthly contributions*, no LXXV, Michaelmas Day 1834; CMS, *Missionary Register*, February 1834: 115–119; CMS,

The symbolic importance of clothes was emphasised most strongly in relation to children. Young people, considered more malleable than their older relatives, were a focus for bodily regimes. In the early 19th century, relatively few Aboriginal children lived permanently with missionaries, and the institutional power exercised on later stations was less apparent; family contact, travelling and ceremonial duties continued. The resulting struggles for control were often expressed in physical terms. When Watson, for instance, recalled his first meeting with the young boy, Billy Black, who died on the journey to Wellington Valley, he emphasised the physical transition that took place.

> When he came to us he was exceedingly filthy and dirty, though well clothed. Mrs Watson cut his hair made him wash himself well all over and as the best means of getting him clean she burnt his linen. His habits in the room where he slept were of too dirty a kind to allow of relation.[32]

John Smithies, who tried increasingly to restrict contact between children in his Perth institution and their parents, stated proudly that the children washed every morning; 'Any omission of this necessary duty should be strictly punished'.[33] Protector Charles Symmons praised Smithies' school for ensuring that the children ate with the missionary's family, implying a vital connection between 'civilised manners' and child custody.[34] A similar link between clothes and custody was made by Port Phillip protector Thomas, who cut the children's hair and dressed them in shirts and frocks when they arrived at his school (noting happily that this made them look like English charity children) but confiscated shirts from children who went travelling with their families.[35] Regimes of clothing and cleanliness were also central to the plans for the Adelaide institution in the 1840s, where the children were to be marched in a daily roll call for physical examination, and where their dormitories (set out like 'a Barrack room') were to demonstrate group conformity but also a certain individualism, with mirrors and personal pegs and shelves. The stated aim of this lifestyle was to 'render a return to bush life intolerable'.[36]

Through correct European clothing, missionaries tried to reshape social, sexual and religious order. Age and gender were differentiated; the Parramatta institution, for example, dressed the boys in linen shirts and knickers and the girls in petticoats and blue striped dresses, while Langhorne's mission dressed

---

*Missionary Register*, August 1839: 388.
32   Watson, journal, 3 October 1832, *WVP*.
33   McNair and Rumley 1981: 47.
34   Hetherington 1992: 51.
35   Thomas, 23 August 1841, *WTP*, ML MSS 214, reel 2, State Library of NSW; William Thomas to GA Robinson, Journal of Proceedings during the months of June, July & August 1841, PROV VPRS4410 unit 3, 1841/70 (reel 2).
36   Estimate and Plan, for the Establishment and Conduct of a Central Government School for Native Children, at Adelaide, c1843, SRSA, GRG24/90, Miscellaneous records of historical interest, no 374.

the younger children in tunics, with trousers for the older boys.[37] Such clothing was intended not only as an outward marker of 'civilisation'; the process of wearing it was meant to alter habits of work and worship, with children instructed to make and repair their own clothes and wash them for the Sabbath.[38] This promoted a more sedentary, privatised working life, especially for the girls. Such institutional conformity, however, points to what the Comaroffs have observed as a broad paradox in mission work: the desire to encourage individualism and consumerism, which coexisted with a wish to stress 'sober sameness and uniformity.'[39]

The bodies of children, when 'civilised', were cited as important signs of philanthropic progress. In 1845–46, Thomas listed amongst the achievements of his Merri Creek school the fact that the children were all dressed in clean shirts, frocks and blankets, 'washed & combed as the children of white parents'.[40] Rev George King made similar pleased remarks to the United Society for the Propagation of the Gospel about his small Aboriginal school in Fremantle.[41] However, the most enthusiastic accounts came from John Smithies' Western Australian Methodist mission, which witnessed a number of youthful conversions in the 1840s. When describing adults visiting their children in his institution, Smithies used bodily imagery to contrast his optimism for the younger generation with the alleged savagery of their elders:

> imagine their coming to the mission establishment draped ... in a few kangaroo skins sewn together not half covering their persons ... these visitors besmeared with grease and oil and wilga [yellow ochre], head and hair clotted and matted with the sauce, their faces glistening and bodies perspiring in the sun ... with as much affection as any other of our common species they hug and kiss their children ... Talk to them about God or Christ or heaven, they seem to have no idea, no feeling, no hope, all is dark, dark, dark.[42]

---

37  Bridges 1978: 165; Brook and Kohen 1991: 73, 205, 209; George Langhorne to Colonial Secretary, 14 August 1837 and 31 December 1837, in Cannon (ed) 1982, *HRV: The Aborigines of Port Phillip, 1835–1839*, vol 2A: 173, 208.
38  McNair and Rumley 1981: 45–47; Langhorne to Colonial Secretary, 31 December 1837, in Cannon (ed) 1982, *HRV*, vol 2A: 208; Matthew Moorhouse to Colonial Secretary, 31 January 1849, SRSA, GRG24/6, Colonial Secretary's Office, Correspondence files, no 242 of 1849; Thomas to Robinson, Journal of Proceedings during the months of June, July & August 1841, PROV VPRS4410 unit 3, 1841/70 (reel 2).
39  Comaroff and Comaroff 1997 vol 2: 220–221.
40  Thomas to Robinson, Journal of Proceedings during the months of June, July & August 1841, PROV VPRS4410 unit 3, 1841/70 (reel 2); Thomas, 14 September 1845, *WTP*, ML MSS 214, reel 8, State Library of NSW.
41  Rev George King to Rev Ernest Hawkins, 15 February 1845, in United Society for the Propagation of the Gospel (USPG), Records, AJCP M1222, SLV.
42  John Smithies to General Secretaries, 25 October 1843, *WMMS*, reel 2, Mp2107, NLA.

This image resonated for Smithies' superiors in the Wesleyan Methodist Missionary Society, who reproduced it in their 1845 report; it also appeared in the 1846 *Missionary Register*.[43] When the *Missionary Register* described the conversion and baptism of some of Smithies' pupils, the passionate and rather physical experience was highlighted, with Indigenous converts portrayed simultaneously as recipients of charity and as joyously included in the Methodist congregation.

> Oh! to behold those once wretched and debased outcasts – these sable Australians – with their shining hair and faces, clad in neat blue garments, and white tippets, made by our Christian Ladies ... Bowing down on their knees to receive their new names ... to behold their tearful eyes, amid the tears and prayers of the Congregation, was a scene not soon to be forgotten.[44]

Efforts to encourage bodily change had important personal and domestic meanings for philanthropists themselves. This topic has been explored in other contexts, including Hawaii by Patricia Grimshaw and North America by Linda Clemmons.[45] The figure of the missionary woman was particularly relevant to regimes of clothing and cleanliness. It was, for instance, the ladies on the Adelaide native school committee who lobbied for proper clothing for the children.[46] The Wellington Valley papers, especially, described Mrs Handt, Mrs Watson and Mrs Günther cutting young men's hair and urging people to wash and wear clothes on Sunday.[47] Here, a vital paradox was evident: proximity to 'dirt' must (by definition) be intolerable to respectable women, yet only such women were qualified to enforce cleanliness. Günther was surprised that his wife Lydia (whose respectability, delicacy and discontent with their inadequate living conditions were stressed in his writings) could stand exposure to young men's bodies during the cleaning process. He commented 'I was surprised that Mrs G. had inclination and ability for it', and 'Mrs G could hardly bear it but observed "I must not mind if I can do the poor men any good".'[48] The contradictory ideal of white missionary femininity – too refined to bear dirt, yet uniquely qualified to eradicate it – was made explicit in a letter to the *Colonist* newspaper in 1839. Praising Wellington Valley mission, the writer remarked:

---

43   CMS, *Missionary Register*, May 1846: 210; 'The Report of the WMMS for the year ending April 1845', Wesleyan Methodist Missionary Society, *Reports of the Wesleyan Methodist Missionary Society*, 1840–1851: 32.
44   CMS, *Missionary Register*, May 1847: 217.
45   Clemmons 1999: 69–91; Grimshaw 1989.
46   Matthew Moorhouse to Colonial Secretary, 23 August 1843, *Protector of Aborigines, Letterbook, 1840–1857*, SRSA, GRG52/7, unit 1.
47   JCS Handt, journal, 5 November 1834 and 26 April 1835, *WVP*; Günther, journal, 25 September 1837, *WTP*; Watson, journal, 3 October 1832, 16 March 1833, *WTP*.
48   Günther, journal, 25 and 29 September 1837, *WVP*.

> I was greatly struck by the neat, clean and orderly appearance of all the children in attendance. While zealous missionaries labour to promote the intellectual, moral and spiritual improvement of the blacks, Mrs Watson and Mrs Günther are no less indefatigable in attending to their personal comforts. The difficulty of performing this latter task can be duly appreciated only by those who have been accustomed to observe the slovenly and filthy habits of savages.[49]

Imposing Evangelical order and purity on young bodies was emblematic of broader challenges inherent in missionary work. For Australian philanthropists of this era – mostly from lower middle-class or artisan backgrounds – projects of Aboriginal 'civilisation' were seen as routes to greater respectability for themselves. At the same time, however, they were also associated with manual labour, and here the domestic strain on their wives was emphasised to show the threat posed to middle-class dignity. Similar tensions have been explored by Anna Cole, in her discussion of Ella Hiscocks, matron of the Cootamundra Girls' Home. Cole portrays the matron exerting harsh power over the children in her care, notably through hygiene regimes – 'Cleanliness, in Hiscocks' world, was next to whiteness'. At the same time, the marginalisation of this white woman through her gender, racial proximity and inferior social class was never far from the surface; 'her futile struggle against dirt symbolises the inevitable exclusion and isolation from mainstream society of both the Aboriginal girls in her care and matron herself.'[50]

Also illuminating was another point that emerged in some unpublished philanthropic writings (although usually obscured in more public accounts): that philanthropists themselves were subject to physical observation and intrusion. En route to Wellington Valley in October 1832, Watson rested at Rebecca's Swamp and distributed provisions to Indigenous men and their shy, reluctant wives. Of the women, Watson wrote:

> I can scarcely ever forget the astonishment they manifested at the dress of the ladies. They pointed at them and laughed and chattered away surprisingly. And they seemed to be much alarmed at my watch. Mrs W. gave her [one woman] the lining of an old bonnet and she was as proud of it as ever a Monarch was of his royal Diadem.[51]

The return of a paternalistic tone in the final sentence could suggest a need to recover authorial control, after the experience of being objects of curiosity and entertainment. Other encounters were more confronting. JCS Handt, whose

---

49   *The Colonist*, 24 December 1839.
50   Cole 2005: 161–163, 169.
51   Watson, journal, 2 October 1832, *WVP*. The 'her' is unidentified; presumably, it refers to one of the women.

pessimistic observations about the 'savagery' of Moreton Bay people were reproduced in the Church Missionary Society's *Missionary Register*, described meeting a group of 50 people at Eagle Farm, who demanded clothes from him, making him fear they might 'strip me, or perhaps do worse.'[52] Chief protector GA Robinson related similar anecdotes from his travels around Port Phillip, meeting people who were aggressively fascinated by his foreignness. In January 1840, he described travelling near Mt Alexander and meeting Daungwurrung people:

> One wanted me to take off my shirt for him, another my trousers, another my shoes, indeed, every article I had on. And so pressing that I scarcely knew whether I was to be left in a state of nudity or not.[53]

Several months later, Robinson recorded another meeting with Daungwurrung people, who demanded food and examined the intruders in disconcerting detail, bringing their physical, sexual and gendered selves into question: 'They felt our arms, neck and thighs and other parts of our persons. They called [the squatter] Mr Stucky a lubra because he had no beard and his hair was done up like a woman's.' They also offered the travellers sexual access to boys, saying 'white fellows on the Goulburn always did that'.[54]

The permeable, vulnerable nature of the European body was made apparent in different ways when Indigenous people offered to treat sick philanthropists. In 1839, Daungwurrung people persuaded protector Dredge to consult the 'native doctor' about his facial tics and depression. The treatment – which Dredge described in terms of sucking and blowing on the affected areas, 'making a whizzing noise with his mouth', and spitting on the ground – did not help Dredge, although he was touched by their concern.[55] Similarly, in 1840, when Thomas became ill at his station and collapsed, three doctors took hold of him, ignoring his servants' protests, and rubbed their faces against his, blowing hard 'to give me life'.[56] Meanwhile, at Buntingdale, Francis Tuckfield described having his infected eyes examined by Wer-e-rup, a man of spiritual authority, who was rumoured to be able to fly and raise the dead.

> He immediately caught my head and began to suck my face under my eyes, after which he took three pieces of she-oak leaf out of his mouth, rubbed them with his fingers and gave them to his wife, who wrapped

---

52   CMS, *Missionary Register*, August 1839: 390.
53   Robinson, *Journals*, vol 1: 132.
54   Robinson, *Journals*, vol 1: 285.
55   Dredge, 9 October 1839, *JDD*, MS11625, MSM534, SLV.
56   Thomas, 8 – 9 November 1840, *WTP*, ML MSS 214, reel 2, State Library of NSW.

them carefully in her rug. The doctor said the pain would leave my eyes and enter the leaves, and if his wife took proper care of them, the cure would be affected.[57]

The tone of such accounts was often more bemused than hostile – although Tuckfield would later accuse Wer-e-rup of witchcraft and deception – and their place in the archive is an intriguing one. The philanthropist, constructed in dominant Evangelical discourse as an expert observer, is revealed to be (at local and personal levels) an object of bodily study, invasion and intimacy himself, reminding the reader of the limits to his power at this time and his uneasy reciprocity with Indigenous people.

## 'Build houses like the white fellows': the privacy paradox

As with the body, so with physical space in general – issues of privacy, autonomy and institutionalisation pervaded philanthropic understandings of labour, leisure and worship. When protector William Thomas praised a Boonwurrung man called Benbow for building himself a hut, and lectured the other people camped by the Yarra that they should do the same, he told them 'that God's book orders man to build houses & inhabit them.'[58] Such assertions were typical. When Archdeacon Broughton, for instance, told the Select Committee on Aborigines (British Settlements) in 1835 that the Indigenous future looked unpromising, one of the reasons cited was fact that 'They have not the most distant conception of a house; they never live in a house: they have no clothing nor houses.'[59] Other, more optimistic writers did not question this association between physical space and Christian enlightenment. The Aborigines Protection Society's *Colonial Intelligencer* (1849–50), for instance, insisted that all races of people were capable of improvement. The journal illustrated this by contrasting the Seneca people's embrace of modern housing with a story of Irish peasants (typically depicted as white savages) refusing to move into clean accommodation, preferring to live in one room with their pigs.[60]

While housing had connotations of hard labour and sedentary life, it was also related to efforts to create a discrete, autonomous self. Missionaries across

---

57 Francis Tuckfield to WMMS, 20 Feb 1839, in Cannon (ed) 1982, *HRV*, vol 2A: 114. For more on Wer-e-rup, see also Francis Tuckfield to General Secretaries, 30 October 1841, *WMMS*, reel 2, Mp2107, NLA.
58 Thomas, 10 May 1846, *WTP*, ML MSS 214, reel 3, State Library of NSW.
59 Archdeacon Broughton, evidence, 3 August 1835, *BPP: Report from the Select Committee on Aborigines (British Settlements) together with minutes of evidence, appendix and index*, Anthropology: Aborigines, vol 1, 1836: 17.
60 Aborigines Protection Society (APS), *The Colonial Intelligencer, or Aborigines' Friend*, vol II, London, 1849–50: 70, in APS, Transactions, c.1839–1909, MIC/o6550, reel 1, (Records the property of Anti-Slavery International).

different parts of the world repeated the claim that native peoples lacked personal boundaries – for example, Joseph Orton's astonished observation that he had seen people in Port Phillip sleeping in groups 'lying in all positions legs over bodies and heads and vice versa like a litter of swine'.[61] In her Hawaiian study, Patricia Grimshaw notes missionaries' similar horror at Hawaiians' communal housing, considered an anathema to civilised privacy, while Michael Harkin observes related concerns about Heiltsuk housing in British Columbia, which defined its residents more as group members than as individuals.[62] Meanwhile, the Comaroffs have examined South African missionaries' desire to remake Tswana housing, to emphasise boundaries both external (fences, doors, windows, symmetrical streets) and internal (rooms designated for specific activities); 'enclosure being both a condition of private property and civilized individualism and an aesthetic expression of the sheer beauty of refinement.'[63] Australian mission housing at this early stage was generally too impoverished to evince such detailed efforts, but concern with establishing order, individualism and boundaries was clear. As Peter Read comments, 'A cottage inhabited by an Aboriginal family was less a shelter than an instrument of management, education and control'.[64]

Only rarely did philanthropic sources mention that some Indigenous societies already lived in houses. The Wesleyan Methodist Missionary Society's *Missionary Notices* (1824) spoke of their hope for mission work amongst a 'new tribe' of people they had heard of at Moreton Bay, supposedly superior because they lived in clean huts, in fishing villages.[65] Similarly, in 1840, protector CW Sievwright reported with fascination his discovery of an 'aboriginal village', with large, solid houses, apparently recently inhabited, between the Wannon and Wando rivers in western Victoria.[66] Given the colonial violence and depopulation which engulfed both these districts, it is perhaps unsurprising that these examples were scarcely mentioned again. Rather, philanthropists vested their hopes in European housing styles.

At Wellington Valley in 1838, James Günther recorded in his diary 'a step, which we long wished to see': three young Wiradjuri men, Jemmy Buckley, George and Fred, announced after their daily lesson 'Now we are going to build a hut'. Günther was delighted, both by the desire for sedentary housing and the

---

61  Joseph Orton, 17 May 1839, Joseph Orton, Journal 1832–1839 and 1840–1841 [hereafter *JOJ*], ML ref A1714–1715, CY reel 1119, State Library of NSW.
62  Grimshaw 1989: 57–63; Harkin 2005: 205–225.
63  Comaroff 1989: 673–674. See also, Comaroff and Comaroff 1997 vol 2: 277.
64  Read 2000: ix.
65  WMMS, *Missionary Notices: relating principally to the Foreign Missions*, vol IV, no 95, November 1824: 363.
66  CW Sievwright, 1 June 1840, Report of the proceedings of Assistant Protector Sievwright, from September 1839 to May 1840, in MacFarlane (ed) 1998, *HRV: Public Finance of Port Phillip, 1836–1840*: 366–367.

hard, independent labour involved; 'the activity & cleverness they displayed, proved quite an enjoyment to us.' He stressed the divisions and boundaries of this housing, symbolising regulation of contact between outer and inner worlds and aspiration to class improvement. He noted, for instance, that Fred wanted separate sleeping and sitting rooms, and that Jemmy wanted a fence around his hut, 'like a gentleman.'[67] Later, Günther added:

> When I have visited George & Jemmy in their new hut after dark and shut the door after me they called out, 'Leave the door open that we may hear the bell for Prayers we shall now go to prayers every evening.'[68]

The Buntingdale missionaries were similarly pleased in 1841, when a man called Karn-karn built himself a house on the mission land, over which he made traditional claims. Tuckfield was careful to note the exact dimensions of the house (14 feet by 7 feet) and the possessions within it – a bed with a straw mattress, 2 plates, 1 fry pan, 2 knives, 1 pot, a table and a stool – interpreted as signs of growing personal autonomy and materialism. By 1844, the WMMS's report stated happily that half the people at Buntingdale were living in houses.[69]

People who made use of European housing may have been motivated partly by a desire for closer, more profitable relationships with philanthropists. Karn-karn, for instance, was rewarded by the missionaries with clothes, food and tools, whereupon several other men announced that they would build houses too.[70] On a more serious note, Dredge recalled being visited in Melbourne after his resignation from the protectorate by Daungwurrung people, who complained about their worsening dispossession. They stressed their wish for a productive relationship with the protectorate in a secure area of their country, and their willingness to adopt European habits to achieve this:

> they said they would look out a good place and would all sit down there, build houses like the white fellows, and plant potatoes ... They said they would build houses for themselves like the white fellows, and a *big one* for me.[71]

Adoption of housing often combined with ongoing traditional practices. Protectors Parker and Robinson complained that people continued to move away

---

67  Günther, journal, 23 March 1838, *WVP*.
68  Günther, journal, 4 April 1838, *WVP*. See also, Günther, journal, 22 March 1838, *WVP*. Note: the bracketed punctuation comes from the edited sources themselves.
69  The Report of the WMMS for the year ending April 1844, in WMMS, *Reports of the Wesleyan Methodist Missionary Society*, 1844: 28, 30; Francis Tuckfield to General Secretary, 30 Oct 1841, *WMMS*, reel 2, Mp2107, NLA; also Tuckfield, 9–11 May 1841, *FTJ*, MS11341, Box 655, SLV.
70  Francis Tuckfield to General Secretaries, 30 October 1841, *WMMS*, reel 2, Mp2107, NLA; also Tuckfield, 9, 11 May 1841, *FTJ*, MS11341, Box 655, SLV.
71  Dredge, 27 November 1841, 4 December 1841, *JDD*, MS11625, MSM534, SLV.

after family members died, refusing to enter their houses again.[72] Meanwhile, Tuckfield, despite his joy at the housing enthusiasm at Buntingdale, was disappointed when two men announced they wanted houses big enough to accommodate their three wives, rejecting Tuckfield's suggestion that 'if they intended to imitate the whites in one thing they should in another and that they were better to get rid of four wives out of six.'[73]

While houses were encouraged as a means and expression of privacy, the most important locale for teaching domestic discipline was the mission house itself. This could be cruelly ironic; efforts to impart 'civilised' private life could involve attacking the family lives of Indigenous people, through attempts to gain custody of children. The separation of families within institutional spaces like workhouses was well established in British philanthropic practice.[74] The first Australian missionaries and protectors – although usually unable to keep children forcibly for long, and frequently obliged to negotiate with families – nonetheless embraced this principle. In 1838, Watson and Günther requested separate boarding facilities for boys and girls, with buildings and fences to isolate the children from contact with their relatives or white servants. Isolation from Europeans – particularly urgent at Wellington Valley, where sexual abuse of young girls occurred – indicated the racial complexities of trying to construct Aboriginal 'privacy' under missionary control, isolated from black and white intrusion. Fenced-in playgrounds – eventually constructed at Wellington Valley, and requested by the schoolteacher at Thomas's station – were also meant to impart the message that leisure should occur in time and space apart from work.[75] Similar regulations were evident at the Methodist mission school in Perth, where the children who worked as servants in white households were banned from loitering or playing marbles in the street, behaviour which blurred the public-private distinction and had connotations of working class vagrancy. Playtime was to occur at the missionary's house only.[76]

There was, however, a paradox at the heart of the mission house: its very use as the epitome of domestic civilisation undermined the private-public distinction. The 'fetish for boundary purity', which Anne McClintock identifies as crucial to Victorian middle-class life, was both present and inadvertently challenged in colonial philanthropic work.[77] Like the discrete, civilised missionary body

---

72   ES Parker, Quarterly Journal, 1 September – 30 November 1841, PROV VPRS4410 unit 2, 1841/59 (reel 2); GA Robinson to CJ La Trobe, 23 October 1839, PROV VPRS10 unit 1, 1839/363 (reel 1).
73   Francis Tuckfield to General Secretaries, 30 October 1841, *WMMS*, reel 2, Mp2107, NLA; also Tuckfield, 9, 11 May 1841, *FTJ*, MS11341, Box 655, SLV.
74   Crowther 1981: 43–44.
75   Bridges, *The Church of England*: 430; James Wilson to GA Robinson, undated (approx 1841), PROV VPRS12 unit 2 (reel 2).
76   Charles Symmons, Regulations and Arrangements relative to the Native Children, enclosed in Gov Hutt to Lord John Russell, 15 May 1841, in *BPP: Papers Relating to Australia, 1844*, vol 8: 387–388.
77   McClintock 1995: 171.

– in fact, an object of fascinated looking and touching – the mission house had to remain open to Indigenous engagement. At Thomas's station in 1841, for example, parents agreed to leave children behind temporarily, but set conditions: they must sleep in the schoolmaster's house for protection from 'Wild Black Fellows', and the girls, for propriety, must be prevented from sitting at the boy's campfire.[78] After leaving the protectorate, James Dredge found his house in Melbourne open at times to Daungwurrung visitors, who crowded inside, greeted his family affectionately and slept on his kitchen floor. Dredge, touched if a little bemused by this, observed 'they came into our house as if they were come home'.[79]

Not all arrivals were so welcome. During 1834, the Wellington Valley missionaries were enraged to discover that young men had been sneaking into the girls' room at night.[80] At Buntingdale in 1841, violence between residents led Dhaugurdwurrung people to seek refuge in the mission house. They woke Tuckfield one Sunday at midnight, banging on the door to tell him they were leaving at once, because they feared violence from people who had just arrived. The following night, a man was murdered. Tuckfield described the scene:

> In a minute the whole of the encampment was in an uproar. The cryes of the children, the screams of the women and the constant threats of the men were indeed awful and as the whole of it were near our houses our situations for the time were any thing but desirable. Great many of our blacks came in about our houses anxious to lay themselves down in our kitchen, School Room etc lest more of them be speared.[81]

Such uses of mission space could highlight the complexities of gender in philanthropic attempts to construct a new Indigenous self, both privatised and institutionalised. The missionary woman, working on food preparation, cleanliness and child care, tried to represent idealised Evangelical femininity, but her very domestic efforts could make her home a space for wider disputes. This was particularly evident at Wellington Valley, due to their zealous efforts to control young people, and to Watson's special enthusiasm for recording his wife's work. Watson frequently described child custody in terms of leaving children with Ann Watson, and in 1836, he mentioned a related incident.

---

78   Thomas, 23 August 1841, *WTP*, ML MSS 214, reel 2, State Library of NSW; James Wilson to GA Robinson, undated (approx 1841), PROV VPRS12 unit 2 (reel 2).
79   Dredge, 10 October 1840, 12 August 1841, *JDD*, MS11625, MSM534, SLV. Note: Dredge identified some of his visitors as 'Woralim', which I have assumed to refer to the group identified by Ian D Clark as Warring-illum Balug, a Taungurong clan from the upper Goulburn River – see Clark 1990: 374–374.
80   Watson, journal, 6 November 1834, *WVP*.
81   Francis Tuckfield to General Secretaries, 30 October 1841, *WMMS*, reel 2, Mp2107, NLA. See also, Tuckfield, 13 June 1841, *FTJ*, MS11341, Box 655, SLV. Note: the new arrivals were not identified in these entries.

> A native female about fourteen years of age came up to the mission house; she is a widow, her husband having died a few months ago ... her father and mother told her to come and live with us. I was not at home when she arrived, and when it was known that she had come to the mission-house Kabon Billy who has two wives already hastened up, and in a very violent rage demanded her. However Mrs Watson took care to secure the door, after which she went round and soon talked Billy into a good humour, and he went quietly away.[82]

Such stories constructed a distinction between the outer (dangerous, savage and masculine) and inner (domestic, civilised and feminine) worlds, while also demonstrating how vulnerable these boundaries were. However, the story serves, too, as a reminder of the complex dynamic between missionary space and the disagreements over custody and kinship occurring between Indigenous people themselves.

Watson's writings showed a recurrent theme of femininised missionary space, inviting Indigenous tutelage yet vulnerable to intrusions by Indigenous men. This became clear in 1836, when a group of people from another district gathered near Wellington Valley, apparently planning revenge attacks. One man, Darby, left the fighting and fled to the mission house for protection. Watson described the scene vividly:

> Our girls on seeing him approach painted all over his face and body, carrying his weapons ... ran to Mrs Watson, 'crying out, Black fellow coming Black fellow coming, running very fast.' Mrs Watson told them to come in ... for she apprehended that the wild natives were coming to attack the Mission House and take away the girls ... what should present itself to her notice but the painted face of a native (between the partly opened door and the door post) and a number of spears and, other weapons half way in. Mrs Watson did not at first recognise him, and she felt some alarm, when, he panting exclaimed, 'Black fellow come up, Black fellow come up, plant, plant, where is Mr Watson.' ... having convinced Mrs Watson as much by his trembling as by his expressions that he wanted to be concealed from the natives who were seeking to kill him, he was put into a private room and shut up... He kept continually rising up and saying 'where is Mr Watson? You go fetch him. No, No, you sit down by me, don't let Black fellow come.' What a scene was this! A stout, able, Savage, seeking for safety, and reposing his confidence for protection in a nervous European female.[83]

---

82   Watson, journal, 2 September 1836, *WVP*.
83   Watson, journal, 17 November 1836, *WVP*.

It is worth noting, again, the significance of paint here, to missionary eyes, as a marker of unfamiliarity and disorder. Two days later, Darby was accused of an incorrect relationship with a woman, and more violence followed. Watson wrote:

> presently our large room which had just been washed and got ready for the Sabbath was nearly filled by about 40 females who had rushed into the kitchen, for refuge, crying and trembling: Then the men came ... for their weapons which the females generally carry. The yinnars [women] ... kept throwing out their weapons saying to Mrs Watson you give that to Bobby and that to Tommy and so on for all their husbands, and it was very well Mrs Watson escaped without injury, for in their fright they threw them down any way.[84]

In the missionary's papers, such descriptions were framed as savage invasions into Christian family space, and were probably intended partly to vindicate the Watsons' policy of separating young girls from their relatives. Yet, other readings are also possible. The account suggests the complex role within mission space of Indigenous men, alternately assumed to be threatening to and dependent on missionary women. And while the nurturing ideal of the missionary woman was reinforced, she was also linked strongly to the tumultuous outside world. This pointed again to the broader paradox of mission privacy: upholding the value of 'civilised' domestic space necessitated extensive engagement with a 'savage' Other. Importantly, of course, such accounts are also suggestive of Wiradjuri people's own use of the space claimed as Mrs Watson's, and the relationships of protection and obligation they tried to build with her.

## Gathering community, enforcing unity

Imposing new divisions between people and stressing the sanctity of the domestic Christian world was only part of philanthropic work. Also important was the reshaping of group selves and attempts to dismantle older divisions between people. Philanthropists designated sites of work, rationing and worship for mass gatherings, where new kinds of social proximity were encouraged. This was presumably seen as part of a long term process to remake Indigenous people as part of a respectable Christian public. However, in the short term, the sense of self missionaries and protectors tried to impart was less that of the legitimate public citizen and more that of the institutional subject.

When gathering communities, protectors and missionaries aimed to dismantle many traditional spatial distinctions between people, and to bring groups together under philanthropic observation and authority. The main settings for

---

84   Watson, journal, 19 November 1836, *WVP*.

this involved communal eating and church services. Thus, a visitor to protector Sievwright's Mt Rouse station described his efforts to feed several hundred people. Sievwright, a former army officer with comparatively little interest in evangelising, emphasised administration and a certain loss of dignity.

> In the morning they [residents] were put into a pen, and run out, one by one, as sheep are when they are counted, when each received a mess of a kind of burgoo, or porridge ... In the middle of the day they were all drawn up in a row, squatted on their heels, and a wheelbarrow, full of pieces of beef, was wheeled around, the overseer giving a piece to each in turn.[85]

The writer did not see Indigenous people as passive participants in this, however, stressing that they scrutinised the food and 'freely gave vent to their feelings of rage and disappointment' when it was inadequate.[86] Missionaries, meanwhile, showed a greater wish to monitor manners. At Wellington Valley, Günther wanted a proper dining hall, where missionaries could observe people, prohibiting greed or the feeding of the undeserving and reminding people of the food's association with God.[87] Later, at Buntingdale, Tuckfield distributed and supervised the meals, claiming clan rivalries made it unwise to allow Indigenous people such responsibility. When residential numbers swelled, the people were instructed to form a circle around the missionaries and the food. After prayers and hymns, breakfast was distributed to each person, along with instructions for the day's work. Here, explicit links were drawn between God, food and labour, in a physical layout that stressed missionary observation and attempted (largely in vain) to flatten distinctions between people, and to establish station residents as a single, orderly community.[88]

However, the most symbolically loaded public space was that of the church service. There is a certain irony here; Evangelical philanthropists viewed conversion as a deeply personal inner transformation and frequently refused to believe that Indigenous people who appeared compliant had 'truly' changed, but they nonetheless cherished the *appearance* of religious community. Tuckfield, when he first arrived in Port Phillip, was pleased by the sedate behaviour of people who attended his services – 'Everything we say on such occasions is to them in an unknown tongue yet they appear to be struck with silent admiration and they invariably listen with breathless attention'.[89] Similarly, Parker doubted the understanding and sincerity of his congregation, but was still pleased by

---

85 Charles Griffith, 1845, *The Present State and Prospects of the Port Phillip District of New South Wales*: 195.
86 Griffith 1845: 195.
87 Günther, journal, 19 December 1837, *WVP*.
88 Tuckfield, 11 January 1840, *FTJ*, MS11341, Box 655, SLV; Francis Tuckfield to General Secretaries, 30 September 1840, *WMMS*, reel 2; Francis Tuckfield to General Secretaries, 30 October 1840, *WMMS*, reel 2, Mp2107, NLA.
89 Francis Tuckfield to General Secretaries, 12 Aug 1838, *WMMS*, reel 1, Mp2107, NLA.

Keeping body and soul together: creating material 'civilisation'

their behaviour in church; 'Their deportment was serious and orderly; they spontaneously followed the example of the whites in standing up, kneeling etc.'[90]

Philanthropists were frustrated and angered, however, by the lasting power of traditional spatial prohibitions. Ironically, the more they tried to engage large numbers in Christian worship, the more pre-colonial practices became visible. At Wellington Valley, young male initiates, forbidden to come near women, sometimes avoided church, explaining 'too much yeener [woman] sit down there.'[91] The missionaries' efforts to accommodate this by seating the older men and children between the young men and women were unsuccessful, forcing them to hold separate services. Similarly, Joseph Orton commented on the difficulties he witnessed at Buntingdale when large groups assembled: 'It is amusing to see them peeping and crouching around the buildings of the station to avoid a casual meeting; and it is sometimes very annoying when they are required to do anything.' He was not so amused when several women refused to enter the church, staying outside and 'peeping and watching every movement of [the] others'.[92] Parker reported particular trouble reconciling church services with the rule forbidding Djadjawurrung women to look upon their future sons-in-law, while his colleague Thomas struggled to make the women sit with the men, who reproved him 'why so stupid you, you know we do not sit together'. Usually, this was resolved by letting the women stand outside, and when it rained they pitched their shelters nearby. Sometimes they still refused to attend, however, complaining that they did not like hiding their faces. Thomas, impatient with the custom, was so irritated when women insisted on sitting with their backs to the men (and to him) that he turned some of them around by force.[93] Efforts to remove older spatial distinctions in mass gatherings were shaped by the Evangelical notion of all worshippers being equal before God, but also by the institutional need to reduce independent identities and make everyone subject to observation.

These early regimes of material 'civilisation' showed contradictions and compromises which might point to weaknesses in philanthropic authority at this time. Certainly, these early protectors and missionaries tended to take a more conciliatory approach than many of their successors would do. However, many of the contradictions of these projects would prove to be both creative and long-standing in Australian mission life. Ideas about physical civilisation were,

---

90   ES Parker, Quarterly Journal, December 1840 – February 1841, PROV VPRS4410 unit 2, 1841/55 (reel 2).
91   Watson, journal, 10 March 1833, *WVP*. Also, Günther, journal, 25 January 1838, 26 January 1838, 18 February 1838, 19 February 1838, 21 February 1838, 4 March 1838, 18 March 1838, *WVP*.
92   Orton, 4 May 1841 and 6 May 1841, *JOJ*, ML ref A1714–1715, CY reel 1119, State Library of NSW.
93   ES Parker, Quarterly Journal, 1 March – 31 May 1841, PROV VPRS4410 unit 2, 1841/61 (reel 2); Thomas, 15 November 1840, 22 November 1840, 29 November 1840, 11 April 1841, 28 May 1841, 30 May 1841, *WTP*, ML MSS 214, reel 2; Thomas, 1 January 1844, *WTP*, ML MSS 214, reel 3, State Library of NSW.

perhaps, inherently paradoxical, seeking to elevate people from the earthly world through bodily regimes. Furthermore, the process of creating autonomous individuals through institutionalisation required some basic tensions, between the Indigenous subject as single and social and the philanthropist as observer, participant and object of observation. Considering such issues helps to further our understanding not only of efforts to change Indigenous societies, but also of the problematic creation of colonial authorities themselves.

# 'Can these dry bones live?' Religious life and afterlife

Writing from the Swan River Methodist mission in Western Australia, John Smithies told his superiors in the Wesleyan Methodist Missionary Society in 1843 that his station was undergoing an unusual atmosphere of revival. Of particular note was the experience of an adolescent girl called Nogyle, who lived with the missionaries. One morning, she declared to an emotional audience of missionaries and students that she had found God, after a vivid and Biblical dream of being visited by the devil.

> He say me your father, you pray to me. Then me look at him, me think he look so miserable, me saying you not my father. My father great and good father, heaven get down … devil take me by my arm and lift me up and show me beautiful Garden and said give me all that if me would pray to him. Me then kneel down and God pray … devil too much wicked.[1]

The delighted missionaries, who may have been used to accounts of spiritual dreams and visions within their own Methodist communities, hailed this as a sign of progress to come, and the school was turned into a spontaneous prayer meeting. However, Nogyle's story would soon take on a tragic, if no less pious, tone in Smithies' papers, when she died young of a lung disease. Again, she explained her journey partly through powerful dreams, claiming to have been visited by an angel who told her of her impending death. She was baptised with the name Mary and died surrounded by the other children, who sang a hymn:

> I am a native child, but Jesus died for me.
> And if I love him, I shall reign with him eternally.
> Oh what a happy thought that when my body dies,
> My saviour will rescue my soul, to dwell above the skies.[2]

In the records of these early missions, Christian exchange and bereavement were often profoundly entwined.

Philanthropic Aboriginal policy at this time rested on the notion that Christianity was integral to the care and elevation of colonised peoples. While evangelising was obviously central to missionary work, it was also built, however controversially, into the mandates of the protectors, who were urged to

---

[1] John Smithies to General Secretaries, 25 October 1843, Wesleyan Methodist Missionary Society, Archive: Australasia 1812–1889 [hereafter *WMMS*], reel 2, Mp2107 (Record ID: 133095), National Library of Australia (NLA).
[2] John Smithies to General Secretaries, 25 October 1843, *WMMS*, reel 2, Mp2107, NLA. See also, Hempton 2005: 63, 65.

promote moral instruction, Christian education and observation of the Sabbath (although their enthusiasm clearly varied).[3] Such priorities were reflected, too, in philanthropic lobbying in Britain. As Elizabeth Elbourne argues, the Select Committee on Aborigines (British Settlements) worked from a belief that the British had a duty to use their power for a higher purpose.[4] This was apparent in the Australian sections of the Committee's report, which included calls for missionary work and pointed to the Crown's 1825 instructions to promote Aboriginal people's Christian instruction. The imperial duty to evangelise was clear in a remark to the Committee by an unnamed clergyman (possibly Cartwright of Black Town), who stressed that colonists owed Christianity to their dispossessed native subjects – 'As through the tender mercy of our God the dayspring from on high has visited us, we are solemnly engaged to impart to them the glorious beams of Gospel truth'.[5]

However, there have been relatively few in-depth discussions of the place of religion on these first missions and protectorate stations. Historical assessments of these projects have tended to downplay religious issues or agree on their spiritual 'failure'. Works by Peter Read, Michael Christie, Jean Critchett, RHW Reece and Michael Cannon on the early colonisation of south-eastern Australia all consider philanthropists' efforts to spread Christianity, but, with their focus on local conflict and resistance, they tend not to debate religion extensively. More recent works by Richard Broome and Henry Reynolds have paid greater attention to the influence of British Evangelical Christianity, but further work remains to be done. Meanwhile, the comparatively small number of works emphasising Indigenous religious participation and cultural change during this period, by historians like Hilary M Carey and Jean Woolmington, have not necessarily focused so much on the wider context of empire.[6]

Certainly, the Australian colonies at this time could not claim widespread evangelical success amongst Indigenous people. Even the Select Committee based their hopes largely on belief in all human beings' capacity for Christian

---

3   Sir George Arthur to Lord Glenelg, 15 December 1837, Cannon (ed) 1982, *Historical Records of Victoria (HRV): The Aborigines of Port Phillip, 1835–1839*, vol 2A: 33; Lord Glenelg to Sir George Gipps, 31 January 1838, in Cannon (ed) 1983, *HRV: Aborigines and Protectors, 1838–1839*, vol 2B: 375.
4   Elbourne 2003: no page numbers.
5   Extract included in Archdeacon Broughton, evidence, 3 August 1835, *British Parliamentary Papers (BPP): Report from the Select Committee on Aborigines (British Settlements) together with minutes of evidence, appendix and index*, Anthropology: Aborigines, vol 1, 1836: 15–16; *BPP: Report from the Select Committee on Aborigines (British Settlements) together with minutes of evidence, appendix and index*, Anthropology: Aborigines, vol 2, 1837: 11, 20.
6   Broome 2005; Cannon 1990; Christie 1979; Carey 2000: 45–61; Carey 1996; Critchett 1990; Read 1988; Reece 1974; Reynolds 1998; Woolmington 1986: 90–98; Woolmington: 283–293; Woolmington 1983: 24–32; Woolmington 1988: 77–92. An exception is Carey and Roberts 2002: 821–869. This considers the Baiame Waganna rituals as a response to colonialism, but the focus remains local.

enlightenment, rather than on any local achievements to date.[7] Meanwhile, local protectors and missionaries were acutely aware of their failures compared to colleagues in other parts of the world, and their papers were marked by claims of spiritual desolation. However, I would argue that these disappointments should not shut down discussion of spiritual topics. Religious exchanges between philanthropists and Indigenous Australians were complex and intriguing, shaped by an array of views about gratitude, guilt, individualism and community. This chapter, therefore, does not set out to evaluate missionaries' 'success' (although I will point to some accounts of baptism that have not received much scholarly attention), so much as to consider how Christian regimes shaped station life. Here, several elements are particularly striking. One concerns philanthropists' committed, if paradoxical, efforts to encourage people to understand Christianity in terms of both impartial observation of individual subjects and conversational two-way ties between mentors and pupils. Indigenous people, in turn, engaged creatively with aspects of Christian belief and practice, while not necessarily treating Christianity as a single, unified system. Also striking to the contemporary reader are the potent meanings of sin, destruction and death. Indigenous people were encouraged, for example, to abandon their alleged fear of mortality through Christian conversion, a process that necessitated warnings of doom and hellfire. Meanwhile, emphasis was placed on stories of the pious deaths of young converts, portrayed in terms of simultaneous grief and religious triumph.

## 'Like the Sun at first rising': private transformation, communal connections

Philanthropists opposed colonial racism through the language of Christianity, asserting that all souls were equally valuable in the eyes of God. As Wellington Valley missionary William Watson commented, to say that Indigenous people were incapable of enlightenment was blasphemous; 'diametrically opposed to the gospel, and derogatory to the honour of the Most High.'[8] Port Phillip protector William Thomas noted proudly in his diary in 1841 that a European visitor to his station, listening to the children singing 'Praise ye the Lord Hallelujah', remarked 'What would the people of England say to hear this from a race that has been designated as not a link from the brute creation [?]'[9] Such stories emphasised not only the ignorant cruelty of settlers who denied human

---

7   Archdeacon Broughton, evidence, 3 August 1835, Dandeson Coates, evidence, 8 June 1836, Rev William Yate, evidence, 13 February 1836, *BPP: Report from the Select Committee on Aborigines (British Settlements)*, vol 1, 1836: 14, 16, 201, 520.
8   William Watson to Colonial Secretary, 3 January 1844, *BPP: Papers Relating to Australia, 1844*, Colonies: Australia, vol 8, 1969: 284.
9   William Thomas, 22 August 1841, William Thomas, Papers, 1834–1868 [hereafter *WTP*], ML MSS 214, reel 2, State Library of NSW.

equality, but also the astonishing power of Christianity to raise Indigenous people from a state which philanthropists themselves considered brutish. Watson, for example, wrote in his journal in 1833 that when he saw Wiradjuri people's illness and degradation he was prompted to ask 'can these dry bones live?' He answered himself 'Thank God we know they can. O that the wind from Heaven might now come and breathe upon these slain that they might rise up an exceedingly great army to praise and glorify God.'[10]

As this suggests, philanthropists, although they compiled information about Indigenous beliefs, ceremonies, taboos, magic and spirits, were not generally sympathetic towards them. Instead, they depicted Aboriginal understandings of the universe as 'superstition', alternately dangerous and ridiculous. Port Phillip protector James Dredge, for instance, reported that Daungwurrung people had no idea 'of a Creator, of the existence of the soul as distinct from the body, or of its future destinies.'[11] Francis Tuckfield of the Buntingdale mission told the Wesleyan Methodist Missionary Society in 1839 that Indigenous people's spiritual notions were 'a rude chaos presenting an awfully distressing vacancy of thought.'[12] Similarly, James Günther claimed that Wiradjuri people had no good spirits to console them, only evil ones to keep at bay.[13] Ideological and linguistic barriers and missionaries' cultural chauvinism stood in the way of greater understanding, as did the guarded and hierarchical nature of Indigenous belief systems, where knowledge was structured and sensitive, and even those who possessed it were not necessarily permitted to share unreservedly. Thus, Joseph Orton, JCS Handt and William Watson all complained they could barely comprehend what they were told about spiritual things and that some people were deliberately vague and reticent.[14] LE Threlkeld's knowledge was probably greatest; he wrote at some length about Awabakal stories and beliefs and claimed to have persuaded a man to show him sacred objects. However, Tricia Henwood still maintains that his access was limited and that he was excluded from initiated men's ceremonies.[15] Whatever partial insights philanthropists developed did nothing to discourage their own religious enthusiasms.

Evangelical aims and moral standards were specific and stringent. Protector ES Parker summarised this in 1850, stating that his sermons focused on 'the fall and

---

10   William Watson, journal, 30 June 1833, in Carey and Roberts (eds) 2002, *The Wellington Valley Project: Letters and Journals Relating to the Church Missionary Society Mission to Wellington Valley, NSW, 1830–42, A Critical Electronic Edition* [hereafter *WVP*]: <http://www.newcastle.edu.au>
11   James Dredge to GA Robinson, 8 November 1839, *WMMS*, reel 1, Mp2107, NLA.
12   Francis Tuckfield to WMMS, 20 February 1839, in Cannon (ed) 1982, *HRV*, vol 2A: 114.
13   James Günther, journal, 13 January 1839, *WVP*.
14   JCS Handt to William Cowper, Annual report of the Church Missionary Society Mission at Moreton Bay for the year 1838, Sir William Dixson, *Documents relating to Aboriginal Australians, 1816–1853*, Dixson Library, ADD 80–82, CY reel 3743, State Library of NSW; Joseph Orton, 29 November 1840, Joseph Orton, Journal 1832–1839 and 1840–1841, ML ref A1714–1715, CY reel 1119, State Library of NSW; Watson, journal, 12 May 1833, 26 October 1834, 19 December 1835, *WVP*.
15   Henwood 1978: 52.

universal corruption of human nature – redemption by the advent and death of our Lord Jesus Christ – the necessity of a change of heart or "new spirit" and of conformity to the will of God.'[16] While Evangelical beliefs varied, they were characterised generally by a stress on the accessibility of scripture, the doctrine of atonement (with Christ's death the only means through which humanity's sins would be forgiven), the radical, defining experience of conversion, and the need to act on one's own salvation by spreading the word to others. The soul – the immaterial, immortal core of one's being – was seen as either dark with sin (an evil predisposition to which all were vulnerable) or pure and enlightened through atonement. Common Evangelical narratives involved childhood religious impressions, a descent into worldliness, an awakening of consciousness, struggles against despair, and repentance and justification in Christ.[17] This was apparent when Methodist missionary Joseph Orton recalled his spiritual experiences. He described to the WMMS his childhood longing to become a preacher, the period of lapse and sin that followed, and his elevation through a 'clear manifestation of the favour of God through Jesus', which rekindled a fervent wish to spread the word.[18] Conversion itself was often described as an intense, transformative experience; a sense of being reborn. This was implied by Benjamin Hurst in 1841, when he reported to the WMMS that while his missionary work amongst Indigenous people at Buntingdale was progressing quite well, 'we are not yet privileged to witness the tears of penitence and the joyful transports of a soul recently transported from the Kingdom of Darkness into the Kingdom of God's dear son'.[19]

Evangelical experiences have also been characterised as personal and introspective, with an emphasis on conscience and self-awareness. (These elements were, of course, in keeping with the growth of inner life, privacy and 'disciplinary technologies' during the Victorian period.) William Watson's papers were particularly notable for their emphasis on interiority, on developing self-consciousness and shame. In 1835, he explained to a Wiradjuri girl 'that the first thing God does in the conversion of a Sinner is causing light to shine into his mind by which he is led to see how very wicked he is.' He told her he had felt this way once, and wept over his sins when he was her age.[20] The following year, he recorded a similarly stern conversation with a girl who had just bathed in the river.

---

16   Edward Stone Parker to GA Robinson, 7 January 1850, Public Records Office of Victoria (PROV) VA512 *Chief Protector of Aborigines*, VPRS4410 unit 2, 1850/65 (reel 2).
17   Armstrong 1973: 49; Bebbington 1989: 2–8; Bradley 1976: 19–25, 71–72, 103; Ditchfield 1998: 26–29; Elbourne 2002: 30, 36–37; Gardner 2006: 27; Hempton 2005: 60–62; Hindmarsh 2001: 72–75; Kent 2005: 67, 70; Roberts 2002: 154–155, 200; Twells 1998: 236.
18   Joseph Orton, 'Answers to Several Questions as to Expertise – Call to Ministry and Theology', 1830, Joseph Orton, Letterbooks 1822–1842, ML ref A1717–A1720, State Library of NSW.
19   Benjamin Hurst to General Secretaries, 16 June 1841, *WMMS*, reel 2, Mp2107, NLA.
20   Watson, journal, 6 January 1835, *WVP*.

> I said to her well have you bathed? She replied 'yes.' Then you are clean now. 'Yes' I said outside; but you don't mind about inside being clean [sic]. You have no desire to have a clean heart. She hung down her head, and said 'yes I do.' I told her in what way she was to obtain a new heart.[21]

When the young man Goongeen (Jemmy Buckley) protested that his prayers had not prompted any action from God, Watson replied that he prayed carelessly and did not really wish to change. He also assured Goongeen that the devil lurked in the hearts of wicked people, and that 'God had always lived and knew everything'.[22] When a youth identified as JM (probably the same person) told Watson he felt miserable for his wicked heart, Watson replied:

> that all good people had been that way at first. That I was miserable once, and that all are born in sin, and that at first the mind was like midnight when there was no moon or stars, all dark, very dark ... but when the spirit of God shone into the mind it was like the Sun at first rising.[23]

Such accounts highlight two important, if paradoxical, aspects of philanthropic experience: the stress on Indigenous people as subjects of observation and monitoring, and the importance of discussion and exchange, of missionaries making their own experiences visible and debatable. Moral observation was certainly significant to mission life. In her study of Coranderrk station, operating in Victoria in the second half of the 19th century, Jane Lydon explores how Western visual cultures privileged seeing over other sensory experiences, emphasising the need to master oneself through a sense of being constantly watched. This contrasted with Indigenous systems of knowledge, which tended to conceptualise thought and understanding in terms of hearing, and which regulated people's behaviour more through public shaming and links to kin than through individual self-control.[24] Philanthropists' concern with the visual world was one reason for the emphasis (discussed in the previous chapter) on physical displays of morality, despite a belief in religious transformation as an inner experience. William Thomas, for example, was pleased when people dressed correctly for Sunday services on his protectorate station, listened politely to his sermons and joined in the hymns. He commented happily 'it really is a pleasure to behold the savages trying I may say persevering by endeavouring to imitate the white man.'[25] Similarly, Günther, who doubted whether Wiradjuri

---

21 Watson, journal, 18 October 1836, *WVP*.
22 Watson, journal, 5 July 1834, *WVP*.
23 Watson, journal, 16 January 1837, *WVP*.
24 Lydon 2005b: 227.
25 Thomas, 28 March 1841, *WTP*, ML MSS 214, reel 2. See also, Thomas, 1 November 1840, 15 November 1840, 22 November 1840, 31 January 1841, 4 April 1841, 11 April 1841, 2 May 1841, *WTP*, reel 2, also 7 July 1844, 10 April 1846, ML MSS 214, reel 3, State Library of NSW.

people understood his sermons, remarked 'Still it always gives me pleasure, to see a number of them at Church: they may at least get some notion & impression of divine ordinances.'[26]

The issue of observation went beyond this, however, as philanthropists' stressed God's omniscient power. In 1833, when he discovered that young Wiradjuri girls had been approached by white men, Watson wrote 'I spoke very seriously to the girls on the subject of God's seeing them, and I would hope they seemed ashamed of their conduct.'[27] Indigenous responses to such campaigns were mixed, but some young people at Wellington Valley appeared to take on these ideas about observation, perhaps out of curiosity, closeness to missionaries, or for strategic reasons. Watson was pleased when the young woman Warrahbin, who lived at the mission sometimes, rebuffed white men's advances by telling them 'the Great God who sits down in Heaven and all about will see and will be angry'.[28] He was also touched when he overheard a group of children talking about how 'Jesus Christ is all over and sees everything'; they named all the places and people they could think of, saying 'and Bathurst too and Sydney too &c &c'.[29]

More seriously, in Port Phillip, protectors Parker and Thomas described how they responded to reports of violent crimes by exhorting people that the 'Great Father' was watching and would punish them. This was Parker's response, for instance, when he was told that a woman called Boougarrapurmun had killed her newborn baby and was ill herself.[30] Perhaps the most dramatic incident occurred in 1840, when Thomas was told that Boonwurrung men from his station had killed other Indigenous people in Twofold Bay, as part of a long-running feud between their societies. A distressed Thomas, after speaking to various witnesses, confronted the men, who had previously insisted on their innocence. They wept and admitted to having speared their enemies and stolen portions of their flesh, after Thomas told them 'My Blackfellows no good, no good, talk me big, big one lie, me know all about my blackfellows, God knows, sees & hears all, me know.' The emphasis here, of course, was not only on God's observation, but also on the protector's.[31]

However, as the intensity of this exchange suggests, European regimes of observation were not being imposed upon Indigenous societies in any simple fashion. Philanthropists' powers were still quite limited, and Indigenous people

---

26   Günther, journal, 26 November 1837, *WVP*.
27   Watson, journal, 27 February 1833, *WVP*.
28   Watson, journal, 7 October 1833, *WVP*.
29   Watson, journal, 11 March 1834, *WVP*.
30   ES Parker, Quarterly Journal, 1 March – 31 May 1841, PROV VPRS4410, unit 2, 1841/61 (reel 2); Thomas, 8 February 1846, *WTP*, ML MSS 214, reel 3, State Library of NSW.
31   William Thomas to CJ La Trobe, 24 June 1840, PROV VPRS11 unit 7 (reel 1); William Thomas to GA Robinson, 6 June 1840, *WTP*, ML MSS 214, reel 4, State Library of NSW.

retained a certain autonomy and mobility. Moreover, Evangelical philanthropy, while stressing self-control and observation by authority figures, also relied on elements of mutuality and exchange. Catherine Hall has noted how ideas about heathen sin shaped British Evangelicals' own sense of moral worth – 'The heathen within constantly threatened at the door, making the imagined lines between self and other psychically and culturally vital'[32] – but a certain crossing of these lines was also a significant, if troubling, experience. For all the importance of watching, speaking was also important; Evangelical life in general involved giving voice to the Word and trying through reasoning and argument to convince people of God's love, and philanthropists' encounters with Aboriginal people commonly centred on conversation and lecturing, to encourage moral development.[33] David Hempton, in his history of Methodism, emphasises the centrality of aural exchange through preaching, exhorting, singing and confessing.[34] Similarly, Jean and John Comaroff have identified the relationship between speaker and audience as a fundamental element of missionary work; 'The preacher was the vehicle of Truth as faithful representation, the believer, its sentient recipient.'[35] In 1849, when protector Parker described church services on his station, it was their spoken qualities he mentioned: not only the liturgy, sermon, prayer, psalms and scriptural translations, but also his addresses 'on some practical topic', where he tried to engage Indigenous people by putting questions to them, 'with a view to excite interest and elicit inquiry in their minds.'[36]

Thus, while Christian transformation was imagined as an inward experience bound up with self-awareness, it was fostered through relationships of mentoring. An understanding of religion in terms of heritage and tutelage was implied by Watson in 1835, when he told a Wiradjuri man called Kabbarin that once upon a time everyone had known about God. This knowledge had been lost, he said, when people neglected to teach their children, 'so those children when they became the heads of families not knowing, or regarding the will of God did not teach their children and this was the reason the heathen did not understand anything regarding Him.'[37] While religious encounters between philanthropists and Indigenous people could be confused or conflicted, this mentoring relationship was nonetheless an important part of station life. This was suggested in several small incidents involving protector Thomas. On one occasion in 1840, Thomas tried to impress upon people the power of religion, by praying fervently over a sick man, singing hymns and lifting his eyes to the sky. The people watching presumably had little knowledge of Christianity at this

---

32  Hall 2002: 304–305.
33  Comaroff and Comaroff 1997 vol 2: 66–72.
34  Hempton 2005: 56, 68.
35  Comaroff and Comaroff 1997 vol 2: 66.
36  ES Parker to GA Robinson, 16 January 1849, PROV VPRS4410 unit 2, 1849/64 (reel 2).
37  Watson, journal, 19 December 1835, *WVP*.

point, but they showed approval at his nurturing behaviour. During another incident, a link between paternalism and Christian knowledge was implied, when one man responded to Thomas's lectures on 'God's seeing & knowing all they did & said', by saying 'no stupid me, my master Mr Dredge tell me long time ago all that'.[38] As Fiona Magowan has noted in her study of Yolngu missions in the 20th century, some missionary behaviour could be assimilated into Indigenous traditions of caring for others and passing on knowledge; sociality and relationality were important to institutional life.[39]

The personal element of evangelising was expressed overtly at Wellington Valley. On several occasions, young people asked the missionaries and their wives to pray and sing with them, and Watson claimed the children would only say their prayers with his wife, Ann.[40] One day in August 1838, a man called Fred, who was ill, surprised James Günther by calling out 'Mr Gunther pray for me!' When questioned by Günther, Fred said he believed in Jesus, adding 'I believe all you say & Mrs G say & I believe all Mr W say & Mrs W say.'[41] The personal link was clearest, however, in Watson's accounts of the conversion and baptism of several young women. In June 1834, Ann Watson told a girl called Nanny that she would be baptised, but cautioned her that when this happened she would belong entirely to Jesus. Nanny responded 'I will never leave you Mrs Watson'.[42] A similar account appeared in Watson's 1843 annual report, which claimed that two women, Sally and Jenny, who had been praying by themselves for some time, brought their children to him to be baptised in church, answering his theological questions satisfactorily, so that 'most of the congregation were deeply moved'. Sally, he said, assented to his warning that she must not take her children 'to live amongst heathens', saying 'I don't want to go away; I shall never leave you till I die'.[43] It can be hard to know how to read such stories, at a time when missionaries were struggling to establish their own authority. However, such dynamics can seem plausible in the context of Indigenous efforts to develop satisfying connections with philanthropists, and philanthropists' own wish for a paternalistic bond.

However, while Indigenous and philanthropic needs coincided in some ways, missionaries remained concerned by their failure to effect widespread conversions. Watson complained gloomily that preaching to Wiradjuri people felt sometimes 'like writing on the sand' or 'like beating the mountains with a

---

38   Thomas, 16 February 1840, *WTP*, ML MSS 214, reel 2, State Library of NSW; William Thomas to GA Robinson, 1 March 1841, PROV VPRS4410 unit 3, 1841/68 (reel 2).
39   Magowan 2005: 162–164.
40   Günther, journal, 2 September 1838, 29 July 1839; Watson, journal, 6 December 1832, 9 October 1833, *WVP*.
41   Günther, journal, 3 August 1838, *WVP*.
42   Watson, journal, 25 June 1834, *WVP*.
43   William Watson to Colonial Secretary, 3 January 1844, *BPP: Papers Relating to Australia, 1844*, vol 8: 285.

rod'.[44] Whilst acknowledging that evangelising always encountered resistance, philanthropists still felt affronted and hurt when their efforts were rejected. Here, their wish for a dynamic of benevolence and gratitude was relevant again. JCS Handt of Wellington Valley, an anxious and sensitive man, was distressed when some people ignored his religious lectures or said he was lying. He concluded 'their hearts seem to be very hard and insensible … a great enmity against the word of truth is manifested.' He prayed that God would 'make these poor people sensible of our desire to do them good!'[45] Günther, similarly, remarked upon 'their indifference towards the means of grace, their idleness, their ingratitude … and the insolence with which they sometimes speak to us'.[46] Thus, missionaries' duty to spread Christianity was translated into Indigenous people's duty to accept it. When the young man Cochrane posed the difficult question of why God had not sent the Bible to Australia long ago, Günther agreed that Europeans may have been to blame for delaying this with their sins. But he illustrated this with a reminder of Wiradjuri people's own culpability.

> Now just look at yourselves, you have had missionaries [a] long time; but you do not believe, nor grow better. If you had become good men, by this time, and could go further on, to other Natives, and, you, too could be missionaries & go all over the bush & preach.[47]

While the possibility of Indigenous preachers was not discussed often, Evangelical philanthropists did see a vital connection between personal salvation and spreading the word. This points to another creative tension in their work: while setting themselves up as spiritual authorities and observers, their sense of their own moral worth rested in many ways on their connections with Aboriginal people. Evangelical cultures in general drew important links between empire, missionary work and personal religious journeys. The London Missionary Society's 1846 *Juvenile Missionary Magazine*, for instance, reminded its young readers that improving their own moral state meant, amongst other things, praying for the heathen and making clothes for heathen children.[48] Similarly, the *Church Missionary Juvenile Instructor* told its readers in 1849:

> When you think of these little [African] slave girls and their troubles, forget not that you yourselves are by nature the slaves of sin and Satan. And if you have not done so already, make haste to come to Jesus, the blessed Redeemer.[49]

---

44  Watson, journal, 1 September 1833, 14 February 1834, *WVP*.
45  JCS Handt to William Jowett, 7 December 1835, *WVP*. Also, JCS Handt, journal, 28 November 1833, 8 March 1834, 16 December 1834, *WVP*.
46  Günther, journal, 27 December 1839, *WVP*.
47  Günther, journal, 15 March 1839, *WVP*.
48  London Missionary Society (LMS), *Juvenile Missionary Magazine*, vol 3, no 26, July 1846: 161, <http://www.nla.gov.au/ferg/issn/14606003.html>, also vol 3, no 20, January 1846: 15.
49  Church Missionary Society (CMS), *Church Missionary Juvenile Instructor*, vol VIII, no 12, December 1849: 358–359.

Thus, sin, redemption and the mission cause became intertwined for both the individual and the empire.

Philanthropists in the Australian colonies related their Indigenous projects to some very personal anxieties. On his way to Wellington Valley in 1832, Watson thanked God for the opportunity to preach to so many people, but worried that:

> I was not more in earnest, felt more love to my Saviour, and more pity for perishing souls. Blessed Redeemer how is it that while thy love is so great to me, mine in return should be so weak so faint so cold. My soul cleareth to the dust quicken thou me O God.[50]

Similarly, at the end of his first year at Wellington Valley, Günther thanked God for His mercies, whilst expressing deep regret for 'my many neglects, ingratitude & transgressions' and longing for 'more zeal & energy, knowledge & wisdom, & especially, faith & patience.'[51] One reason why Indigenous people's alleged sins were so distressing was because they were seen as reflecting badly on missionaries' own moral state. At Wellington Valley in 1834, when boys were caught sneaking into the girls' dormitory, Watson reflected that this was a warning to the missionaries not to be proud or assume that they alone could change people's hearts; 'God will have all the glory of His Grace.'[52] In 1837, he mused again on his failures, concluding that some deficiency on his part must be keeping the Holy Spirit from triumphing amongst the Wiradjuri. He wrote 'We daily pray Search us O God and try us and see if there be any wicked way in us.'[53]

Such concerns also surfaced in the papers of protectors Dredge and Thomas. James Dredge, an introspective and frequently unhappy man, wrote in his diary on his birthday in 1838 'numerous have been the Lord's mercies, and great my unfaithfulness. O that my spared life may be *more* devoted to God!'[54] Two years later, he marked another birthday by writing anxiously 'I feel myself to have been an unprofitable servant. May the Lord accept my thanks for his goodness to me – forgive me – and save henceforth!'[55] An account by Thomas drew a clearer connection between colonial work and personal redemption. One night in 1841, Thomas wrote in his diary that he had dreamed of his own death. '[T]he first thing my Saviour ask'd me was about the Poor Dark Blks if any was bowing to the mighty God.' When Thomas replied that they were not, the response

---

50   Watson, journal, 3 October 1832, *WVP*.
51   Günther, journal, 31 December 1837, *WVP*.
52   Watson, journal, 6 November 1834, *WVP*. See also, 3 October 1835.
53   Watson, journal, 3 January 1837, *WVP*.
54   James Dredge, 6 October 1838, James Dredge, Diaries, Notebook and Letterbooks, ?1817–1845 [hereafter *JDD*], MS11625, MSM534, State Library of Victoria (SLV).
55   James Dredge, 6 October 1840, *JDD*, MS11625, MSM534, SLV.

was 'did you tell them of the Cross [?] ... then how expect that they can come for there is but one access to God.' Feeling both humbled and revived, Thomas vowed 'methinks the Gates of Hell cannot prevail against me.'[56]

Philanthropists recounted most of these stories in their journals. It is not clear that they shared these anxieties with Indigenous people (although, as noted earlier, some did talk about their earlier lives as sinners seeking redemption). Nor did such expressions of humility and repentance feature much in missionary society publications, which preferred to highlight promising signs of Indigenous conversion. Nonetheless, moral self-interrogation was an important part of Evangelical life, and such passages are suggestive of philanthropists' need to make sense of their work and its relevance to their own selves. Religious soul-searching could also enable the airing of feelings that were otherwise unacceptable. On his birthday in 1838, James Günther described his guilt that his excessive secular duties on the station prevented him from engaging in meditation and prayer, 'to review my past life with the mercies I have experienced, the sins I have committed, the neglects I have become guilty of.' This apparent self-criticism in fact conveyed a double message, as Günther had been urging the Church Missionary Society in vain to send more aid to Wellington Valley.[57] Thus, when we consider how Christian morality was lived in practice, it was characterised by an interplay of watching, speaking and listening, of individualism and relationality, and of troubled attempts to construct subjects and authorities.

## 'Black fellows knew a great deal': Christianity received and explored

Philanthropists' anxious appraisals of their shortcomings have no doubt contributed to the general historical assessment of them as failures. However, while they certainly had many weaknesses, this assumption of Christian failure can be challenged. For one thing, some Indigenous conversions were reported, on stations where the missionaries were unusually keen or the circumstances unusually conductive. Wiradjuri country became one site for this, following Watson's split from the Church Missionary Society. While his colleague Günther had rigorously refused to baptise people whose conversions seemed uncertain, Watson was less hesitant. When Governor Gipps visited in 1840, he noted that one child (living with Watson) had been baptised, an eight-year-old boy called William Campbell.[58] Baptisms subsequently increased. The missionaries had been hopeful about a girl called Jane since one night in 1837, when they found

---

56 Thomas, journal, 17 August 1841, *WTP*, ML MSS 214, reel 2, State Library of NSW.
57 Günther, journal, 12 May 1838, *WVP*.
58 Memoranda, enclosed in Sir George Gipps to Lord John Russell, 5 April 1841, *BPP: Papers Relating to Australia, 1844*, vol 8: 70.

her sitting up, wanting to pray and feeling distressed about 'her soul, her sin, & her wicked heart'. Jane, who had been molested by white men and had a baby at a young age, became understandably attached to the relative security and affection of mission life. It was probably Jane to whom Watson was referring, when he described in an 1841 report a young woman whose Christian beliefs made her confident to refuse the approaches of white men, answering their taunts about her sexual history by replying 'I did not then know the Bible'. Watson baptised Jane in 1845; with an intriguing mixture of sexism and religious severity, he asked permission of her husband, Jemmy, but would not baptise Jemmy himself because he was not yet saved.[59] In 1849, Watson informed Governor Fitzroy that he had baptised seven people at Wellington Valley and 25 at his new Apsley station.[60] It is hard to know what to make of this. Watson, a prickly and obsessive character, no doubt wished to defy his neighbours and colleagues by asserting the success of his lone endeavours. However, his relationships with Wiradjuri people seem to have been fairly enduring, presumably helping some people to remain in their country after the official mission closed.

While Watson's isolated efforts did not receive much public praise, British missionary societies publicised some encouraging reports from John Smithies' Swan River mission in Western Australia in the 1840s. The WMMS reported with delight his account of young Indigenous people 'bathed in tears, broken in heart, and crying "Jesus save me! O Lord save me!"'[61] *Papers Relative to the Wesleyan Missions* (1848) rejoiced at the fact that 18 youths had been baptised at Swan River and 30 or 40 people 'converted'.[62] These accounts are indicative of Smithies' personal connections to young mission residents, but perhaps also of the impact of his efforts to integrate his pupils into white society as servants. This lifestyle may have made Christianity seem more relevant to these youths; perhaps it also helped them cope with circumstances which could be alienating and exploitative. This was suggested in the religious visions of a young girl called Wobart, who was converted at the same time as Nogyle. Wobart became a Christian after sitting up late one night at the house where she worked, feeling anxious and depressed, minding the baby of her white employers who had gone out to a party. She dreamed of black and white sinners being condemned on Judgement Day, where 'white lady and gentleman go dancing down to hell'.[63]

---

59  Günther, journal, 10 September 1837, *WVP*; William Watson, First Report of the Aboriginal Mission, Murrung gallang, Wellington, c1841, in Sir William Dixson, *Documents relating to Aboriginal Australians*; Woolmington 1985: 286.
60  William Watson to Gov Charles Fitzroy, 31 December 1849, 9th Annual Report of the Apsley Aboriginal Mission, in Sir William Dixson, *Documents relating to Aboriginal Australians*.
61  WMMS, *Report of the WMMS for the year ending April 1845*, April 1846: 30–31; CMS, *Missionary Register*, May 1847: 217.
62  WMMS, *Papers Relative to the Wesleyan Missions, and to the State of Heathen Countries*, no cxi, March 1848.
63  John Smithies to General Secretaries, 25 October 1843, *WMMS*, reel 2, Mp2107, NLA.

It is curious that missionary historians, who have explored other projects in such depth, have not paid more attention to these accounts. John Harris, for example, does not explore the claims of individual conversions at Wellington Valley and gives only a brief outline of the Swan River 'revival'. William McNair and Hilary Rumley also give an oddly cursory description of Smithies' baptisms of numerous children, while Neville Green's chapter on Swan River omits the subject.[64] Presumably the early deaths of many of these converts discouraged further examination, although, as I will discuss later, missionaries themselves did not necessarily read such tragedies in terms of meaningless failure at all.

Assumptions of Evangelical failure can also be challenged in other respects. Even the rarity of baptisms deserves closer analysis. Missionaries' exacting standards of conversion meant that even when Indigenous people expressed interest in Christianity, this was often greeted with suspicion and interrogation. Awabakal man Biraban (or John M'Gill), for example, was an important translator, guide and companion to LE Threlkeld for years, but when he helped Threlkeld translate in a court case in 1838, the missionary informed Justice Burton that Biraban had not been baptised; his character, particularly his drinking, was incompatible with Christian life.[65] Similarly, at Wellington Valley in 1835, Handt reported that while the children's scriptural knowledge was good and they took part readily in Christian discussions, he could not call them converts; 'no real spiritual mindedness has yet manifested'.[66] Günther, similarly, told Governor Gipps that he would not baptise any children who were still living with their families, and when a man called Fred asked to be baptised (possibly because he wanted to marry one of the mission girls), Günther refused, lecturing him 'that he did not truly believe as yet, that he was too wicked still.'[67] This must be kept in mind when evaluating these projects. As Paul Landau has warned in his African study, some historians have been too quick to accept the stark divisions missionaries drew between converts and heathens, a distinction which may have had less meaning for native peoples themselves.[68]

On the first Australian missions, there were certainly some supposedly non-Christian people who engaged in articulate, interesting discussions about Christianity. This was the main area – indeed, virtually the only area – where British publications actually recounted Indigenous people's opinions, albeit partially. Stories published from Wellington Valley mentioned religious conversations and arguments, children practising hymns and prayers, and

---

64 Green 1988: 156–157; Harris 1990: 60, 63, 67, 275–277; McNair and Rumley 1981: 97–102.
65 LE Threlkeld, 'Correspondence and Early Reports Relating to the Aboriginal Mission 1825–1841', in Gunson (ed) 1974 vol 2: 271.
66 JCS Handt, 1835 Report, *WVP*.
67 Günther, journal, 13 August 1838, *WVP*; Memoranda, enclosed in Sir George Gipps to Lord John Russell, 5 April 1841, *BPP: Papers Relating to Australia, 1844*, vol 8: 68–70.
68 Landau 1999: 11.

people behaving well in church.⁶⁹ Methodist publications, too, emphasised religious discussions and battles against sin, notably an anecdote from Buntingdale about a senior Indigenous man who rebuked a settler for not going to church, threatening that he would go to hell, and a comment from a young man, Hoymonaneau, who claimed to feel sorry for his sins: 'I have two spirits within me, the good spirit and the bad spirit, and they are talking to me every day'.⁷⁰ It is unsurprising that official publications emphasised such stories, given their 'Christianity first' focus. However, it also draws our attention to the fact that Indigenous views on more systemic colonial issues – notably the loss of land and resources – could be muffled in Evangelical publications, which considered Christianity the justification for empire.

Local records are suggestive of how Indigenous people tried to understand Christian elements within the colonial world. Wiradjuri people watched with interest the baptisms of white children, and missionaries at Wellington Valley and Buntingdale were asked questions about heaven: how large it was, what they would eat, whether there would be trees, cattle and rivers, whether they would have to work like white men, and whether there would be racial distinctions.⁷¹ Some queries took the missionaries by surprise. Günther, for example, was nonplussed when the young man Cochrane, who alternately told the missionaries that he wanted to become a Christian and that he did not have the patience for it, asked 'What the devil say to them when they come to hell?' Günther finally replied that the devil would tell sinners they were foolish for not repenting.⁷²

Here, it is helpful to consider the work of Peggy Brock, who has cautioned historians not to naturalise missionaries' assumption that their faith must oppose and replace native beliefs. In her portrayal of First Nations Tsimshian convert Arthur Wellington Clah, Brock argues that Tsimshian people saw Christianity as providing new elements of knowledge to improve their lives, mingling with local beliefs and dynamics.⁷³ At mission stations in the early Australian colonies, some people participated in aspects of Christian life without abandoning other beliefs. Goongeen (Jemmy Buckley), for instance, whose long conversations about Christianity the Wellington Valley missionaries recorded eagerly, was

---

69  CMS, *Church Missionary Paper*, London, CMS, no LXXIV, Christmas, 1836. Also, CMS, *Missionary Register*, November 1835: 515–520; CMS, *Missionary Register*, June 1836: 296–301; CMS, *Missionary Register*, September 1836: 427–430; CMS, *Missionary Register*, August 1838: 372–373; CMS, *Missionary Register*, September 1838: 423–425; CMS, *Missionary Register*, August 1839: 387–389.
70  CMS, *Missionary Register*, May 1846: 210; WMMS, *Report of the Wesleyan Methodist Missionary Society for the year ending April 1840*, 1840: 32; WMMS, *Report of the WMMS for the year ending April 1845*, 1845: 30–31.
71  Günther, journal, 26 November 1837, WVP; JCS Handt, journal, 27 September 1835, WVP; Francis Tuckfield to General Secretaries, 30 October 1841, WMMS, reel 2, Mp2107, NLA.
72  Günther, journal, 5 August 1838, WVP. Also, 27 December 1839.
73  Brock 2000: 78, 90.

nonetheless offended by their lectures against heathen superstition. He told Günther 'Black fellows knew a great deal', and spoke 'with feelings of veneration, & with a great degree of self sufficiency.'[74] During a conversation with Watson in 1834, Goongeen talked about Christian ideas of heaven, hell and angels, then tried to tell the missionary that shooting stars were portents of death. When Watson scoffed at this, Goongeen replied 'you won't believe Black fellow, Black fellow won't believe you.'[75] The missionaries were especially baffled by one incident that year, when Goongeen shut himself in the blacksmith's shop and performed a church service, complete with hymns, prayers, Benediction and sermon, before running away when he realised he was being watched. Watson wondered if he was mocking them, but felt that the time and energy Goongeen expended suggested something more. While it is not possible to know exactly what happened here, it seems plausible that some people were interested in exploring Christian knowledge, although not always submitting to missionary authority.[76]

Some particularly intriguing stories emerged of people undergoing Christian dreams and visions. Unlike Nogyle, not all these people were identified as converts, nor did they accept missionary guidance so compliantly. To assume, though, that they were simply less Christian is perhaps to take the missionaries' own assumptions too much for granted. It might be better to read these visions in a context of varied efforts to negotiate social and spiritual change. At Wellington Valley, a young man called Oorimbildwally, who was ill and nearly blind, became rather dependent on the missionaries and attended church enthusiastically for a time. The fascinated missionaries described Oorimbildwally as a doctor, with the power to hunt Buggeen, 'the devil'; he suffered from strange seizures and his relatives told William Watson that he was troubled by ghosts. In 1833, he claimed to have had several dreams about the missionaries' God. In one, he was in a large building full of windows, where he saw God but did not speak to him, and in another he was pulled by a kurrajong cord through the window into God's house, where he saw God and Jesus in long white coats and thousands of people reading books. When he announced that he was sure to go to heaven when he died, however, Watson was uneasy, seeing Oorimbildwally as over-confident and not sufficiently worried about his sins.[77] Protector Thomas recorded similar scepticism and hope when a Boonwurrung man, Benbow, who was ill, told Thomas that while he was asleep God had touched his chest and told him he would not die. Thomas, although unconvinced, did not wish to discourage this line of thought.[78] These issues were echoed at Buntingdale in

---

74   Günther, journal, 9 July 1833, *WVP*.
75   Watson, journal, 5 July, 1834, *WVP*.
76   Watson, journal, 21 December 1834, *WVP*.
77   Watson journal, 19 April 1833, 12 May 1833, 20 May 1833, 21 July 1833, 10 February 1834, *WVP*.
78   Thomas, 14 March 1847, *WTP*, ML MSS 214, reel 3, State Library of NSW.

1841, when a man called Wer-e-rup, who was attributed with powers to heal the sick and raise the dead, made a conciliatory gesture towards Christianity, after several unpleasant scenes with Francis Tuckfield, who called him an impostor. Wer-e-rup announced that he had flown to heaven to retrieve the soul of a dead child and spoken to the Great Spirit the missionaries talked about. This baffled Tuckfield, who was unsure how to respond when young men cried out during his sermons 'It is true! "Wer-e-rup" has said so!' He concluded that the doctor's power must be diminishing, making Wer-e-rup want to 'shelter under our wing.'[79] However, such accounts might suggest efforts by influential men to reinforce their own status and knowledge, as well as engaging more broadly with Christian imagery and beliefs.

Here, it is useful to keep in mind Landau's argument that Africans did not view Christianity initially as a single, coherent phenomenon (as missionaries assumed it to be), but rather experienced it in fragmented, piecemeal ways.[80] When Indigenous Australians expressed hostility towards Christian ideas, this was in relation to specific topics, which may or may not have affected their religious feelings in other contexts. The greatest problem stemmed from missionaries' insistence on talking about death and the afterlife. When JCS Handt persisted in lecturing a man called Jacky about death, despite his protests, he was crestfallen when Jacky answered his question 'whether he did not love the Saviour of men?' with a blunt 'No.'[81] Mentions of recently deceased people caused particular offence and distress. When a young man called Billy of Ngannima died at Wellington Valley, the missionaries took aside Billy's kinsman, Tommy, seeing this as an opportunity to 'exhort and warn him'. The resulting scene was unpleasant.

> When Mr W. pointed out hell fire, Tommy grew angry & called out: 'Don't you talk that way! you were in fire. When that fire come from in your house? [Referring to a recent accidental fire in Watson's study.] … Godder (God) made it; he badly with you (angry), he make fire.'

Günther, taken aback, reflected 'the Natives understand & know more of what the missionaries tell them than we are sometimes led to suppose.'[82] Thomas recorded a similar scene in 1846, when an old man died. Thomas addressed the mourners 'upon Death, Sin, Heaven & Hell & shew'd to them that God's Book was our only light … & Christ would at the resurrection try us by it'. One man retorted that his kinsman had died because he stopped too long by Thomas's Narre Narre Warren school and ceased to visit his country in Melbourne.[83] On

---

79  Francis Tuckfield to General Secretaries, 30 October 1841, *WMMS*, reel 2, Mp2107, NLA.
80  Landau 1999: 11.
81  Handt, journal, 15 June 1835, *WVP*.
82  Günther, journal, 10 July 1838, *WVP*.
83  Thomas, 29 April 1846, *WTP*, ML MSS 214, reel 3, State Library of NSW.

such occasions, even people who had been interested in Christianity in other contexts could take offence. Jemmy Buckley (Goongeen), for instance, became furious when the missionaries interrupted his dancing at a ceremony to warn him about sin. He burst out 'You always come & tell us this! What you always come to the Camp for & tell us we should go to hell [?] ... Don't you go to hell?' Günther noted 'The poor fellow appeared almost ready to beat us.'[84] Such incidents may have signified inner spiritual struggles (this was presumably the missionaries' view) but it is also possible that Indigenous observers saw this as inappropriate and offensive behaviour, rather than a reflection on a whole spiritual system.

## 'A brand plucked from the burning?' Triumphs and tragedies

The deaths of Indigenous people sparked some passionate controversies during this period. This was especially so because of the significance of death to Evangelicals, who believed strongly in the judgement to come, when the unsaved would be bound for hellfire. This led to a keen (if perhaps contradictory) approach: philanthropists asserted that Indigenous Australians, being unsaved sinners, were excessively afraid of death, but the way to change this involved stressing to people the dangers of damnation. The shadow of death was assumed to hang particularly heavy in Australia, given Aboriginal depopulation and supposed 'savagery'. Indigenous mourning rituals, especially body paint and self-mutilation, were depicted with horror, partly because missionaries associated them with 'dirt', but also because such elaborate mourning was taken as a sign of despair, of people trapped in the earthly world. In 1842, John Smithies contrasted what he considered a dignified mission funeral, where the children dressed neatly and sang hymns, with Indigenous burial rites, where they 'sorrow, wail, ring the air & lacerate themselves and of course have none of the consolation of religion.'[85] Günther, likewise, watched relatives of a dead man cutting themselves and crying over his grave, and was moved to shed tears himself, reflecting 'this occasion proved to me so strikingly & affectingly, that they are without God & without hope.'[86]

Indeed, Indigenous people's very reluctance to talk about death was taken as proof of their enslavement to it. When a man called Eramdiul urged Watson to stop warning him about sin and dying, Watson replied that he would not be afraid to die if he knew God and Christ; 'through fear of death they are all their lifetimes subject to bondage.'[87] However, philanthropists often tried

---

84 Günther, journal, 3 March 1838, *WVP*.
85 John Smithies to General Secretaries, 1 May 1842, *WMMS*, reel 2, Mp2107, NLA.
86 Günther, journal, 26 June 1838, *WVP*.
87 Watson, journal, 16 March 1834, *WVP*.

to encourage this transformation by speaking at length about the afterlife. As Handt remarked 'Their fear of death is very great, and they are loath to hear anything on the subject; and yet it is difficult to speak on religious matters without touching this point.'[88] Similarly, in 1845, protector Thomas described how he moved around the camp, 'endeavouring to make them more familiar with Death & to drive away their superstitions'.[89] Elsewhere, he elaborated on his methods, telling chief protector Robinson that he warned people about 'the awful end and suffering of the wicked White and Black', and 'punishment hereafter to the wicked'.[90] Thomas regretted that he did not have the language to reiterate constantly to people the threat of sin and judgement after death.[91]

However, Evangelical views on death went beyond threats and fears, as they struggled to deal with an issue considered both painful and strangely elating: the fact that their rare Indigenous converts often died young. While the missionaries were saddened and downcast by their pupils' deaths, they did not explain this in terms of failure. Instead, these losses were portrayed according to 19th century understandings of 'good death': slow, dignified, comparatively painless, allowing sufferers to put their lives in order and be reconciled with God. Pat Jalland has stressed the centrality of deathbed scenes to Victorian Evangelical cultures, where a person's manner of dying could provide vital proof of their salvation, as they gave assurance of their nearness to heaven.[92] Such ideas affected missionaries around the world; Patricia Grimshaw's Hawaiian study and Michael Harkin's examination of missions amongst the Heiltsuk note the importance missionaries attached to joyous 'good deaths', especially of children, whose helplessness epitomised humanity's status in relation to God.[93]

Such ideas were certainly apparent in the Australian colonies. Watson spoke optimistically of the 1839 death of one of his most promising pupils, the girl called Nanny. She had requested and received baptism and confessed her faith in Jesus, and Watson claimed to have observed 'a real change of heart in her.' (His refusal to invite his colleague Günther to be present at her baptism and death suggests the bitter animosity between the two men, as well as the personal claims missionaries made over such triumphs.)[94] Of the seven people Watson baptised at Wellington Valley, three passed away early in such a virtuous state, and he mentioned the deaths of several young people 'in the faith of Jesus Christ' as a hopeful sign for the beginning of his Apsley mission.[95]

---

88  Handt, 1835 Report, *WVP*.
89  Thomas, 9 November 1845, *WTP*, ML MSS 214, reel 3, State Library of NSW.
90  William Thomas to GA Robinson, 6 October 1840, PROV VPRS11 unit 7, 1840/335 (reel 1); William Thomas to GA Robinson, 2 March 1844, PROV VPRS4410 unit 3, 1844/79 (reel 2).
91  Thomas, 26 September 1847, *WTP*, ML MSS 214, reel 3, State Library of NSW.
92  Jalland 1996: 20–23, 33.
93  Grimshaw 1989: 148; Harkin 1993: 8–10.
94  Günther, journal, 26 July 1839, *WVP*.
95  William Watson, First Report of the Aboriginal Mission, Murrung gallang, Wellington, c1841, in Sir William Dixson, *Documents relating to Aboriginal Australians*; William Watson to Governor Charles Fitzroy, 31

Anecdotes of hope and demise were also recounted in Western Australia. Anglican clergyman Rev George King told the United Society for the Propagation of the Gospel in 1846 that he had baptised five Indigenous children. Perhaps strangely, this does not seem to have been discussed widely, perhaps because King added that he could not state for certain whether the children had experienced proper repentance and faith. In the same year, he reported that two of his students had recently died. Their families attended the funerals; one child, who was 'in a probationary state', was permitted an Indigenous burial, while the other, whom he described as a clever, educated girl, was laid to rest in the churchyard. King claimed with some pride that this was the first such event in Australia.[96]

More emphatic stories of both conversion and deathbed piety emerged from the neighbouring Methodist mission, where an epidemic of unspecified 'mesentery' (intestinal) disease, carried away many young people in the mid-1840s. As noted earlier, the 1843 conversions of the young girls Nogyle and Wobart were followed by sorrow when Nogyle died soon afterwards. Wobart, to everyone's surprise, went on to marry the mission's white overseer, John Stokes; they lived happily together and had three children. This was short-lived, however; four years into her marriage, Wobart died of influenza. According to Smithies, all those around her were impressed by her piety, as she farewelled her family, saying 'God loves me'.[97] Smithies' reports were full of such tales of youthful tragedy. He described the slow, wasting death of a young boy, Birgee, in 1843; 'there was a meekness and patience and hope in the lad that made him lovely in his last days. He was frequently amidst much pain found on his knees praying to God to bless him.'[98] Two years later, a 10-year-old girl, Caroline Barrett, also died after delighting the missionaries with her devotion. She told them 'If Caroline in bush now too much frightened about death coming soon, but now I love Jesus ... me want to die and be with my dear Saviour ... friends leave me but Jesus never leave me.' Smithies reflected with mournful approval 'Many die as young in our fatherland but not so well.'[99]

There is no reason to doubt the sadness and regret of the missionaries, who had invested high hopes and perhaps real affection in their young residents, only to nurse them through terminal illness. A wish to understand these losses not in terms of failure and destruction, but as bittersweet triumphs, is scarcely

---

December 1849, 9th Annual Report of the Apsley Aboriginal Mission, Sir William Dixson, *Documents relating to Aboriginal Australians*.
96   George King to Ernest Hawkins, 1 January 1846, Rev George King to Rev E Hawkins, 22 June 1846, Rev George King to the Bishop of Australia, 9 April 1846, United Society for the Propagation of the Gospel, Records, AJCP M1222, SLV.
97   McNair and Rumley 1981: 104–106; John Smithies to General Secretaries, 21 September 1845, *WMMS*, reel 2, Mp2107, NLA.
98   John Smithies to General Secretaries, 10 January 1843, *WMMS*, reel 2, Mp2107, NLA.
99   John Smithies to General Secretaries, 21 September 1845, *WMMS*, reel 2, Mp2107, NLA.

surprising. However, the trope of the good death was also a literary device, popular in missionary society publications. This was apparent in accounts by Watson and the CMS. In 1836, the CMS's *Church Missionary Paper* included an anecdote about the good death of a young boy called Dicky Marshall. Watson had made earlier, optimistic mention of him, partly because of his very willingness to discuss threats of spiritual destruction. Walking in the bush together one evening in 1833, Watson prompted him by asking 'where wicked children would go when they died?' Dicky responded 'to that very bad place'.

> I then asked him who were wicked children? He replied, 'those that are disobedient, say naughty words, play or bathe on a Sunday'. He spoke this in so simple and artless a manner as made it very pleasing. Tears often run down his cheeks when we speak to him on religious subjects.[100]

Dicky's own pious death was cited as cause for hope by the CMS, who repeated Watson's conclusion '*Is this not a brand plucked from the burning?*'[101]

When Smithies' accounts appeared in missionary magazines, the relationship between hope and doom was even more confronting. His reports of a revival amongst black and white residents of his district were initially published with great enthusiasm. However, by 1849 the *Missionary Register* was stating that Smithies' main job might be to prepare the ground for later success. They added that it was uplifting to observe the 'ingatherings of a few juvenile Converts to the Lord Jesus, and especially to the heavenly state above, for they early blossomed, early ripened, and as early sickened and died; but they have commenced an early and glorious immortality.'[102] Ironically, at the same time as the mission itself was in decline, the *Wesleyan Juvenile Offering* (1853) keenly recounted tales of Indigenous Christianity. The story of Mary Nogyle was reported with particular enthusiasm, focusing on her conversion and dreams about devils and angels. She was described as gentle, pure and lovely; the journal explained that the missionaries kept her original name because it sounded appropriately like 'no guile'. The author wrote happily 'it seemed necessary to look at the sable colour of her skin, and listen to her broken English, in order to be convinced that she was indeed the child of these poor wandering denizens of the forest.'[103] The sad early end to Nogyle's life was a key element in this story; juvenile religious magazines frequently told tales of virtuous children meeting their deaths with saintly acceptance.

---

100  Watson, journal, 5 April 1833, *WVP*.
101  CMS, *Church Missionary Paper*, no LXXIV, Christmas 1836.
102  CMS, *Missionary Register*, May 1849: 218–219. Also, WMMS, *Report of the WMMS for the year ending April 1845*, 1845: 32–33.
103  WMMS, *Wesleyan Juvenile Offering*, London, Wesleyan Mission House, September 1853: 98–101; also WMMS, *Wesleyan Juvenile Offering*, August 1853: 87.

For Evangelical philanthropists, an intense awareness of death, and its relation to judgement, sin and salvation, was in keeping with their wider religious discourse. Yet, for the contemporary reader, it is hard not to associate it with the growing colonial portrayals of Indigenous Australians as a doomed race, whose depopulation was not the result of dispossession or preventable poverty, but of evolutionary 'progress'. It would be unwise to draw any simplistic correlation here; Evangelical Christianity, with its aim of universal salvation, could challenge colonists' claims that Indigenous people were hopeless. Furthermore, many of the above-mentioned descriptions of faith and death came from philanthropists who continued to hold hopes for the Aboriginal future. Nonetheless, in a setting of Indigenous dispossession and high mortality, some readers might well have begun to naturalise these stories of mission deaths. The relative weakness of Evangelical interest in Indigenous Australia could not have helped here; joyous accounts of deathbed faith might appear almost as the pinnacle of Australian missionary achievement. This was, perhaps, the dark side of a discourse which understood Indigenous welfare in terms of philanthropy, which focused strongly on doom and salvation, and which saw Christian instruction as both compensation for and consolidation of British imperialism. These elements affected philanthropists in complex ways, as they found their rare Christian victories to be temporary, transient and framed by loss.

# 'This bitter reproach': destruction, guilt and the colonial future

In 1841, LE Threlkeld wrote to Colonial Secretary E Deas Thomson to report on the imminent closure of his Lake Macquarie mission. The mission had been marked by controversy virtually from the beginning, due to Threlkeld's angry public statements about colonial violence and his disputes with powerful local figures – firstly, with missionary advocate Samuel Marsden (which contributed to the London Missionary Society's decision to remove their funding in 1828) and later with outspoken politician John Dunmore Lang (which furthered the removal of government funding).[1] Throughout these tumultuous years, Threlkeld had contributed to the production of ideas about Indigenous Australia. He had set himself up as an expert on Awabakal language and society, promoted the need for missionary work, and objected passionately to what he believed was a culture of frontier violence. However, he also came to see the final disappearance of Indigenous societies as probable and perhaps unavoidable. Threlkeld's final report encapsulated some of these complexities. He reported with pride that King William IV had accepted a copy of his linguistic work for the Royal Library, but made clear that this was more about memorialising a dying race than supporting a living one. Threlkeld asserted that his mission was closing because so few Awabakal people remained, and expressed hope that this tragedy would not dissuade the government from supporting future philanthropy. Indigenous opinions on the mission's closure were not discussed, and his morose conclusion suggested a certain temptation to hold them responsible for his disappointments and their own mortality:

> It is a melancholy fact that, although much has been done in the way of translation, there are now scarcely any Aborigines left to learn to read, and the few who remain appear determined to go in the broad road to destruction.[2]

In fact, Threlkeld's mission was one of the first to close; others, in southern and western Australia, had barely begun. His comments, however, drew attention to – and perhaps exacerbated – the pessimism that surrounded many Australian philanthropic efforts, even at their inception. By 1855, all of the first missions and protectorate stations had shut (most had dwindled long before). Meanwhile, Aboriginal people across all the colonies were suffering from loss of land and resources, erosion of cultural life, and depopulation through illness, poverty, low

---

1   Johnston 2006: 59, 73–77.
2   LE Threlkeld to E Deas Thomson, 'The final report of the mission to the Aborigines, Lake Macquarie, New South Wales, 1841', PMS1847, Australian Institute of Aboriginal and Torres Strait Islander Studies (AIATSIS).

birth rates and violence. Philanthropists reported this destruction frequently but felt largely powerless to prevent it. This chapter traces the humanitarian collapse, while also attempting to go beyond the common assessment of these missions and protectorates as simple failures. In a setting where Evangelical philanthropists consistently stressed that nothing but their own Christian efforts could save Indigenous people, the closure of their projects had important implications for future policy-making. Intertwined with these changes was a growth in popular settler portrayals of Indigenous people as naturally doomed, a topic which brings to the fore the ambiguous place of philanthropists within empire, as they alternately opposed such racist attitudes and became implicated in them.

## 'An eternal memento': Indigenous deaths and philanthropic collapse

The spectre of Indigenous death and disappearance had been present in philanthropic discourse from at least the 1820s, with Christian intervention portrayed as the only solution. The Wesleyan Methodist Missionary Society's *Missionary Notices* (1825), for example, reported 'exterminating conflict' occurring in Bathurst, and called for a mission to be established nearby. Accompanying this was a quotation from the *Sydney Gazette*:

> it is horrible to think, that, at a moment when all the civilized world is united for the abolition of the (abominable) slave trade, that even one man could be found cruel enough to think it necessary to exterminate the whole race of these poor misrepresented people.[3]

Similarly, the Church Missionary Society's *Missionary Register* (1831) anticipated that the government would support the proposed Wellington Valley mission in order to avoid the devastation that had occurred in other British colonies.[4] In 1838, when the Colonial Church Society promoted the need for stronger religious life in the colonies, one reason cited was the need to prevent Indigenous destruction. Otherwise, the 'New Hollanders', along with native peoples of Africa and America, would remain degraded and 'vitiated', 'melting away from existence'.[5]

While the claim that only missionaries could save Indigenous people was understandable and in some respects valid, it conveyed some mixed messages. This was especially so when Indigenous people were described as so degraded

---

3 Wesleyan Methodist Missionary Society (WMMS), *Missionary Notices*, no 116, August 1825: 499.
4 Church Missionary Society (CMS), *Missionary Register*, January 1831: 118–119.
5 Colonial Church Society (CCS), *The Second Report of the Australian Church Missionary Society, now formed into the Colonial Church Society*, 1838: 19.

that missionary success seemed near-impossible. For instance, the WMMS's *Papers Relative to the Wesleyan Missions* (1822) gave derogatory descriptions of Indigenous Australians and asserted that 'left to themselves' they would soon become 'extinct'.

> Shall these tribes go on diminishing in numbers until they become extinct for want of food, which we can teach them to raise? and shall this bitter reproach be written in our history, that we suffered them thus to perish from the face of the earth, without an effort to save either their bodies or their souls? God forbid![6]

This, however, raised the implicit question of what would happen to Indigenous people should their missionaries fail.

This question assumed immediate relevance by the 1830s, as philanthropists reported high Aboriginal mortality and depopulation. Threlkeld had urged the London Missionary Society as early as 1828 that greater action was needed to prevent 'their speedy extinction'.[7] By the mid-1830s, as his work became controversial and unpopular, his Lake Macquarie reports had assumed a grim tone. In 1836–37, Threlkeld warned that Awabakal numbers were shrinking; he cited the low birth rate and venereal disease, asserting 'the decrease of the Black population is not local and temporary, but general and annual'.[8] In 1839, two years before the mission was finally defunded, he told Colonial Secretary Thomson that deaths were outnumbering births in his region; 'in the elapse of a very few years, humanly speaking, the race will become extinct in these parts'.[9]

This concern had become apparent in British philanthropic advocacy by the late 1830s, and it permeated the work of the Select Committee on Aborigines (British Settlements). The Church Missionary Society's *Missionary Register* set the tone in 1836, praising TF Buxton's efforts to push for enquiries into native conditions throughout the empire, and commenting 'It is not very creditable to the general policy of our Colonial Settlements, that wherever we establish Colonies, there the Aboriginal Population begins rapidly to disappear.'[10] This was a major theme in the Committee's 1837 report. An overview stated that the original peoples of Newfoundland and the Caribbean had been exterminated, that Native Americans had suffered from cruelty and depopulation but were

---

6 WMMS, *Papers Relative to the Wesleyan Missions and to the State of the Heathen Countries*, no IX, September 1822.
7 LE Threlkeld, 'London Missionary Society. Mission to the Aborigines, New South Wales. Circular', 8 October 1828, London Missionary Society, Records [hereafter *LMS*], AJCP M73, State Library of Victoria (SLV).
8 LE Threlkeld, Annual Reports, 1836 and 1837, in Gunson (ed) 1974 vol 1: 133–135.
9 LE Threlkeld to E Deas Thomson, Annual Report of the Mission to the Aborigines, Lake Macquarie, 1839, in L.E. Threlkeld, Papers 1815–1862, ML ref A382, CY reel 820, State Library of NSW.
10 CMS, *Missionary Register*, January 1836: 5.

helped by missionaries, that native peoples in British Guinea were disappearing through government neglect, and that 'Hottentots' and 'Bushmen' in the Cape Colony had died in great numbers through dispossession and genocidal violence.[11]

Within this context, the Australian sections were distinguished not so much by their threats of Aboriginal 'extermination', as by the relatively minor attention and future planning they received. Certainly, Indigenous Australians were described as neglected and abused, diminishing in numbers and needing humanitarian intervention. Rev Walter Lawry stated 'White men, on the spot, generally think that the black will become extinct within the colony. I think so too, and this will be very much through the vices of the Europeans.'[12] However, some of the Australian testimonies contained mixed messages. Archdeacon Broughton, for instance, described Aboriginal decline thus:

> wherever the Europeans meet with them, they appear to wear out, and gradually to decay ... within a very limited period, those who are very much in contact with Europeans will be utterly extinct; I will not say exterminated, but they will be extinct.[13]

He blamed this largely on alcoholism and loss of resources (downplaying colonial violence) but added in the more mystical tone which would come to characterise the 'doomed race' discourse: 'there is something in our manner and state of society which they appear to decay before'.[14]

The report's section on Van Diemen's Land showed some particularly equivocal views on destruction and responsibility. The exile of Indigenous people to Flinders Island was described as tragic but unavoidable, on the grounds that settlers, angered by Aboriginal attacks, would exterminate them otherwise. A comment from Governor Arthur was included, lamenting the need to drive away 'a simple, but warlike, and, as it now appears, noble-minded race'. While their banishment was portrayed as necessary, their imminent doom was still taken largely for granted. (The unofficial survival of Indigenous people in the sealing islands of Bass Strait was ignored.) Also featured was a remark from former Secretary of State for the Colonies, Sir George Murray, that 'the adoption of any line of conduct, having for its avowed or secret object that extinction of the native race, could not fail to leave an indelible stain upon the British

---

11  *British Parliamentary Papers (BPP): Report from the Select Committee on Aborigines (British Settlements) with minutes of evidence, appendix and index*, Anthropology: Aborigines, vol 2, 1837: 6–10, 25–29.
12  *BPP: Report from the Select Committee on Aborigines (British Settlements)*, Anthropology: Aborigines vol 1, 1836: 498. Also, *BPP: Report from the Select Committee on Aborigines (British Settlements)*, vol 2: 10–11.
13  Archdeacon Broughton, evidence, 3 August 1835, *BPP: Report from the Select Committee on Aborigines (British Settlements)*, vol 1: 17.
14  Archdeacon Broughton, evidence, 3 August 1835, *BPP: Report from the Select Committee on Aborigines (British Settlements)*, vol 1: 17.

Government.'[15] Thus, the colonial government was both blamed and excused, the possibility of Indigenous survival was neglected, and Van Diemen's Land was held up as a warning to other colonies. No doubt the authors hoped this would prompt more humane policies on the mainland, but the use of Tasmanian examples may have also fed inadvertently into a darker discourse. As Lyndall Ryan has argued, portrayals of Tasmania as an aberrant, exceptionally brutal district have served historically to obscure the oppression which occurred in other colonies, less notoriously but on a wider scale.[16]

By this stage in New South Wales, reports from Wellington Valley combined predictions of Indigenous tragedy with mixed assertions that missionaries were both crucial to Indigenous survival and unequal to the task. From the start, the Church Missionary Society had framed their official commentary on Wellington Valley with gloomy warnings, highlighting a quotation from missionary JCS Handt that the people around Sydney were 'fast wasting away, wherever the Whites get a footing'.[17] By 1835, CMS lay secretary Dandeson Coates was admitting to Lord Glenelg, Secretary of State for the Colonies, that initial failures and frustrations were evident at Wellington Valley, but maintained that mission work was always problematic at first and would improve.[18] However, by the late 1830s, with few signs of Christian triumph and a severe drought damaging the station, support from the CMS declined. This was not helped by the loathing between missionaries William Watson and James Günther. As William Cowper, secretary of the CMS's Sydney corresponding committee, complained 'one needs a better temper and the other needs more energy'. The abrasive Watson was urged in vain to 'cultivate a meek and quiet spirit, which in the sight of God, is of great price.'[19] He was eventually dismissed in 1840 and left, furiously, to start a private mission at Apsley nearby. The missionaries were also feuding with neighbouring magistrate Henry Fysche Gisbourne, who told the New South Wales Executive Council that they were inefficient and deceptive.[20]

Throughout these struggles, the missionaries continued to warn of Indigenous destruction. Handt claimed in 1835 that more Wiradjuri people were dying than were being born, a statement repeated by Günther in 1838. When Watson and Günther complained to the colonial secretary, E Deas Thomson, about the

---

15  *BPP: Report from the Select Committee on Aborigines (British Settlements)*, vol 2: 13–14, 121–122.
16  Ryan 1981: 5, 259–260.
17  CMS, *Church Missionary Paper: for the use of weekly and monthly contributions*, no LXXV, Michaelmas-Day 1834; CMS, *Missionary Register*, January 1831: 118–19; CMS, *Missionary Register*, April 1832: 238.
18  Dandeson Coates to Lord Glenelg, 17 December 1835, *BPP: Papers Relating to Australia, 1844*, vol 8, 1969: 59–60.
19  William Cowper to Dandeson Coates, 26 December 1838, Church Missionary Society, Records [hereafter *CMS*], reel 40, AJCP M212, SLV; CMS Corresponding Committee, New Holland, 28 November 1838, *CMS*, reel 40, AJCP M212, SLV.
20  Henry Fysche Gisbourne to the Executive Council, 17 April 1839, *BPP: Papers Relating to Australia, 1844*, vol 8: 40–42; Rev Richard Taylor to Rev William Cowper enclosed in William Cowper to William McPherson, 26 April 1839, *BPP: Papers Relating to Australia, 1844*, vol 8: 45.

need for their station to be better supported and isolated from Europeans, they warned that the Wiradjuri might be destroyed by the bad colonial influences which had already wrecked other communities.[21] Again, the centrality of mission work to any viable Indigenous future was stressed; as the CMS's *Missionary Register* stated in 1839, 'nothing but Missionary Effort can save these wretchedly-corrupted Natives from becoming extinct.'[22] However, at the same time as mission life was portrayed as the only hope for Indigenous people, the flimsiness of such hopes was becoming clear. In 1839, the CMS Corresponding Committee admitted they had few hopes for the mission's success; a key reason for continuing their support (for the moment) was that they feared the government would not support any future missionaries if this project collapsed.[23] State support was certainly declining; in 1840, Governor Gipps commented to Lord John Russell, Secretary of State for the Colonies, that the mission seemed ineffective and possibly hopeless.[24] The government refused to increase their support, and the CMS decided in 1842 to close the station.

Meanwhile, the German stations at Moreton Bay were reporting even less success. Christopher Eipper and JCS Handt (at his new posting) asserted in 1841 that Indigenous numbers were decreasing, due largely to introduced diseases and the low birth rate, and that the people showed little interest in Christianity.[25] The following year, their colleague Karl WE Schmidt complained that the government was withdrawing its support,

> since everybody, believers and unbelievers alike, despairs of the conversion of the Australian aborigines and regards our work amongst the children of the bush (which are viewed not as people but as a race between people and monkeys, orangoutangs) as hopeless.[26]

This situation worsened when Governor Gipps demanded that they shift location in 1842, some 80 miles inland, in response to the expansion of the nearby Moreton Bay settlement. Government funding was removed in 1844. The missionaries continued working with funds raised in Berlin, their new station at Zion Hill closed down in 1849.

---

21  JCS Handt, 1835 Report, in Carey and Roberts (eds) 2002, *The Wellington Valley Project: Letters and Journals Relating to the Church Missionary Society Mission to Wellington Valley, NSW, 1830–42, A Critical Electronic Edition* [hereafter *WVP*]: <http://www.newcastle.edu.au>; James Günther, journal, 8 February 1838, *WVP*; William Watson and James Günther to Colonial Secretary E Deas Thomson, 12 March 1838, *CMS*, reel 40, AJCP M212, SLV.
22  CMS, *Missionary Register*, August 1839: 387.
23  CMS Corresponding Committee, New Holland, 23 August 1839, *CMS*, reel 40, AJCP M212, SLV.
24  Sir George Gipps to Lord John Russell, 7 May 1840, *BPP: Papers Relating to Australia, 1844*, vol 8: 33.
25  Evans 1992: 22–24.
26  Karl WE Schmidt, *Report on an Expedition to the Bunya Mountains in search of a suitable site for a mission station*, Accession 3522, Box 7072, State Library of Queensland (SLQ): 15.

Southern projects attracted little more optimism. In 1839, Joseph Orton had warned the Wesleyan Methodist Missionary Society that Indigenous people were dying because of dispossession and corrupt European influences and would eventually become 'extinct', 'leaving only an eternal memento of a blot upon the justice – equality & benevolence of our Christian Government.'[27] Such advocacy led to the funding of Buntingdale mission, but discussions of missionary work continued to overlap with pessimistic predictions. In 1840, his work barely commenced, Buntingdale missionary Francis Tuckfield warned the WMMS that he feared dispossession, poverty and frontier violence would lead to 'the final and utter extinction, of at least, some of the Aboriginal tribes'.[28] Three years later, he warned that the Colac people (apparently Gulidjan and Dhaugurdwurrung) were being victimised by neighbouring groups and might be dead soon. His colleague, Benjamin Hurst, agreed, stating that the local population had decreased by 15 per cent between 1840–41, citing venereal disease and the low birth rate. In 1842 Hurst reiterated his complaints about disease, violence and government inefficiency, asserting flatly that 'most of the natives are dead and others are dying'.[29] Missionary society reports and publications expressed occasional hopes for Buntingdale during the mid-1840s, when some Indigenous people took up labouring jobs and sedentary housing, and when neighbouring settlers became more supportive. However, by the end of the decade, these publications were declaring the mission a failure. In contrast to their local employees, the missionary societies placed greater blame on Indigenous people, citing their alleged apathy, violence and nomadic life.[30]

The Port Phillip protectors also voiced fears of Indigenous doom and their own weakness. By 1840, protector ES Parker was already predicting that dispossession and frontier violence would expose Indigenous people to 'rapid and certain destruction'. During 1841–42, he reported a death rate in Mt Macedon, the Western District, Campaspe and the Pyrenees that significantly outstripped births, adding that he believed the country west of the Pyrenees to South Australia had seen worse losses, at a rate of perhaps 20 per cent over the previous

---

27 Joseph Orton to General Secretaries, 13 May 1839, Wesleyan Methodist Missionary Society, Archive: Australasia 1812–1889 [hereafter *WMMS*], reel 1, Mp2107 (Record ID: 133095), NLA.
28 Francis Tuckfield to General Secretaries, 30 September 1840, *WMMS*, reel 2, Mp2107, NLA.
29 Benjamin Hurst to CJ La Trobe, 22 December 1841, Public Records Office of Victoria (PROV) VA512 *Chief Protector of Aborigines*, VPRS10 unit 3, 1841/2027 (reel 1); Benjamin Hurst to General Secretaries, 21 January 1842, *WMMS*, reel 2, NLA; Benjamin Hurst to J McKenny, 8 March 1842, *WMMS*, reel 2, Mp2107, NLA; Benjamin Hurst to General Secretaries, 23 June 1842, *WMMS*, reel 2; Francis Tuckfield, Report on the Wesleyan Missionary Society's Mission to the Aborigines of the Sub District of Geelong, Port Phillip, August 1843, *WMMS*, reel 2, Mp2107, NLA.
30 CMS, *Missionary Register*, May 1843: 238; CMS, *Missionary Register*, April 1844: 227; CMS, *Missionary Register*, May 1845: 210; CMS, *Missionary Register*, May 1849: 218–19; Minutes of the Annual Meeting of the Australian District, 31 July 1845 and 30 July 1846, Methodist Missionary Society, Records [hereafter *MMS*], reel 5, AJCP M122, SLV; WMMS, *Papers Relative to the Wesleyan Missions, and to the State of Heathen Countries*, no CXI, March 1848; WMMS 1848, *Report of the Wesleyan Methodist Missionary Society for year ending April 1848*: 34–39.

two years.[31] Chief protector GA Robinson, reporting to the Select Committee on the Condition of the Aborigines in 1845, estimated that the Indigenous numbers in occupied districts had decreased over the past six years by about a fifth.[32] Meanwhile, between 1839–48, protector William Thomas produced alarming census reports from the Yarra and his Narre Narre Warren station, reporting significantly higher deaths than births. In 1848, he remarked morosely that if he survived his allotted three score years and ten, 'this Protector may outlive the whole of his charge.'[33]

BURIAL OF ONE OF THE NATIVES OF AUSTRALIA.

**Fig 4. By the 1840s, philanthropists' reports were becoming pessimistic. As this choice of illustration in a missionary journal shows, Indigenous Australians were increasingly portrayed as hopeless and doomed.**

'Burial of one of the natives of Australia', Wesleyan Missionary Society, *Papers Relative to the Wesleyan Missions, and to the State of Heathen Countries*, no CXI, March 1848, London. National Library of Australia, Petherick NK5726.

---

31   Edward Stone Parker to GA Robinson, 1 April 1840, in Cannon (ed) 1983, *Historical Records of Victoria (HRV): Aborigines and Protectors, 1838–1839*, vol 2B: 695–696; Edward Stone Parker to GA Robinson, Returns of Deaths and Births, 1 January – 30 June 1841, 1 March – 31 August 1841, PROV VPRS4410 unit 2 (reel 2); ES Parker, Quarterly Journals, 1 March – 31 May 1841, 1 June – 31 August 1842, PROV VPRS4410 unit 2 (reel 2).
32   GA Robinson, Evidence to the Select Committee on the Condition of the Aborigines, 1845, in Frauenfelder (ed) 1997: 51.
33   William Thomas to GA Robinson, 31 August 1848, PROV VPRS4410 unit 4, 1848/109 (reel 2). Also, William Thomas to GA Robinson, 20 November 1839, William Thomas, Papers, 1834–1868 [hereafter *WTP*], ML MSS 214, reel 7, State Library of NSW; William Thomas to GA Robinson, 6 January 1840, *WTP*, ML MSS 214, reel 4; William Thomas to GA Robinson, 29 February 1840, PROV VPRS4410 unit 3, 1840/66 (reel 2); William Thomas to GA Robinson, Journal of the Proceedings during the months of June, July & August 1841, PROV VPRS4410, unit 3, 1841/70 (reel 2); William Thomas to GA Robinson, 24 May 1842, PROV VPRS4410 unit 3, 1842/71 (reel 2); William Thomas to GA Robinson, Journal of Proceedings, 1 December 1842 – 1 March 1843, PROV VPRS4410 unit 2, 1843/87 (reel 2); William Thomas to GA Robinson, 1 June 1846, PROV VPRS4410 unit 4, 1846/87 (reel 2); William Thomas to GA Robinson, 31 May 1848, PROV VPRS4410 unit 4, 1848/106 (reel 2); William Thomas to GA Robinson, 1 December 1847, PROV VPRS4410 unit 4, 1847/102 (reel 2).

Such comments were not welcomed by settlers or local officials, whose evaluations of the protectorate were damning. As early as 1840, Colonial Secretary Thomson wrote brusquely that the protectors were demanding and inefficient; 'From the beginning he [the governor] observed in them all, a disposition to complain a great deal and in their chief to write a great deal.'[34] During 1841, superintendent CJ La Trobe complained that the protectors were inefficient and their duties problematic; Governor Gipps was also disparaging about their personal failings.[35] Certainly, the combination of scandals and administrative problems that marked the protectorate could not have enhanced its standing – protector CW Sievwright's furious disputes with neighbouring settlers over accusations of frontier violence, and his eventual dismissal on grounds of sexual immorality, comprised the most notorious example. However, the protectorate's slow collapse was not anomalous within wider Indigenous governance. Funding was reduced in 1843, the 1845 Select Committee reached negative conclusions, and in 1847 Governor Fitzroy commented to Earl Grey that the system had achieved almost nothing.[36] It was abandoned in 1849, and as Jane Lydon has observed 'The failure of the protectorate came to be seen in terms of the innate wretchedness of Aboriginal people, justifying colonialism and underwriting humanitarian management of the survivors.'[37]

Any assessment of the 1840s as a period of philanthropic decline should be tempered by acknowledgement of the greater official support for comparable projects in Western Australia and South Australia. As noted, missionary society publications voiced optimism about John Smithies' Swan River Methodist mission, and Western Australia was singled out as a hopeful site for Indigenous policy by Lord Stanley in 1843, and South Australia by Earl Grey to 1848.[38] However, such hopes were tied, to some extent, to these institutions' greater willingness to make Indigenous pupils useful to colonists as servants. Furthermore, they still did not last. In 1849, Western Australian protector Charles Symmons was retitled pointedly Guardian of Natives and Protector of Settlers. This protectorate, which had long been more of a policing operation than a philanthropic one, was phased out as Symmons assumed other government roles. George King's Fremantle school closed in 1851, with the children transferred to Smithies' institution, but this did not endure either. It declined in the early 1850s, due to disease and Indigenous resentment at being

---

34   E Deas Thomson to CJ La Trobe, 24 April 1840, enclosed in James Dredge to Jabez Bunting, 31 July 1840, *WMMS*, reel 1, Mp2107, NLA.
35   Christie 1979: 102–104.
36   Sir Charles Fitz Roy to Earl Grey, 17 May 1847, *Historical Records of Australia (HRA)*, 1925, series 1, vol xxv, April 1846 – September 1847: 558.
37   Lydon 2005: 215.
38   Lord Stanley to Gov Grey, 10 July 1843, *BPP: Papers Relating to Australia, 1844*, vol 8: 341; Report of the Wesleyan Methodist Missionary Society for year ending April 1848: 34–39 (in *Reports of the Wesleyan-Methodist Missionary Society*, 1840–51).

pressed to move to a new station in the York district, and it closed in 1855.[39] Meanwhile, South Australian missions were also in decline. The *Colonial Church Chronicle, and Missionary Journal* (1849–50) blamed Indigenous people for this, for refusing to merge their communities into one area, adding that the failure of such projects gave ammunition to opponents of philanthropy.[40] The transfer of young people to the new Poonindie station from 1850, however, signalled a future cycle of South Australian mission life.

There was undoubtedly a connection between the decline in philanthropic efforts and the alarming drop in the Indigenous population. Dispossessed people could not have benefited from losing the (limited) land and resources philanthropists had secured for them, and, in turn, it became hard to justify mission funding when the target population was vanishing. However, the correlation between evangelising and Indigenous survival was also a conceptual one, created partly by philanthropists themselves. Observing how single-minded religious conviction both drove and hindered the career of New Zealand missionary Thomas Kendall, Judith Binney has observed of missionaries 'A profound sense of their infallibility was to guide their actions. As instruments of Divine Will they could not fail.'[41] The frequent assertion that missionary work alone could save Indigenous people, combined with the apprehension that had surrounded these projects from the start, meant that their ultimate closure brought into question the value of philanthropy and the future of Aboriginal policy. The implication that white advocates' failures proved the hopelessness of Indigenous people themselves has, I would suggest, left a long and troubling legacy.

## 'While we hesitate they die': the threat and allure of destruction

Henry Reynolds and Elizabeth Elbourne have argued that many philanthropists saw Indigenous suffering as a national sin, for which Britain and the colonies would be held accountable.[42] When faced with their own collapse, some local missionaries and protectors endorsed this view strongly. They tended to portray governments as inert and neglectful rather than deliberately malicious, while blaming colonists as much for their callousness, greed and sinful habits as for their outright acts of violence. Here, the angriest accusations were voiced by James Dredge. Upon resigning from the Port Phillip protectorate in 1840, he reflected furiously on Indigenous suffering, writing to Methodist leader Jabez Bunting 'while we hesitate they die. Their condition is indescribably awful and perilous. As colonization extends their misery is enhanced, and their existence

---

39   Hasluck 1970: 79–80; McNair and Rumley 1981: 60, 134–143.
40   CMS, *The Colonial Church Chronicle, and Missionary Journal*, vol III, July 1849 – July 1850: 278.
41   Binney 1968: 13.
42   Elbourne 2003; Reynolds 1998: 41–45.

endangered.' He warned of the possibility of 'exterminating conflict', like that which had 'well nigh blotted out' Indigenous Tasmanians. Reflecting on his failure in 1841, Dredge repeated that only 'a few years will be required to blot them from the living.'[43] In such accounts, official negligence was not excused or portrayed as benign misunderstanding, but rather implicated deeply in the destruction of a people. Similar concerns were voiced by missionary advocates in Britain. The Colonial Church Society, for example, worried about the sinful behaviour of colonists, given their imperial responsibilities; 'God has given us all this dominion, all this wealth, all this population'.[44] Similarly, the *Church Missionary Intelligencer* (1850) warned its readers of the fall of past empires because of their selfish glory or religious decline, thus demonstrating 'that God ever bestows great empires for the *truest and highest* good of the governed; and that whenever that good is not stedfastly [sic] pursued, such a kingdom carries with it the sure seed and element of decay.'[45]

However, it was the oppression and destruction of Indigenous people *in a state of heathenism* that distressed philanthropists; colonial suffering and the absence of Christianity could not easily be disentangled. The London Missionary Society, for instance, warned its supporters during the 1830s that millions of Indians ('British subjects') had not yet received the Gospel; '*God will not hold us guiltless of their blood*'.[46] Similarly, the Colonial Church Society remarked in 1839 on the need to promote missions – 'Only as our Government and nation thus maintain the true faith of Christ throughout the land, they approve themselves in the sight of the Supreme Governor of the world, and obtain his favour.'[47] Such comments were both authoritative and anxious. As indicated in the previous chapter, Evangelical advocates constructed themselves as observers and moral judges of empire and native peoples, whilst also seeing this role as critical to their own (and their country's) salvation.

A mingling of ideas about death, heathenism and colonial guilt was apparent in some accounts from Wellington Valley. Watson, for example, remembered sharing tea and a conversation about God with a group of people in 1832, and realising how puny his efforts were, given the scale of the challenge. He observed:

---

43  James Dredge to Jabez Bunting, 31 July 1840, *WMMS*, reel 2; James Dredge to Jabez Bunting, 10 May 1841, *WMMS*, reel 2, Mp2107, NLA.
44  CCS, *Report of the Australian Church Missionary Society, now formed into the Colonial Church Society*, 1839: 20.
45  CMS, *The Church Missionary Intelligencer, A Monthly Journal of Missionary Information*, vol 1, no 3, July 1849: 51–52.
46  *Evangelical Magazine and Missionary Chronicle*, vol XII, London, Westley and Davis, August 1834: 317. Also, London Missionary Society (LMS), *Missionary Magazine and Chronicle*, vol 1, London, LMS Directors, June 1836 – December 1837: 280.
47  CCS, *Report of the Australian Church Missionary Society, now formed into the Colonial Church Society*, 1839: 17–18.

> One of them, a very old man with no hair on his head, ripe for death, on the verge of eternity, altogether ignorant of every moral and religious truth … For one of the human race to be in this condition is lamentable beyond description, but it is not the case with one alone, it is the state of families, tribes, yea doubtless of all the Black Natives of this colony.[48]

Again, in 1837, his colleague Günther recalled visiting a woman called Sally, who was seriously ill. He concluded 'It is a melancholy sight, to see these poor creatures dying apparently without God, without hope, ignorant of the Saviour of Sinners.'[49] Such remarks drew attention to philanthropists' deep unease at the outcomes of colonialism, but also their reliance on imperial expansion to further their aims. The relationship between enlightenment and governance was made more explicit by James Dredge, who lobbied Jabez Bunting on the need for Indigenous projects to be better supported and placed under missionary control. He drew attention to both the physical and spiritual damage caused by mishandled colonialism.

> I know not how to repress the struggling fire in my bones – while a witness of the awful tragedy in course of performance around me and which, while the natives are the immediate sufferers cannot fail, sooner or later, to entail the righteous retribution of insulted heaven upon the European innovators and oppressors.[50]

While such views had a certain political resonance during the 1830s, they did not remain popular for long, especially in the Australian colonies. Rather, philanthropists found themselves in an environment where Indigenous deprivation and death were increasingly portrayed in terms of 'progress' – natural, inevitable and ultimately positive. Russell McGregor, who has dubbed this the 'doomed race theory', traces its development throughout the late 19th and early 20th centuries, but its origins were older still.[51] The influential 18th century idea that all living creatures were arranged in a hierarchical sequence called the Great Chain of Being lent itself easily to the ranking of human societies from superior to inferior, with the lowest races placed one link above apes (a belief that endured into 19th century evolutionary science). This sat fairly comfortably beside Enlightenment theories describing human societies developing through progressive stages, with savages portrayed as retarded or childlike. Peter Bowler argues that ideas of human development as hierarchical and purposeful became significant in the 19th century because they helped to rationalise imperial expansion and to console Europeans, themselves unsettled

---

48  William Watson, journal, 27 November 1832, *WVP*.
49  Günther, journal, 17 September 1837, *WVP*.
50  James Dredge to Jabez Bunting, 10 May 1841, *MMS*, reel 55, AJCP M172, SLV.
51  McGregor 1997.

by rapid industrialisation and social change.⁵² Moreover, the naturalising of extermination can be associated with a form of settler-colonialism which sought to supplant Indigenous people with an overwhelmingly large white population, relying on the absence of Indigenous people from the physical, political and cultural landscape.

Such beliefs had entered public debate in the colonies by the time the first philanthropists arrived. One correspondent to the *Sydney Herald* wrote in 1836 'it is in the order of nature that, as civilization advances, savage nations *must* be exterminated'.⁵³ The *Australian* published a similar claim in 1838:

> The approaches of the Europeans among the savages ... has ever been the signal for their rapid and final disappearance. In North America, in South America, in Africa and in Australia, the black has always retreated before the footsteps of the white man.⁵⁴

Again, in 1846, the *Geelong Advertiser* declared:

> the perpetuation of the race of Aborigines is not *to be desired* ... they are an inferior race of human beings ... the probable extinction of the race from natural causes is proof of this ... it is no more desirable that any inferior race should be perpetuated, than that the transmission of a hereditary disease, such as scrofula or insanity, should be encouraged.⁵⁵

In her analysis of the northern frontier in the late 19th century, Deborah Bird Rose asserts that Indigenous depopulation (which she sees as occurring largely through neglect and unofficial cruelty) was rationalised by a colonial belief in 'the agency of history', leading to a form of dispossession that was haphazard and complacently vicious; 'If the tide of history doomed Aboriginal people, complicit whitefellows hastened that history along.'⁵⁶ This understanding of history as an impersonal force of progress via destruction had its origins in earlier decades, and it is important to consider philanthropists' role in challenging, negotiating or reinforcing it.

Philanthropists usually opposed attempts to naturalise Indigenous death. They insisted that it was a barbaric affront to Christianity to suggest that a race of human beings were destined for annihilation. Quaker missionary travel writer James Backhouse commented in his 1834 work on Australia that he was disturbed by the common view that indigenous destruction in Australia and

---

52  Bowler, 1984: 90–92; Bowler 1989: 1–13. See also, Lovejoy 1960[1936]: 184, 190, 197, 235; McGregor 1997: ix, 1–9; Meek 1976: 2, 12–13, 16–17, 22.
53  *Sydney Herald*, 26 December 1836.
54  *Australian*, 27 December 1838.
55  *Geelong Advertiser*, 2 May 1846.
56  Rose 2001: 153.

North America was unavoidable.[57] Port Phillip chief protector GA Robinson was similarly perturbed. In 1846 he gave an indignant account of remarks by colonists, which hinted at simultaneous guilt and displacement of responsibility: 'Well Mr Robinson I admit their situation is a hard one and I should be sorry to see them injured but then sir really I do think under all circumstances the sooner they are got rid of the better.'[58] He repeated in his 1848 report that many colonists saw Indigenous people as doomed. Robinson commented 'such unhappily has been the case but such is not a natural consequence ... if the White man could but do to the coloured as he would be done unto all would be well.'[59] Similarly, former protector ES Parker claimed in 1854 that Aboriginal extinction, while possible, was not 'the inscrutable decree – of Divine Providence'; such theories, he said, were impious.[60] The Aborigines Protection Society made a lengthier protest against Social Darwinist ideas in the late 1840s:

> Such a theory is a libel upon the mercy, the beneficence, and the wisdom of God. It is a crying impiety to urge it; it is a slander upon Christianity to perpetuate it; it is the foulest iniquity to advocate it.[61]

Nonetheless, philanthropists did not only oppose the 'doomed race theory'; their relationships to this belief were more complex. For one thing, it was rare for them to confront head-on the question of whether Indigenous destruction might be linked inherently to settler colonialism itself – what Ann Curthoys has called 'the murderous desires that underlie colonisation, the taking of someone else's land'.[62] For proponents of humane colonialism, this dilemma could not be acknowledged easily. As Elbourne has observed, the focus on sin and virtue by the Select Committee, for instance, could serve to obscure the wider structural issues of dispossession.[63] When philanthropists did address these broader questions of guilt, they did so equivocally. The Aborigines Protection Society's 1840 report, for instance, contained an angry article about the destruction caused by Australian dispossession and the weakness of official protection; 'Justice is hard to administer, where famine is decreed to one party, and the fruits of spoliation to the other'.[64] This did not detract much, though, from the APS's generally pro-imperial view. Indeed, their *Papers and Proceedings* for the following year briefly described most of the Indigenous Tasmanians as

---

57  James Backhouse 1843, *A Narrative of a Visit to the Australian Colonies*: 532.
58  GA Robinson 2001, '1846 Annual Report', in *The Papers of George Augustus Robinson, Chief Protector, Port Phillip Aboriginal Protectorate*, Clark (ed) vol 4: 116.
59  Robinson 2001, '1848 Annual Report', in *The Papers of George Augustus Robinson,* Clark (ed) vol 4: 152.
60  ES Parker 1967, 'The Aborigines of Australia', 10 May 1854, in *Frontier Life in the Loddon Protectorate: Episodes from Early Days, 1837–1842*: 30.
61  Aborigines Protection Society (APS), Annual Report, 3 May 1848: 42–44, in *APS Transactions, c1839–1909*, MIC/o6550, reel 3 (Records the property of Anti-Slavery International). Also, APS, *The Colonial Intelligencer, or Aborigines' Friend*, vol II, 1849–50, APS, Transactions, reel 3: 67–69.
62  Curthoys, Veracini and Docker 2002: 5.
63  Elbourne 2003.
64  APS, 3rd Annual Report, 23 June 1840, APS, Transactions, reel 1: 31–33.

'swept from the earth', but did so amidst broad praise for the benefits of empire. Colonial violence, in this context, came across as horrifying but anomalous.[65] Similarly, chief protector GA Robinson touched on a more radical understanding of imperialism when he mused in his journal in 1847:

> We carry what we call our civilisation into savage lands, but we carry our vices and our diseases along with it and I am not sure that savages are not better without us … They are free, they are strong, they are healthy … the utmost we do for them is to instil wants into them which when they cannot supply, they become miserable.[66]

Such uncomfortable thoughts, however, did not discourage Robinson from pursuing a profitable career in colonial government.

Moreover, philanthropists' warnings about Indigenous destruction and missionary hardship could be appropriated by some hostile commentators to argue that Aboriginal philanthropy was useless. In an 1840 report to James Stephen (permanent under-secretary of the Colonial Office), the Colonial Land and Emigration Office commented that there was no point in increasing funding to Wellington Valley, as the missionaries had not shown enough success to warrant greater resources or control over land. (Wiradjuri rights to land were ignored.) Here, the findings of the 1835 Select Committee, which had used evidence from Wellington Valley to support Evangelical claims, were cited to prove that Australian missions were futile. The office drew attention to philanthropic disappointments mentioned by the Committee – notably, the depopulation occurring on the supposedly humane Flinders Island, and the failures of protectorates amongst the allegedly more advanced First Nations people in Canada – in order to prove that Wellington Valley would probably fail. If Evangelical warnings of Indigenous disaster and death were meant to inspire missionary work, some less sympathetic observers could merge these claims with disturbing ease into a discourse of Aboriginal doom.[67]

Philanthropists may not have been responsible for how their writings were reinterpreted, but even their own publications conveyed some mixed messages. In 1848, *Papers Relative to the Wesleyan Missions* published an article calling for further missionary work. While asserting that all people were blessed in Christ, the author wrote:

> no race of men have been considered more hopelessly ignorant of religion than the aboriginal inhabitants of New South Wales. The difficulties in

---

65  APS, *Extracts from the Papers and Proceedings of the Aborigines' Protection Society*, vol II, no III: 89–91.
66  GA Robinson 2000, *Journals: Port Phillip Aboriginal Protectorate*, Clark (ed) vol 5: 169.
67  T Frederick Elliot, Robert Torrens and Edward C Villiers to James Stephen, 17 July 1840, in Church Missionary Society, Papers 1840, MS4153, NLA: 3–13, 17–22, 35–36, 40–45.

the way of instructing them have appeared almost insuperable; and the Church of God is called to special prayer, and special exertion, in their behalf.[68]

These apprehensive remarks were accompanied, somewhat ominously, by illustrated descriptions of Aboriginal funeral rites. A similar mixture of hope and gloom was voiced by the CMS's *Missionary Register* in 1850, which noted the loss of residents at Buntingdale but also the possibility of Christian marriages at John Smithies' Swan River mission. A quotation from the WMMS committee was included, stating that Indigenous Australians were the most ignorant and hopeless of all the colonised peoples of the world – 'Yet even these are not without the pale of Divine Compassion, nor beyond the reach and influence of patient evangelical labour.'[69] Such messages were no doubt meant to remind the reader of God's extraordinary power and the heroic labours of missionaries. However, the stress on Aboriginal degradation, in a context of reduced support for Australian projects, meant that such accounts might also be read as preludes to surrender.

In this context, even philanthropists' claims that God alone could save the heathen (conventional enough, on one level) may have started to take on a double meaning. They helped to renew confidence in a painful, frustrating situation, but they may have also contributed to a certain refusal of responsibility. Thus, at Wellington Valley in 1834, the none-too-optimistic JCS Handt assured himself 'God is well able to enliven and to raise these dry bones, though there may at present be no appearance of it. He works in a mysterious way, and performs his wonders so, as to secure the glory to himself.'[70] His colleague James Günther, describing Wiradjuri people as sinful and apathetic, wrote 'the more I see of the Aborigines of this country the more I feel convinced of the need of the Almighty's powerful display of his saving mercy as the only means to effect what human efforts must despair of.'[71] Such notions were reiterated by protector Thomas in 1843. Depressed at Kulin peoples' insistence on visiting Melbourne, which he considered a sinful locale, he remarked that this dampened his zeal; 'I am led to conclude under present circumstances that physical means will ever prove abortive, and that nothing short of supernatural agency of the Holy Spirit will change their condition'.[72] Such comments reaffirmed missionary faith, whilst also coming close to acknowledging (and perhaps exaggerating) their helplessness. This was certainly implied in 1844, when William Cowper, of

---

68  WMMS, *Papers Relative to the Wesleyan Missions, and to the State of Heathen Countries*, no CXI, March 1848.
69  CMS, *Missionary Register*, May 1850: 218.
70  Handt, journal, 8 March 1834, *WVP*.
71  Günther, journal, 31 December 1837, *WVP*.
72  William Thomas to GA Robinson, Journal of Proceedings, 1 December 1842 to 1 March 1843, PROV VPRS4410 unit 3 (reel 2).

the CMS corresponding committee, wrote to society secretary Dandeson Coates, reflecting morosely on the failure of every mission and protectorate in eastern Australia. He concluded 'Yet I would indulge the hope, that hereafter some of the Aborigines of this part of the earth, will be made partakers "of the Salvation, which is in Christ Jesus with eternal glory".'[73] Here, the Indigenous future was reduced from a prospect to be worked towards, to a faint hope to be indulged.

Indigenous people's own views on the depopulation and destruction of their people were scarcely mentioned. While British publications ignored Indigenous opinions on a range of subjects, this particular omission from local records is a startling one, given that missionaries and protectors did highlight Aboriginal statements on other topics. Only a handful of remarks from Port Phillip stand out. In 1843, protector Thomas talked to Woiwurrung leader Billibellary about his fear that infanticide was occurring, and urged him to take action to prevent it. Billibellary's response was grim: 'Black Lubras say now no good children, Black fellow say no country now for them ... no more come up Pickaniny.' The following year, Thomas told Robinson that the birth rate was low. He suspected that people did not see the point in raising children, telling him 'No good Pickaninnys now no country'.[74] Parker repeated this claim in 1846: 'The blacks say they have now no country and are therefore unwilling to keep their children'.[75] Such comments hint at a deep and chilling despair, but how pervasive it was can be hard to say now, given the paucity of the sources. Philanthropists' apparent lack of interest in Indigenous opinions indicates how Aboriginal people were rendered passive within a discourse of racial doom. It also suggests, perhaps, that without a strong enthusiasm for mission life, Indigenous people's views on their future were not considered to be of much value.

Certainly, some philanthropists' papers reflected a transition from outrage at Indigenous destruction to a final naturalising of it. Ironically, LE Threlkeld, the most vocal opponent of racial science and one of the most outspoken protesters against frontier violence, also became the most inclined to cite mysterious reasons for Indigenous demise. As Anna Johnston has commented, these two sides of his personality are enigmatic and hard to reconcile.[76] When Threlkeld reported to the LMS in 1826, he wrote of his distress not only at colonists' cruelty but also at their belief that Indigenous people were hopeless.[77] By 1837, however, he had changed his tune. He wrote in his annual report:

---

73 William Cowper to Dandeson Coates, 27 February 1844, *CMS*, reel 40, AJCP M212, SLV.
74 Thomas, journal, 7 October 1843, *WTP*, ML MSS 214, reel 3, State library of NSW; William Thomas to GA Robinson, 1 December 1843, PROV VPRS4410 unit 3, 1843/78 (reel 2); William Thomas to GA Robinson, 31 November 1844, PROV VPRS4410 unit 3, 1844/82 (reel 2).
75 ES Parker, 1846, *The Aborigines of Australia*: 14.
76 Johnston 2003: 183.
77 LE Threlkeld, Second Half Yearly Report of the Aboriginal Mission Supported by the London Missionary Society, 21 June 1826, *LMS*, AJCP M73, SLV.

> He who 'Increaseth the nation', or 'Destroys that there should be no inhabitant', has visited the land, and the Meazles, the hooping cough and the influenza have streched [sic] the Black victims in hundreds on the Earth ... Many suffered from the ire of human vengeance ... but the most died by the act of God.[78]

His final report, in 1841, concluded despondently 'The thousands of Aborigines ... decreased to hundreds; the hundreds have lessened to tens, and the tens will dwindle into units, before a very few years shall have passed away.' This, he attributed largely to 'the wrath of God'.[79] In his 1850 publication, *A Key to the Structure of the Aboriginal Language*, Threlkeld reminisced about Awabakal life in the old days. The romantic language and imagery he employed would, over the following century, become a key part of the doomed race discourse.

> [T]he once numerous actors, who used to cause the woods to echo with their din, now lie mingled with the dust, save some few solitary beings who here and there still stalk abroad, soon, like their ancestors, to become 'a tale that is told'.[80]

A similar, if less dramatic, transition was also apparent in James Günther's writing. In 1841 he described to William Cowper his regret at Wellington Valley's imminent closure; it was distressing to think that 'these poor Aborigines should be given up, not so much because they have proved unworthy of Christian charity, but because our mission has almost proved unworthy of its name & design'.[81] However, by 1846, having left the district in resentment and despair, Günther had hardened his views. He had been especially chagrined to discover a clandestine affair between mission agriculturalist William Porter and a woman called Noamilly, whom the Günthers had considered a promising pupil. The resentment some Wiradjuri people voiced at Günther's dismissal of Porter, and the refusal of most of them to accompany him to his new home in Mudgee, left him embittered. He told the Legislative Council's committee investigating Aboriginal conditions that 'very little or nothing can be done for these Aborigines, who seem to care less for any kind of improvement, and are more devoid of reflection, than any other known races.' Here, the assertion of God's mysterious power merged with a refusal of personal responsibility. 'Unless it should please God, to change their disposition, in some marvellous manner, or to raise some extraordinary man to labor, as missionary, among them ... their Case Seems to be hopeless.'[82]

---

78 LE Threlkeld, Annual Report 1837, in Gunson (ed) 1974 vol 1: 137.
79 LE Threlkeld, Annual Report 1841, in Gunson (ed) 1974 vol 1: 169.
80 LE Threlkeld, 1850, *A Key to the Structure of the Aboriginal Language*, in LE Threlkeld, 1892, *An Australian Language as Spoken by the Awabakal, the People of Awaba or Lake Macquarie*, Fraser (ed): 89.
81 James Günther to William Cowper, 12 June 1841, *CMS*, reel 40, AJCP M212, SLV.
82 James Günther, Reply to a Circular Letter Addressed to the Clergy of all Denominations, 1846, in Bridges 1978: 733; James Günther to Richard Taylor, 12 November 1842, *N.S.W. Archival Estrays: N.S.W. Royal*

Threlkeld's and Günther's views were not universal amongst their colleagues, but they do point to some broader concerns. Belief in the regenerative power of Christianity and the philanthropic role of state and church had, of course, driven Evangelical advocacy in the first place, but it also limited this process. Local disappointments, combined with philanthropists' basic support for imperialism and their tying of Indigenous survival to charitable gratitude, could occasionally steer them perilously close to a sense that Indigenous destruction might be unavoidable after all.

## Despair, resistance, continuity? Possibilities for understanding this period

It is unsurprising that historians have often described the first missionaries and protectors as failures, emphasising their inability to make converts, protect people from violence and deprivation, alter Indigenous customs, succeed in farming, or work effectively with one another. Emphasis has been placed, variously, on philanthropists' personal shortcomings (as in Vivienne Rae-Ellis's biography of GA Robinson), their helplessness against mass dispossession (as in works by Peter Corris and Michael Cannon), and their cultural conflicts with Indigenous people (as in Michael Christie's emphasis on Aboriginal Victorians' refusal to comply with protectorate agendas, and Peter Read's portrayal of Wellington Valley within a narrative of Wiradjuri resistance).[83] Of course, all of these interpretations can be borne out, to varying degrees. Nonetheless, I would emphasise that philanthropic declarations of failure and despair were by no means neutral or straightforward. Here, some additional challenges to the failure thesis have been posed. Hilary Carey, for example, has suggested that missionary understandings of failure may have had more to do with personal and spiritual disappointments than with the (expected) challenges of station life.[84] Moreover, as Richard Broome has pointed out, too much of a failure focus can detract from accounts of Indigenous continuity and endurance.[85]

While Indigenous views on the future were rarely sought, philanthropists' records do yield some sense of the (limited) directions left available to Aboriginal people. Despite the grief and depression hinted at by Thomas, some anecdotes challenge the dominant sense of Indigenous helplessness and philanthropic disappointment. For one thing, Indigenous people were unlikely to understand

---

*Commission into Crime in the Braidewood District [Journal 1836–1865 of Rev. James Günther]*, ML MSS 508, item 10, CY reel 872. (Accessed copy at AIATSIS library, ref MF294); James Günther to the Lord Bishop of Australia, 17 November 1843, *NSW Archival Estrays*, ML MSS 508, item 10, CY reel 872.
83   Arkley 2000; Cannon 1990; Christie 1979; Corris 1968; Rae-Ellis 1988; Read 1988.
84   Carey 2000: 45–61.
85   For a discussion of the protectorate that highlights Aboriginal agency and continuity rather than philanthropic failings, see Broome 2005: 35–53.

the situation strictly in terms of Evangelical 'failure', given that they never fully endorsed philanthropists' aims in the first place. In some cases, a sense of disloyalty may have been more relevant. For instance, when the Günthers left Wellington Valley, Noamilly shouted furiously after them that they had ruined the station by allowing all the land and cattle to be given away. She may have disliked Günther because of his sacking of William Porter, but her response also suggests Günther's betrayal of his obligations to Wiradjuri people and country.[86]

Other Indigenous people retained friendlier relationships with their former missionaries, and indeed may have experienced the post-mission period more in terms of continuity than rupture. Some Wiradjuri people opted to continue a mission life on Watson's station, where he carried on with religious instruction and baptisms. Günther also kept receiving some visits by younger Wiradjuri people; Cochrane, his wife Maria and their child even lived with the Günthers for a while.[87] Similarly, Francis Tuckfield of the Buntingdale mission remained in his district as a private grazier until 1850, retaining contact with Indigenous people.[88] Even the pessimistic Threlkeld continued with some Aboriginal preaching whilst running his Newcastle coal mine and working as a minister of the Bethel Union; the few surviving Awabakal people were living in their country nearby, working as fishermen, washerwomen, servants and sailors.[89] Such accounts can point, also, to the primacy of ties to country; a philanthropist's presence need not be the key factor determining people's residence in a district. In the 1840s, for instance, there were ongoing reports of Indigenous people living at Dredge's and Sievwright's abandoned protectorate stations.[90]

Furthermore, Indigenous responses to the decline of the Port Phillip protectorate demonstrated the need for political contacts, as well as personal ones. When James Dredge left the Goulburn River in 1840, Daungwurrung people seemed distressed, and later visited his house in Melbourne four times, complaining to Dredge about his successor, William Le Souef, and urging him to return to their country, promising to build him a house and work on his farm. While Dredge's

---

86   James Günther to Richard Taylor, 12 November 1842, *NSW Archival Estrays*; James Günther to the Lord Bishop of Australia, 17 November 1843, *NSW Archival Estrays*, ML MSS 508, item 10, CY reel 872.
87   Bridges 1978: 733; James Günther, 13 August 1842, *NSW Archival Estrays*; James Günther to the Lord Bishop of Australia, 17 November 1843, *NSW Archival Estrays*, ML MSS 508, item 10, CY reel 872.
88   Greenwood 1956: 16–19.
89   Niel Gunson, 'Introduction', in Gunson (ed) 1974 vol 1: 28–29; Henwood 1978: 42; LE Threlkeld, 'Memoranda', in Gunson (ed) 1974 vol 1: 166–167.
90   Cannon 1990: 130–131; James Horsburgh to GA Robinson, Return of the numbers of Aborigines daily present at the Goulbourn Aboriginal Station, April 1846 – December 1848, PROV VPRS12 unit 7, 1848/30 (reel 3); ES Parker to GA Robinson, Return of the number of Aborigines daily present, Goulbourn River, April – December 1845, PROV VPRS12 unit 6, 1845/25 (reel 3).

own political role had collapsed (he lamented 'Poor fellows, I can do nothing for them'), the political efforts of the people he had been sent to protect were growing.[91]

Circumstances at ES Parker's protectorate station were particularly interesting. Parker's final report in 1850 struck an intriguingly optimistic note, stating that he had never been more hopeful of Indigenous people's working and religious improvement: 'Success seems to have dawned, and I most earnestly pray ... nothing will occur to blight or destroy the work so begun on this establishment.'[92] While he may have been hoping for future financial support, Parker's relationships with Djadjawurung and Djabwurung people did outlast the protectorate's closure. He retained the land, and set himself up as a pastoralist with an Aboriginal school, which continued to operate at Franklinford till the Board closed it in 1864. He also boasted that several young men whom he had known for years were running successful farms and living as Christians; Parker's son claimed some of these people were still farming around Mt Franklin in the 1870s. Many of them died young, however, or were forced off their land by colonists; some moved eventually to the new Coranderrk station.[93]

Perhaps the most politically charged philanthropic link maintained by Indigenous people in Victoria was with William Thomas, in his new capacity as Guardian of the Aborigines. Their dealings with Thomas were not always happy; his papers in the early 1850s depict the small numbers of people left around Melbourne as impoverished, depressed and alcoholic, and he began to advocate forcible removal of their children. However, Thomas's role was by no means negligible to Aboriginal people. They discussed with him Earl Grey's plans to set aside reserves for them in 1849, and various Kulin and Gunnai delegations lobbied him for assistance to secure farming land in their country. Thomas was surprised and pleased by their new enthusiasm for agriculture, but the ultimate results made clear where colonial power really lay; the land he had helped them reserve was seized by neighbouring settlers.[94]

---

91  James Dredge, 11 June 1840, 10 October 1840, 18 March 1841, 27 November 1841, 4 December 1841, James Dredge, Diaries, Notebook and Letterbooks, ?1817–1845 [hereafter *JDD*], MS11625, MSM534, SLV; James Dredge to J Harding, 31 October 1840, *JDD*, MS11625, MSM534, SLV.
92  ES Parker to GA Robinson, 7 January 1850, PROV VPRS4410 unit 2, 1850/65 (reel 2).
93  Christie 1979: 149; Lewis 1987: 19; Morrison 2002a: 84; Rhodes 1995: 13; Morrison 2002b: 235–242; O'Connor 1991: 12; Parker, 'The Aborigines of Australia': 23; ES Parker to Colonial Secretary, 1 March 1853 in William Thomas 1854, *Aborigines: A Return to Address Mr Parker – 21 October 1853*: 29.
94  Attwood 2003: 7; Barwick 1998: 34; Christie 1979: 138; Peter Dean Gardner 1979, *W. Thomas and the Aborigines of Gippsland*, PMS3118, Australian Institute of Aboriginal and Torres Strait Islander Studies (AIATSIS): 7; William Thomas to CJ La Trobe, 9 September 1850, PROV VPRS2893 unit 1, 1850/57 (reel 3); William Thomas to CJ La Trobe, 2 December 1850, VPRS2893 unit 1 (reel 3); Thomas 1854, *Aborigines: A Return to Address*: 17, 29; William Thomas to the Commissioner of Lands and Survey, 4 March 1859, in Attwood and Markus 1999: 41–42; William Thomas to Sir Redmond Barry, 21 October 1861, in William Thomas Papers – Correspondence, 1861, PMS681, AIATSIS: 125–126.

To summarise philanthropic work as a simple failure can be problematic. It can imply too great a sense of collapse and ruin – the above accounts of Indigenous endurance challenge this somewhat – but it can also minimise the impact of these projects. This point is highlighted by Deborah Bird Rose in her study of the Daly River Jesuit mission. Rose points to the rich and violent complexity of these supposedly fruitless mission projects, and observes that it can be dangerous to accept a sense of missionary helplessness at face value.

> To sum this [missionary work] up as a failure to have an impact, or to assume that the impacts had only been superficial, is to set up the parameters of the frontier: presence described as absence. Denial of impact was also a denial of accountability and responsibility. The missionaries and everyone else could rest assured that their departure had no consequences because their presence had had no effects.[95]

It is not my intention to downplay the sense of loss and tragedy conveyed in philanthropic records. Indigenous suffering pervades these sources, and although it fed into various forms of Evangelical rhetoric, it also has a painful immediacy: philanthropists were witnesses to physical and social destruction, which they deplored but could not prevent and, in some ways, ended up reinforcing. Questions of responsibility here are both urgent and problematic. If philanthropists voiced the loudest protests over dispossession, they also demonstrated some of the complexities of this response. Their papers suggest how models of Evangelical Protestantism, imperialism and charity were both necessary and limiting to the expression of compassion, grief and guilt.

---

95   Rose 1998: 27.

# Conclusion

Christian philanthropic work amongst Indigenous Australians was a form of governance considered unlikely and limited from its earliest manifestations, a view that philanthropists themselves alternately challenged, utilised or reinforced. A final impression of missionary failure may have triumphed in these early decades, although, as demonstrated, we can still trace alternative Indigenous views, as well as interrogating exactly what failure meant to the missionaries themselves. Furthermore, the closure of the first missions and protectorates did not signal an end to Christian and government intervention in Indigenous issues; quite the contrary. Subsequent decades saw a growth in new missions and government stations, including Poonindie, Bethesda and Hermannsburg in South Australia; Ebenezer, Ramahyuck, Coranderrk and Framlingham in Victoria; Maloga and Warangesda in New South Wales; Fraser Island in Queensland; and Camfield in Western Australia. In the first 'civilising' projects, considered here, we can trace the origins of later (often more powerful) agendas, whilst also observing how they were shaped by varied circumstances of governance, advocacy, material power and control over land and cultural life. Mission and protectorate histories, when viewed from different angles, can appear in terms of particularity and disruption, or of tenacious continuity. Ongoing controversies over the history of church and state power in Indigenous people's lives – most notably in the forced removal of Aboriginal children – indicate the relevance of this area of research.

Scholarly interest in Australian philanthropic history appears to be strong and ongoing. Works in this field over the past decade have focused on topics as diverse as educational approaches in mission schools, visual and spatial regimes on missions, cultural exchanges between Christianity and older Indigenous beliefs, and the relationships of paternalism, authority and obligation that developed between philanthropists and Indigenous people.[1] The breadth of these studies is suggestive of how historians' approach to mission history has changed from fairly straightforward admiration or condemnation, to a greater interest in missions as sites of personal, cultural and imperial encounters. Helen Bethea Gardner, in her work on missions in Oceania, has commented 'Perhaps the recent explosion of anthropological research of Oceanic Christianity is a sign that Christianity is now so foreign to most in the West that it can be studied as an alien institution'.[2] Certainly, Australian missionaries' own beliefs and behaviours have become problematised and considered legitimate subjects of enquiry and critique, often by secular scholars. This does not indicate a lack of

---

1   For example, Barry 2006, pp.169–182; Broome 2006: 43.1–43.16; Carey and Roberts 2002: 821–869; Lydon 2005: 211–234; Magowan 2005: 157–175; Reed 2004: 87–99; Scrimgeour 2006: 35–46; Van Gent 2005: 227–248.
2   Gardner 2006: 13.

immediacy or relevance, however. A number of historians of early philanthropy – notably, Henry Reynolds, Elizabeth Elbourne and Anna Johnston[3] – have linked it strongly to contemporary debates over colonialism, humanitarianism and Reconciliation. The greater visibility of philanthropists as subjects of debate is also indicative of more nuanced understandings of whiteness, imperialism and governance.

I was drawn to this project by an initial interest in tracing early humanitarian movements in the Australian colonies, including the lineage of white support for Aboriginal rights. While this is undoubtedly an important task, it has also led me to a realisation of the need to interrogate this lineage closely. From the start, philanthropists were implicated crucially in governing Indigenous Australians and recreating them as subjects of empire. Their support for Indigenous people's rights derived from understandings of Aboriginal Australians as colonised groups with traditional identities and claims to land, but also as British subjects whose futures must be shaped by the adoption of agriculture, individualist work ethics and Evangelical Christianity. Concepts of Indigenous entitlements were shaped, therefore, by beliefs about religion, paternalism and the civilising obligations of empire, as well as relationships with Indigenous people themselves, whose own ideas about obligation and exchange could not be ignored. At a time when Aboriginal rights (and indeed broader notions of human rights) are both highly visible and contested in Australian public life, it is valuable to consider the historical development of such ideas in greater detail.

Also important were creative paradoxes inherent in attempts to remake Indigenous Australians as British subjects. Current debates over Aboriginal policy have tended to assume a polarity between individualism and communal dependence on the state, but a study of early missions highlights the fact that individualist labour, self-awareness and personal religious struggles were being encouraged within a context of institutional life, where Indigenous people were understood as colonised, subordinate *groups*. This was apparent across issues as intimate as housing and hygiene, to wider discussions of Indigenous people's legal and sovereign status. While philanthropists promoted British subjecthood as a path to assimilation and (some) equality, their ideas about governance also sought to inscribe Aboriginal difference. This was further complicated by local conditions and the need to negotiate and build relationships with Indigenous people. Governance, in its day-to-day forms, could be a shifting, improvised process. As Heather Goodall has observed, 'Seen across time, invasions come to look like simple, two-sided struggles. When underway, colonial invasions were more likely to appear confused, riven with antagonisms within the contending camps and frayed with doubts.'[4]

---

3   For example, Elbourne 2003; Johnston 2006 58–87; Johnston 2003: 102–113; Henry Reynolds 1998.
4   Goodall 1990: 260.

## Conclusion

A sense of missionary colonialism as both a significant, enduring heritage and an unstable, ambiguous process also emerges when we consider its legacy for the Australian nation-state. As observed, philanthropists were in some ways passionate advocates of greater governance, and yet their most vivid debates occurred over issues of imperial authority and local contests. 'Australia', per se, did not exist in its current form and issues of colonial self-government were treated ambivalently by Evangelical commentators. This appears challenging in a contemporary context, where Aboriginal dispossession (and the small but significant protests made by white humanitarians) have become seen as part of a national legacy. While the history of colonialism undoubtedly has a powerful relevance for Australia's identity and future, it is nonetheless important to continue debating how this history should be conceptualised, and how it has been shaped by ideas of nation and empire. More work remains to be done, for instance, on the place of Indigenous affairs within the development of Australian self-government and national identity. Such research will no doubt be facilitated by the growing scholarly interest in re-evaluating Australia's place within the British empire, after several decades of more isolated national history-writing. Furthermore, when we consider Australia's history of Indigenous dispossession and resistance – a continuing source of pain, pride, shame and controversy – it is important to keep questioning how beliefs about national inheritance and responsibility themselves have developed over the past two centuries. The sense of evangelism, sin, imperial duty and uneasy paternalism voiced by the first philanthropists may seem, to the contemporary reader, distant and foreign, yet still unnervingly relevant.

# Bibliography

## Primary sources

### Manuscripts

Aboriginal Missions and Reserves Historical Database, University of Newcastle, Newcastle.

Carey, Hilary M, and David A Roberts (eds) 2002, *The Wellington Valley Project: Letters and Journals Relating to the Church Missionary Society Mission to Wellington Valley, NSW, 1830–42, A Critical Electronic Edition (WVP)*, <http://www.newcastle.edu.au/group/amrhd/wvp/>

Roberts, DA, HM Carey and Vicki Grieves (eds) 2002, *Awaba: A Database of Historical Materials Relating to the Aborigines of the Newcastle – Lake Macquarie Region*, University of Newcastle, <http://www.newcastle.edu.au/group/amrhd/awaba/>

### Australian Institute of Aboriginal and Torres Strait Islander Studies (AIATSIS), Canberra

Gardner, Peter Dean 1979, *W. Thomas and the Aborigines of Gippsland*, Ensay, Vic, PMS3118.

Parker, J, *Boyish Recollections of Victoria 70 years ago*, PMS2675.

William Thomas Papers – Correspondence, 1861, PMS681.

LE Threlkeld to E Deas Thomson, 'The final report of the mission to the Aborigines, Lake Macquarie, New South Wales, 1841', PMS1847.

### National Library of Australia, Canberra

Church Missionary Society, Papers 1840, MS4153.

John Dunmore Lang, Papers 1811–1887, vol 30, reel 18, mfmG24821.

Wesleyan Methodist Missionary Society, Archive: Australasia 1812–1889, Mp2107 (Record ID: 133095).

Wesleyan Methodist Missionary Society, Records, 1819–1874, mfmG3726 (Record ID: 1040441).

## Public Records Office of Victoria, Melbourne

VA512 Chief Protector of Aborigines, 1838–1849 – series VPRS 10–12, 2893–95, 4399, 4410, 4414 (filed as Aboriginal Affairs Records, mfm, VPRS4467, reel 1 – 3).

## State Library of New South Wales, Sydney

Sir William Dixson, Documents relating to Aboriginal Australians, 1816–1853, Dixson Library, ADD 80–82, CY reel 3743.

*N.S.W. Archival Estrays: N.S.W. Royal Commission into Crime in the Braidewood District [Journal 1836–1865 of Rev. James Günther]*, ML MSS 508, item 10, CY reel 872. (Accessed copy at AIATSIS library, ref MF294.)

Joseph Orton, Journal 1832–1839 and 1840–1841, ML ref A1714–1715, CY reel 1119. (Accessed copy at AIATSIS library, ref MF302.)

Joseph Orton, Letterbooks 1822–1842, ML ref A1717–A1720. (Accessed copy at AIATSIS library, ref MF303.)

William Thomas, Papers, 1834–1868, ML MSS 214/1–28. (Accessed copy at AIATSIS library, ref MF323.)

LE Threlkeld, Papers 1815–1862, ML ref A382: CY reel 820. (Accessed copy at AIATSIS library, ref MF324.)

LE Threlkeld, Papers 1817–1871, ML MSS 2111/1–2: CY reel 341. (Accessed copy at AIATSIS library, ref MF329.)

## State Library of Queensland, Brisbane

Schmidt, Karl WE, May 1842, *Report on an Expedition to the Bunya Mountains in Search of a Suitable Site for a Mission Station*, Accession 3522, Box 7072.

## State Library of Victoria, Melbourne

Church Missionary Society, Records, AJCP M212, M218, M238.

James Dredge, Diaries, Notebook and Letterbooks, ?1817–1845, MS11625, MSM534.

London Missionary Society, Records, AJCP M11, M73–74.

Methodist Missionary Society, Records, AJCP M118–122, M126, M150, M166, M172.

Parker Family Papers, MS8174, MSB423.

WM Tennant, Letters 1837–1883, MS12699, Box 3504/9 (1–40).

Francis Tuckfield, Journal, 1837–1842, MS11341, Box 655.

Francis Tuckfield to General Secretaries, 29 January 1840, MS10623, MSB281.

United Society for the Propagation of the Gospel, Records, AJCP M1222.

## State Records of South Australia, Adelaide

GRG 24/1, Colonial Secretary's Office, Letters and other communications received, 1837–1841.

GRG 24/4, Colonial Secretary's Office, Letters sent, 1838–1847.

GRG 24/6, Colonial Secretary's Office, Correspondence files, 1842–1850.

GRG 24/90, Miscellaneous records of historical interest, 1843–1844.

GRG 52/7, Protector of Aborigines, Letterbook 1840–1857, vol 1.

## University of Melbourne

Aborigines Protection Society, Transactions, c1839–1909, MIC/o6550, Reel 1, 3. Records the property of Anti-Slavery International.

## Published sources

Aborigines Protection Society 1841, *Extracts from the Papers and Proceedings of the Aborigines' Protection Society*, vol II, no III, April 1841, William Ball & Co, London.

Aborigines Protection Society 1838, *First Annual Report, 16 May 1838*, W Ball, London.

Backhouse, James 1843, *A Narrative of a Visit to the Australian Colonies*, Hamilton, Adams and Co, London.

*British Parliamentary Papers (BPP): Correspondence and Other Papers Relating to Aboriginal Tribes in British Possessions 1834*, Irish University Press, Shannon, 1968.

*BPP: Papers Relating to Australia, 1830–36*, Colonies: Australia, vol 4, Shannon, Irish University Press, 1970.

*BPP: Papers Relating to Australia, 1837*, Colonies: Australia, vol 5, Shannon, Irish University Press, 1970.

BPP: *Papers Relating to Australia, 1844*, Colonies: Australia, vol 8, Shannon, Irish University Press, 1969.

BPP: *Papers Relating to Australia, 1850*, Colonies: Australia, vol 12, Shannon, Irish University Press, 1969.

BPP: *Papers Relating to Australia, 1851–52*, Colonies: Australia, vol 13, Shannon, Irish University Press, 1969.

BPP: *Report from the Select Committee on Aborigines (British Settlements) together with minutes of evidence, appendix and index*, Anthropology: Aborigines, vol 1, Shannon, Irish University Press, 1836.

BPP: *Report from the Select Committee on Aborigines (British Settlements) together with minutes of evidence, appendix and index*, Anthropology: Aborigines, vol 2, Shannon, Irish University Press, 1837.

BPP: *South Australia*, Colonies: Australia, vol 2, Shannon, Irish University Press, 1968.

Cannon, Michael (ed) 1982, *Historical Records of Victoria (HRV): the Aborigines of Port Phillip, 1835–1839*, vol 2A, Victorian Government Printing Office, Melbourne.

—— (ed) 1983, *Historical Records of Victoria (HRV): Aborigines and Protectors, 1838–1839*, vol 2B, Victorian Government Printing Office, Melbourne.

——, and Pauline Jones (eds) 1981, *HRV: Beginnings of Permanent Government*, vol 1, Victorian Government Printing Office, Melbourne.

Church Missionary Society (CMS) 1835–1839, *Annual Report of the Australian Church Missionary Society*, William Jones, Sydney.

—— 1850–1853, *Church Missionary Intelligencer, A Monthly Journal of Missionary Information*, vols 1–4, Seeleys, London.

—— 1848–1850, *Church Missionary Juvenile Instructor*, Seeleys, London.

—— Michaelmas 1834 – Christmas 1836, *Church Missionary Paper: for the Use of Weekly and Monthly Contributions*, nos LXXIV–LXXV, Church Missionary Society, London.

—— 1847–1850, *The Colonial Church Chronicle, and Missionary Journal*, vols 1–3, Francis and John Rivington, London.

—— 1831–1850, *Missionary Register*, Seeley & Sons, London.

Colonial Church Society (CCS) 1838, *Colonial Church Record*, vol 1, no 3, CCS, London.

— 1838–1840, *Report of the Australian Church Missionary Society, now formed into the Colonial Church Society*, A Macintosh, London.

Dredge, James 1845, *Brief Notices on the Aborigines of New South Wales*, James Harrison, Geelong.

— 1998, 'A Letter from Port Phillip', *LaTrobe Journal* 61, Autumn: 27–32.

Eipper, Christopher 1975, 'Statement of the origin, condition and prospects of the German Mission to the Aborigines at Moreton Bay', in *Brisbane Town in Convict Days, 1824–1842*, JG Steele, University of Queensland, St Lucia: 281–293.

*Evangelical Magazine and Missionary Chronicle*, August 1834 – July 1836, vols XII–XV, Frederick Westley and AH Davis, London.

*Evangelical Magazine and Missionary Chronicle*, July 1837 – April 1838, vols XV–XVI, Thomas Ward & Co, London.

Griffith, Charles 1845, *The Present State and Prospects of the Port Phillip District of New South Wales*, William Curry, Dublin.

Hale, Horatio 1846, *United States Exploring Expedition During the Years 1838, 1839, 1840, 1841, 1842 – Ethnography and Philology*, C Sherman, Philadelphia.

*Historical Records of Australia (HRA)*, series 1, vol xiii, July 1843 – September 1844, Library Committee of the Commonwealth Parliament, Sydney, 1920.

*HRA*, series 1, vol xix, July 1838 – January 1839, Library Committee of the Commonwealth Parliament, Sydney, 1923.

*HRA*, series 1, vol xx, February 1839 – September 1840, Library Committee of the Commonwealth Parliament, Sydney, 1924.

*HRA*, series 1, vol xxii, April 1842 – June 1843, Library Committee of the Commonwealth Parliament, Sydney, 1924.

*HRA*, series 1, vol xxv, April 1846 – September 1847, Library Committee of the Commonwealth Parliament, Sydney, 1925.

*HRA*, series 1, vol xxvi, October 1847 – December 1848, Library Committee of the Commonwealth Parliament, Sydney, 1925.

Hodgkindon, Clement 1845, *Australia from Port Macquarie to Moreton Bay; with descriptions of the natives, their manners and customs; the geology, natural productions, fertility, and resources of that region*, T&W Boone, London.

Lang, John Dunmore 1839, *Appeal to the Friends of Missions on Behalf of the German Mission to the Aborigines of New South Wales*, JD Lang, Sydney.

— 1847, *Cooksland in North-Eastern Australia; the Future Cotton-field of Great Britain: Its Characteristics and Capabilities for European Colonization*, Longman, Brown, Green and Longmans, London.

London Missionary Society (LMS) 1836, *Missionary Magazine and Chronicle*, vol 1, nos 1–4, June – September, The Society, London.

LMS, *Juvenile Missionary Magazine*, June 1844 – Dec 1850, <http://www.nla.gov.au/ferg/issn/14606003.html>

LMS 1837–1849, *The Missionary Magazine and Chronicle*, vols 1–13, published by the LMS directors, London.

MacFarlane, Ian (ed) 1998, *HRV: Public Finance of Port Phillip, 1836–1840*, Melbourne University Press, Melbourne.

*New South Wales Government Gazette*, 1850, no 19, Government Printer, Sydney.

Nique, Peter 1841, 'Aborigines: diary of Messrs Nique and Hartenstein of the German Mission to the Aborigines', *Colonial Observer* 1(4–5).

NSW Parliament, Legislative Council 1838, *Report from the Committee on the Aborigines Question, with Minutes of Evidence*, J Spilsbury, Sydney.

Orton, Joseph, 1836, *The Aborigines of Australia*, Thomas, London.

Parker, Edward Stone, 1846, *The Aborigines of Australia*, William Clarke, Melbourne.

Parker, Edward Stone 1967, 'The Aborigines of Australia', 10 May 1854, in *Frontier Life in the Loddon Protectorate: Episodes from Early Days, 1837–1842*, Edgar Morrison (ed), Melbourne: 1–30.

Robinson, George Augustus, 1966, *Friendly Mission: The Tasmanian Journals and Papers of George Augustus Robinson, 1829–1834*, NJB Plomley (ed), Halstead Press, Kingsgrove.

— 1998, *Journals: Port Phillip Aboriginal Protectorate*, vols 1–4, Ian D Clark (ed), Heritage Matters, Melbourne.

— 2000, *Journals: Port Phillip Aboriginal Protectorate*, vol 5, Ian D Clark (ed), Heritage Matters, Melbourne.

— 2001, '1846 Annual Report', in *The Papers of George Augustus Robinson, Chief Protector, Port Phillip Aboriginal Protectorate*, vol 4, Ian D Clark (ed), Heritage Matters, Clarendon: 108–119.

— 2001, '1848 Annual Report', in *The Papers of George Augustus Robinson, Chief Protector, Port Phillip Aboriginal Protectorate*, vol 4, Ian D Clark (ed), Heritage Matters, Clarendon: 139–156.

— 2001, 'Brief report of an expedition to the Aboriginal tribes of the interior over more than two thousand miles of country during the five months commencing March to August 1846', in *The Papers of George Augustus Robinson, Chief Protector, Port Phillip Aboriginal Protectorate*, vol 4, Ian D Clark (ed), Heritage Matters, Clarendon: 55–69.

— 2001, 'A Report of an Expedition to the Aboriginal Tribes of the Western Interior during the months of March, April, May, June, July and August, 1841', in *The Papers of George Augustus Robinson, Chief Protector, Port Phillip Aboriginal Protectorate*, vol 4, Ian D Clark (ed), Heritage Matters, Clarendon: 14–24.

Salvado, Dom Rosendo 1977[1851], *The Salvado Memoirs*, EJ Storman (ed), University of Western Australia Press, Nedlands.

Society for the Propagation of the Gospel 1846, *The Church in Australia: Two Journals of Visitation to the Northern and Southern Portions of his Diocese, by the Lord Bishop of Australia, 1843*, Society for the Propagation of the Gospel, London.

Thomas, William 1854, *Aborigines: A Return to Address Mr Parker – 21 October 1853*, Government Printing Office, Melbourne.

Threlkeld, LE 1828, *A Statement Relating to the Formation and Abandonment of a Mission to the Aborigines of New South Wales: Addressed to the serious consideration of the Directors of the London Missionary Society*, R Howe, Sydney.

— 1832, *Specimens of a Dialect, of the Aborigines of New South Wales: Being the first attempt to form their speech into a Written Language*, Arthur Hill, Sydney.

— 1836, *An Australian Spelling Book in the Language as spoken by the Aborigines in the vicinity of Hunter's River, Lake Macquarie, New South Wales*, Stephens and Stokes, Sydney.

— 1892, *An Australian Language As Spoken by the Awabakal, the People of Awaba or Lake Macquarie*, Government Printer, Sydney. (Includes LE Threlkeld, 1850, 'A Key to the Structure of the Aboriginal Language'.)

— 1974, 'Correspondence and Early Reports Relating to the Aboriginal Mission 1825–1841', in *Australian Reminiscences and Papers of L. E. Threlkeld, Missionary to the Aborigines, 1824–1859*, vol 2, Niel Gunson (ed), Australian Institute of Aboriginal Studies, Canberra: 177–306.

— 1974, 'Memoranda', in *Australian Reminiscences and Papers of L.E. Threlkeld, Missionary to the Aborigines, 1824–1859*, vol 1, Niel Gunson (ed), Australian Institute of Aboriginal Studies, Canberra: 83–170.

— 1974, 'Reminiscences 1825–1826', in *Australian Reminiscences and Papers of L. E. Threlkeld, Missionary to the Aborigines, 1824–1859*, vol 1, Niel Gunson (ed), Australian Institute of Aboriginal Studies, Canberra: 43–71.

Tiechelmann, Christian Gottlieb 1841, *Aborigines of South Australia: Illustrative and Explanatory Notes of the Manners, Customs, Habits and Superstitions of the Natives of South Australia*, SA Wesleyan Methodist Auxiliary Missionary Society, Adelaide.

Ullathorne, William Bernard 1963[1837], *The Catholic Mission in Australasia*, Rockliff & Duckworth, Liverpool.

Wesleyan Methodist Missionary Society (WMMS), November 1823 – December 1838, *Missionary Notices: relating principally to the Foreign Missions*, vol IV, no 95–276, Wesleyan Mission House, London.

—, *Papers Relative to the Wesleyan Missions and to the State of the Heathen Countries*, London, Wesleyan Missionary Society, no.IX, September 1822 and no CXI, March 1848.

— 1821–1828, *Reports of the Wesleyan Methodist Missionary Society*, Howe, Sydney.

— 1833–1835, *Reports of the Wesleyan Methodist Missionary Society*, Sydney, Stephen & Stokes.

— 1840–1851, *Reports of the Wesleyan Methodist Missionary Society*, PP Thoms, London.

— 1980, *Synod Minutes, 1822–1855*, ICP, Zug.

— 1847–1853, *Wesleyan Juvenile Offering: a Miscellany of Missionary Information for Young Persons*, Wesleyan Mission House, London.

## Newspapers

*Australian*

*The Colonist*

*Geelong Advertiser*

*Inquirer* (Perth)

*Moreton Bay Courier*

*Perth Gazette*

*Sydney Herald*

*Sydney Morning Herald*

## Secondary sources

Arkley, Lindsey 2000, *The Hated Protector: the Story of Charles Wightman Sievwright, Protector of Aborigines, 1839–42*, Orbit Press, Mentone.

Armstrong, Anthony 1973, *The Church of England, the Methodists and Society, 1700–1850*, University of London Press, London.

Arneil, Barbara 1996, *John Locke and America: the Defence of English Colonialism*, Clarendon Press, Oxford.

Atkinson, Alan 1988, 'Time, place and paternalism: early conservative thinking in New South Wales', *Australian Historical Studies* 23(90), April: 1–18.

— 1994, 'Towards independence: recipes for self-government in colonial New South Wales', in *Pastiche I: Reflections on Nineteenth-Century Australia*, Penny Russell and Richard White (eds), Allen & Unwin, St Leonards: 85–102.

Attwood, Bain 1989, *The Making of the Aborigines*, Allen & Unwin, North Sydney.

— 2003, *Rights for Aborigines*, Allen & Unwin, Crows Nest.

— and Andrew Markus (eds) 1999, *The Struggle for Aboriginal Rights: a Documentary History*, Allen & Unwin, Sydney.

Baker, Gwenda 2005, 'Crossing boundaries: negotiated space and the construction of narratives of missionary incursion', *Journal of Northern Territory History* 16: 17–28.

Bank, Andrew 1990, 'Losing faith in the civilizing mission: the premature decline of humanitarian liberalism at the Cape, 1840–60', in *Empire and Others: British Encounters with Indigenous Peoples, 1600–1850*, Martin Daunton and Rick Halpern (eds), University of Pennsylvania Press, Philadelphia: 364–383.

Barnes, John, 1998, 'Annotation: a letter from Port Phillip', *La Trobe Journal* 61, Autumn: 27–32.

Barry, Amanda 2006, '"A matter of primary importance": comparing the colonial education of indigenous children', in *Rethinking Colonial Histories: New and Alternative Approaches*, Penelope Edmonds and Samuel Furphy (eds), RMIT publishing, Melbourne: 169–182.

Barwick, Diane E 1998, *Rebellion at Coranderrk*, Aboriginal History Inc, Canberra.

Bebbington, DW 1989, *Evangelicalism in Modern Britain: a History from the 1730s to the 1980s*, Unwin Hyman, London.

Bell, Duncan 2007, *The Idea of Greater Britain: Empire and the Future of World Order, 1860–1900*, Princeton University Press, Princeton and Oxford.

Benton, Laura 2002, *Law and Colonial Cultures: Legal Regimes in World History, 1400–1900*, Cambridge University Press, Cambridge.

Binney, Judith 1968, *The Legacy of Guilt: a Life of Thomas Kendall*, Oxford University Press, Christchurch.

Blaskett, Beverley A 1979, 'The Aboriginal Response to White Settlement in the Port Phillip District, 1835–1850', MA thesis, University of Melbourne, Melbourne.

Bourne, HRF 1899, *Aborigines Protection Society: Chapters in its History*, PS King & Son, Westminster.

Bowler, Peter J 1984, *Evolution: the History of an Idea*, University of California Press, Berkeley.

— 1989, *The Invention of Progress: the Victorians and the Past*, Basil Blackwell, Oxford.

Bradley, Ian 1976, *The Call to Seriousness: the Evangelical Impact on the Victorians*, Jonathon Cape, London.

Bremner, Robert H 1994, *Giving: Charity and Philanthropy in History*, Transaction Publishers, New Brunswick.

Bridges, Barry John 1978, 'The Church of England and the Aborigines of New South Wales, 1788–1855', PhD thesis, University of New South Wales, Sydney.

Brock, Peggy 1995, 'South Australia', in *Contested Ground: Australian Aborigines under the British Crown*, Ann McGrath (ed), Allen & Unwin, St Leonards: 208–239.

— 2000, 'Building bridges: politics and religion in a First Nations community', *The Canadian Historical Review* 81(1): 67–97.

— 2005, 'New Christians as Evangelists', in *Missions and Empire* (companion to the Oxford History of the British Empire), Norman Etherington (ed), Oxford University Press, Oxford: 132–152.

Brook, J and JL Kohen 1991, *The Parramatta Native Institution and the Black Town: a History*, University of New South Wales Press, Kensington.

Broome, Richard 1994, 'Aboriginal workers on south–eastern frontiers', *Australian Historical Studies* 26(103), October: 202–220.

— 2001, *Aboriginal Australians: Black Responses to White Dominance, 1788–2001*, Allen & Unwin, St Leonards.

— 2005, *Aboriginal Victorians: a History since 1800*, Allen & Unwin, Crows Nest.

— 2006, ' 'There were vegetables every year Mr Green was here': right behaviour and the struggle for autonomy at Coranderrk Aboriginal reserve', *History Australia* 3(2): 43.1–43.16.

Buchan, Bruce 2001, 'Subjecting the natives: Aborigines, property and possession under early colonial rule', *Social Analysis* 45(2): 143–162.

— 2007, 'Traffick of empire: trade, treaty and *Terra nullius* in Australia and North America, 1750–1800', *History Compass* 5(2): 386–405.

Butcher, Barry 1994, 'Darwinism, social Darwinism, and the Australian Aborigines: a reevaluation', in *Darwin's Laboratory: Evolutionary Theory and Natural History in the Pacific*, Roy MacLeod and Philip F Rebock (eds), University of Hawai'i Press, Honolulu: 371–394.

Byrne, Geraldine 1981, *Valiant Women: Letters from The Foundation Sisters of Mercy in Western Australia, 1845–1849*, Polding Press, Melbourne.

Cannon, Michael 1990, *Who Killed the Koories?*, Heinemann, Port Melbourne.

Carey, Hilary M 1996, *Believing in Australia: a Cultural History of Religions*, Allen & Unwin, St Leonards.

— 2000, '"Attempts and attempts": responses to failure in pre and early Victorian missions to the Australian Aborigines', in *Mapping the Landscape: Essays in Australian and New Zealand Christianity*, Susan Emilsen and William Emilson (eds), Peter Lang, New York: 45–61.

— and David A Roberts 2002, 'Smallpox and the Baiame Waganna of Wellington Valley, New South Wales, 1829–1840: the earliest Nativist movement in Aboriginal Australia', *Ethnohistory* 49(4): 821–869.

Christie, MF 1979, *Aborigines in Colonial Victoria, 1835–86*, Sydney University Press, Sydney.

Clark, Ian D 1990, *Aboriginal Languages and Clans: an Historical Atlas of Western and Central Victoria, 1800–1900*, Monash Publications in Geography, Melbourne.

— 1998, *'That's My Country Belonging to Me': Aboriginal Land Tenure and Dispossession in Nineteenth Century Western Victoria*, Heritage Matters, Melbourne.

— 2001, *The Papers of George Augustus Robinson, Chief Protector, Port Phillip Aboriginal Protectorate*, 4 vols, Heritage Matters, Clarendon.

Clemmons, Linda 1999, '"Our children are in danger of becoming little Indians": Protestant missionary children and Dakotas, 1835–1862', *Michigan Historical Review* 25(2), Fall: 69–91.

Clouten, Keith H 1967, *Reid's Mistake: the Story of Lake Macquarie from its Discovery until 1890*, Lake Macquarie Shire Council, Sydney.

Cochrane, Peter 2006, *Colonial Ambition: Foundations of Australian Democracy*, Melbourne University Press, Carlton.

Cole, Anna 2005, '"Would have known it by the smell of it": Ella Hiscocks', in *Uncommon Ground: White Women in Aboriginal History*, Anna Cole, Victoria Haskins and Fiona Paisley (eds), Aboriginal Studies Press, Canberra: 153–171.

Comaroff, Jean 1991, 'Missionaries and mechanical clocks: an essay on religion and history in South Africa', *Journal of Religion* 71(1): 1–17.

— and John Comaroff 1991, *Of Revelation and Revolution: Christianity, Colonialism and Consciousness in South Africa*, vol 1, University of Chicago Press, Chicago and London.

Comaroff, John L 1989, 'Images of empire, contests of conscience: models of colonial domination in South Africa', *American Ethnologist* 16(4), November: 661–682.

— and Jean Comaroff 1997, *Of Revelation and Revolution: Christianity, Colonialism and Consciousness in South Africa*, vol 2, University of Chicago Press, Chicago and London.

Cooke, Raymond M 1965, 'British Evangelicals and the issue of colonial self-government', *Pacific Historical Review* 34: 127–140.

Corris, Peter 1968, *Aborigines and Europeans in Western Victoria*, Australian Institute of Aboriginal Studies, Canberra.

Critchett, Jan 1990, *A 'Distant Field of Murder': Western District Frontiers, 1834–1848*, Melbourne University Press, Burwood.

Crowther, MA 1981, *The Workhouse System, 1834–1929: the History of an English Social Institution*, Batsford Academic and Educational, London.

Curthoys, Ann 2002, *Freedom Ride: a Freedom Rider Remembers*, Allen & Unwin, Crows Nest.

— 2007, 'Self-Government and Indigenous Dispossession: Linked fates, separate histories, long shadows', conference paper, *Governing by Looking Back*, 14 December 2007, Research School of Social Sciences, Australian National University.

— 2008, 'The Humanitarians versus Colonial Self-Government: the Australian Colonies in the mid nineteenth century', conference paper, *Race, Nation, History: A Conference in Honour of Henry Reynolds*, 29–30 August 2008, National Library of Australia, Canberra.

Curthoys, Ann, in conversation with Lorenzo Veracini and John Docker 2002, 'Genocide and colonialism', *Australian Humanities Review* 27, September: unpaginated.

Damousi, Joy 1997, *Depraved and Disorderly: Female Convicts, Sexuality and Gender in Colonial Australia*, Cambridge University Press, Cambridge.

Davies, Susanne 1987, 'Aborigines, murder and the criminal law in early Port Phillip, 1841–1851', *Historical Studies* 22(88), April: 313–335.

De Moor, Martina, Leigh Shaw-Taylor and Paul Warde 2002, 'Comparing the historical commons of north west Europe: an introduction', in *The Management of Common Land in North West Europe, c.1500–1850*, Martina de Moor, Leigh Shaw-Taylor and Paul Warde (eds), Turnhout, Brepols: 15–33.

Ditchfield, GM 1998, *The Evangelical Revival*, UCL Press, London.

Douglas, Mary 1966, *Purity and Danger: an Analysis of the Concepts of Pollution and Taboo*, Routledge, London.

Driver, Felix 1993, *Power and Pauperism: the Workhouse System, 1834–1884*, Cambridge University Press, Cambridge.

Dyer, Richard 1997, *White*, Routledge, London and New York.

Edmonds, Penelope 2006, '"The inconvenience and immorality of Aborigines in the town": racialised spaces in colonial Melbourne, 1836–1860', in *Sharing Spaces: Indigenous and Non-Indigenous Responses to Story, Country and Rights*, Gus Worby and Lester-Irabinna Rigney (eds), Australia Research Institute, Perth: 171–195.

Elbourne, Elizabeth 1997, 'Combating spiritual and social bondage: early missions in the Cape', in *Christianity in South Africa: a Political, Social and Cultural History*, Richard Elphick and Rodney Davenport (eds), James Curry, Oxford: 31–50.

— 2002, *Blood Ground: Colonialism, Missions and the Contest for Christianity in the Cape Colony and Britain, 1799–1853*, McGill-Queen's University Press, Montreal.

— 2003, 'The sin of the settler: the 1835–36 Select Committee on Aborigines and debates over virtue and conquest in the early nineteenth-century British white settler empire', *Journal of Colonialism and Colonial History* 4(3), (online through Project Muse).

Elias, Norbert 1978, *The Civilizing Process*, Blackwell, Oxford.

Englander, David 1998, *Poverty and Poor Law Reform in 19th Century Britain, 1834–1914*, Longman, London and New York.

Evans, Julie 2002a, 'Re-reading Edward John Eyre: race, resistance and repression in Australia and the Caribbean', *Australian Historical Studies* 33(118): 175–198.

— 2002b, 'Safer as subjects than citizens: privilege and exclusion in the transition to nationhood in Australia and Natal', in *Writing Colonial Histories: Comparative Perspectives*, Tracey Banivanua Mar and Julie Evans (eds), Melbourne University Conference and Seminar Series, Melbourne: 165–185.

— 2004, 'The formulation of privilege and exclusion in settler states: land, law, political rights and indigenous peoples in nineteenth-century Western

Australia and Natal', in *Honour Among Nations? Treaties and Agreements with Indigenous People*, Marcia Langton, Maureen Tehan, Lisa Palmer and Kathryn Shain (eds), Melbourne University Press, Carlton: 69–82.

—, Patricia Grimshaw, David Phillips and Shurlee Swain 2003, *Equal Subjects, Unequal Rights: Indigenous peoples in British settler colonies, 1830–1910*, Manchester University Press, Manchester.

Evans, Raymond 1992, 'The mowgi take mi-an-jin: race relations and the Moreton Bay penal settlement 1824–42', in *Brisbane: the Aboriginal Presence 1824–1860*, Rod Fischer (ed), Brisbane History Group, Papers no 11: 7–30.

Eves, Richard 1996, 'Colonialism, corporeality and character: the Methodist missions and the refashioning of bodies in the Pacific', *History and Anthropology* 10(1): 85–138.

Frauenfelder, Peter (ed) 1997, *Aboriginal Communities: the Colonial Experience, Port Phillip District*, Education Centre of the State Library of Victoria, Melbourne.

Gardner, Helen Bethea 2006, *Gathering for God: George Brown in Oceania*, Otago University Press, Dunedin.

Goodall, Heather 1996, *Invasion to Embassy: Land in Aboriginal Politics in New South Wales, 1770–1972*, Allen & Unwin, St Leonards.

— 1999, 'Authority under challenge: Pikampul land and Queen Victoria's law during the British invasion of Australia', in *Empire and Others: British Encounters with Indigenous Peoples, 1600-1850*, Martin J Daunton and Rick Halpern (eds), UCL Press, London: 260–279.

Green, Neville 1988, 'The cry for justice and equality: some exceptional Protestant missionaries in Western Australia', in *Aboriginal Australians and Christian Missions*, Tony Swain and Deborah Bird Rose (eds), Australian Association for the Study of Religions, Bedford Park: 156–173.

Greenwood, GW 1956, 'Reverend Francis Tuckfield's magnificent failure at Bunting Dale', *Heritage* 1(2): 3–21.

Griffiths, Gareth 2005, '"Trained to tell the truth": missionaries, converts, and narration', in *Missions and Empire* (companion to the Oxford History of the British Empire), Norman Etherington (ed), Oxford University Press, Oxford: 153–172.

Grimshaw, Patricia 1989, *Paths of Duty: American Missionary Wives in Nineteenth-Century Hawaii*, University of Hawai'i Press, Honolulu.

Gunson, Niel (ed) 1974, *Australian Reminiscences and Papers of L.E. Threlkeld, Missionary to the Aborigines, 1824–1859*, 2 vols, Australian Institute of Aboriginal Studies, Canberra.

— (ed) 1978, *Messengers of Grace: Evangelical Missionaries in the South Seas, 1797–1860*, Oxford University Press, Melbourne.

Haebich, Anna 2000, *Broken Circles: Fragmenting Indigenous Families, 1800–2000*, Fremantle Arts Centre Press, Fremantle.

Hall, Catherine 1992, *White, Male and Middle-Class: Explorations of Feminism and History*, Polity Press, Cambridge.

— 2002, *Civilising Subjects: Colony and Metropole in the English Imagination, 1830–1867*, University of Chicago Press, Chicago and London.

Harkin, Michael 1993, 'Power and progress: the Evangelic dialogue among the Heiltsuk', *Ethnohistory* 40(1): 1–33.

— 2005, 'The house of longing: missionary-led changes in Heiltsuk domestic forms and structures', in *Indigenous Peoples and Religious Change*, Peggy Brock (ed), Brill, Leiden: 205–225.

Harris, John 1990, *One Blood: 200 Years of Aboriginal Encounter with Christianity: a Story of Hope*, Albatross Books, Sutherland.

Hasluck, Paul 1970, *Black Australians: a Survey of Native Policy in Western Australia, 1829–1897*, Melbourne University Press, Carlton.

Hempton, David 2005, *Methodism: Empire of the Spirit*, Yale University Press, New Haven & London.

Henwood, Tricia 1978, 'Rev. L.E. Threlkeld and the Awabakal Aborigines: An Example of Cultural Interaction, 1824–1841', Hons thesis, LaTrobe University, Melbourne.

Hetherington, Penelope 1992, 'Aboriginal children as a potential labour force in Swan River Colony, 1829–1850', *Journal of Australian Studies* 33: 41–55.

— 2002, *Settlers, Servants and Slaves: Aboriginal and European Children in Nineteenth-Century Western Australia*, University of Western Australia Press, Crawley.

Hindmarsh, D Bruce 2001, 'Patterns of conversion in early Evangelical history and overseas mission experience', in *Christian Missions and the Enlightenment*, Brian Stanley (ed), Wm B Eerdmans, Surrey: 71–98.

Hirst, John B 1988, *The Strange Birth of Colonial Democracy: New South Wales, 1848–1884*, Allen & Unwin, Sydney.

— 2002, *Australia's Democracy: a Short History*, Allen & Unwin, Crows Nest.

Hofmeyr, Isabel 2005, '"Inventing the world": transnationalism, transmission, and Christian textualities', in *Mixed Messages: Materiality, Textuality, Missions*, Jamie S Scott and Gareth Griffiths (eds), Palgrave MacMillan, New York: 19–36.

Howell, PA 1986, 'The South Australia Act, 1834', in *The Flinders History of South Australia*, Dean Jaensch (ed), Wakefield Press, Netley: 26–51.

Hunter, Ann 2004, 'The boundaries of colonial criminal law in relation to inter-Aboriginal conflicts ('*Inter Se* Offences') in Western Australia in the 1830s-1840s', *Australian Journal of Legal History* 8(2): 215–236.

Irving, Terry 2006, *The Southern Tree of Liberty: the Democratic Movement in New South Wales before 1856*, Federation Press, Sydney.

Jalland, Pat 1996, *Death in the Victorian Family*, Oxford University Press, Oxford.

Jenkins, Paul 2000, 'The Church Missionary Society and the Basel Mission: an early experiment in inter-European cooperation', in *The Church Mission Society and World Christianity, 1799–1999*, RE Frykenbeg and Brian Stanley (eds), Curzon Press, Richmond: 43–65.

Johnston, Anna 2003a, *Missionary Writing and Empire, 1800–1860*, Cambridge University Press, Cambridge.

— 2003b, 'The well-intentioned imperialists: missionary textuality and (post) colonialists politics', in *Resistance and Reconciliation: Writing in the Commonwealth*, Bruce Bennett, Susan Cowan, Jacqueline Lo, Sutendra Nandan and Jennifer Webb (eds), Association for Commonwealth Literature and Language Studies, Canberra: 102–113.

— 2006, 'A blister on the imperial antipodes: Lancelot Edward Threlkeld in Polynesia and Australia', in *Colonial Lives Across the British Empire: Imperial Careering in the Long Nineteenth Century*, David Lambert and Alan Lester (eds), Cambridge University Press, Cambridge: 58–87.

Johnstone, SM 1925, *A History of the Church Missionary Society in Australia and Tasmania*, Church Missionary Society, Sydney.

Kenny, Robert 2007, *The Lamb Enters the Dreaming: Nathanael Pepper and the Ruptured World*, Scribe, Carlton North.

Kent, Eliza F 2005, 'Books and bodices: material culture and protestant missions in colonial South India', in *Mixed Messages: Materiality, Textuality, Missions*, Jamie S Scott and Gareth Griffiths (eds), Palgrave MacMillan, New York: 67–87.

Kociumbas, Jan 2001, '"Mary Ann", Joseph Fleming and "Gentleman Dick": Aboriginal-convict relationships in colonial history', *Journal of Australian Colonial History* 3(1), April: 28–54.

Kumar, Krishan 2003, *The Making of the English National Identity*, Cambridge University Press, Cambridge.

Laidlaw, Zoë 2002, 'Integrating metropolitan, colonial and imperial histories – the Aborigines Select Committee of 1835–37', in *Writing Colonial Histories: Comparative Perspectives*, Tracey Banivanua Mar and Julie Evans (eds), Melbourne University Conference and Seminar Series, Melbourne: 75–92.

— 2007, 'Heathens, slaves and Aborigines: Thomas Hogkin's critique of missions and anti-slavery', *History Workshop Journal* 64(1), Autumn: 133–161.

Lakic, Mira, and Rosemary Wrench (eds) 1994, *Through Their Eyes: an Historical Record of Aboriginal People in Victoria as Documented by the Officials of the Port Phillip Protectorate, 1839–1841*, Museum of Victoria, Melbourne.

Landau, Paul 1999, '"Religion" and Christian conversion in African history: a new model', *The Journal of Religious History* 23(1), February: 8–31.

Le Couteur, Howard 1998, 'The Moreton Bay Ministry of the Reverend Johann Handt: a re-appraisal', *Journal of the Royal Australian Historical Society* 84(2): 140–151.

Lester, Alan 2005, 'Humanitarians and white settlers in the nineteenth century', in *Missions and Empire* (companion to the Oxford History of the British Empire), Norman Etherington (ed), Oxford University Press, Oxford: 64–85.

— 2006, 'Colonial networks, Australian humanitarianism and the history wars', *Geographical Research* 44(3): 229–241.

Lewis, Rosalind Jane 1987, 'Edward Stone Parker: Protector of Aborigines, Missionary and Visionary', Hons thesis, Deakin University.

Lourandos, Harry 1977, 'Aboriginal spatial organization and population: south western Victoria reconsidered', *Archaeology and Physical Anthropology in Oceania* 12(3): 202–225.

Lovejoy, Arthur 1960[1936], *The Great Chain of Being: a Study of an Idea*, Harper Torchbooks, New York,

Lydon, Jane 2005, *Eye Contact: Photographing Indigenous Australians*, Duke University Press, Durham and London.

— 2005a, '"Men in black": the Blacktown Native Institution and the origins of the 'Stolen Generations'', in *Object Lessons: Archaeology and Heritage in Australia*, Jane Lydon and Tracy Ireland (eds), Australian Scholarly Publishing, Melbourne: 201–224.

— 2005b, '"Our sense of beauty": visuality, space and gender on Victoria's Aboriginal reserves, south-eastern Australia', *History and Anthropology* 16(2), June: 211–234.

Magowan, Fiona 2005, 'Experiencing the spirit: religious processes of interaction and unification in Aboriginal Australia', in *Indigenous Peoples and Religious Change*, Peggy Brock (ed), Brill, Leiden: 157–175.

Main, JC 1986, 'The foundation of South Australia', in *The Flinders History of South Australia*, Dean Jaensch (ed), Wakefield Press, Netley: 1–26.

Mackenzie-Smith, John 1992, 'The Kilcoy poisonings: the official factor 1841–43', in *Brisbane: The Aboriginal Presence 1824–1860*, Rod Fischer (ed), Brisbane History Group, Papers no 11: 58–68.

Mann, Michael 2004, '"Torchbearers upon the path of progress": Britain's ideology of a "moral and material progress" in India', in *Colonialism As Civilizing Mission: Cultural Ideology in British India*, Harald Fischer-Tine and Michael Mann (eds), Anthem Press, London: 1–28.

Massola, Aldo 1975, *Coranderrk: a History of the Aboriginal Station*, Lowden, Kilmore.

McClintock, Anne 1995, *Imperial Leather: Race, Gender and Sexuality in the Colonial Context*, Routledge, New York and London.

McGrath, Ann 1987, *Born in the Cattle: Aborigines in Cattle Country*, Allen & Unwin, Sydney.

McGregor, Russell 1997, *Imagined Destinies: Aboriginal Australians and the Doomed Race Theory, 1880–1939*, Melbourne University Press, Carlton South.

McKenna, Mark 1996, *The Captive Republic: a History of Republicanism in Australia, 1788–1996*, Cambridge University Press, Cambridge.

McLay, Anne 1992, *Women out of their Sphere: a History of the Sisters of Mercy in Western Australia*, Vanguard Press, Northbridge.

McLisky, Claire 2005, '"Due observation of justice, and the protection of their rights": philanthropy, humanitarianism and moral purpose in the Aborigines Protection Society circa 1837 and its portrayal in Australian historiography', *Limina* 11: 57–66.

McMahon, John T 1943, *Bishop Salvado: Founder of New Norcia*, Patersons Printing Press, Perth.

McNair, William and Hilary Rumley 1981, *Pioneer Aboriginal Mission: the Work of Wesleyan Missionary John Smithies in the Swan River Colony, 1840–1855*, University of Western Australia Press, Nedlands.

Meaney, Neville 2001, 'Britishness and Australian identity: the problem of nationalism in Australian history and historiography', *Australian Historical Studies*, 32(116): 76–90.

Meek, Ronald L 1976, *Social Science and the Ignoble Savage*, Cambridge University Press, Cambridge.

Mingay, GE 1997, *Parliamentary Enclosure in England: an Introduction to its Causes, Incidence and Impact, 1750–1850*, Longman, London and New York.

Mitchell, Don 2003, *The Right to the City: Social Justice and the Fight for Public Space*, Guildford Press, New York and London.

Mitchell, Jessie 2009a, '"Are we in danger of a hostile visit from the Aborigines?" Dispossession and the rise of self-government in New South Wales', *Australian Historical Studies* 40(3): 294–307.

— 2009b, '"The galling yoke of slavery": race and separation in colonial Port Phillip', *Journal of Australian Studies* 33(2): 125–137.

— 2009c, '"The Gomorrah of the Southern Seas": population, separation and race in early colonial Queensland', *History Australia* 6(3), December: 69.1–69.15.

Moreton-Robinson, Aileen 2004, 'Whiteness, epistemology and Indigenous representation', in *Whitening Race: Essays in social and cultural criticism*, Aileen Moreton-Robinson (ed), Aboriginal Studies Press, Canberra: 75–88.

Morrison, Edgar 2002a, 'Early days in the Loddon Valley: memoirs of Edward Stone Parker', in *A Successful Failure: the Aborigines and Early Settlers*, Geoff Morrison (ed), Graffiti Publications, Maryborough: 6–110.

— 2002b, 'The Loddon Aborigines: Tales of Old Jim Crow', in *A Successful Failure: the Aborigines and Early Settlers*, Geoff Morrison (ed), Graffiti Publications, Maryborough: 174–279.

Neeson, JM 1993, *Commoners:Common Right, Enclosure and Social Change in England, 1700–1820*, Cambridge University Press, Cambridge.

O'Brien, Anne 2008, '"Kitchen fragments and garden stuff": poor law discourse and Indigenous people in early colonial New South Wales', *Australian Historical Studies* 39(2): 150–166.

O'Brien, Jean 1999, '"They are so frequently shifting their place of residence": land and the construction of social place of Indians in colonial Massachusetts', in *Empire and Others: British Encounters with Indigenous Peoples, 1600–1850*, Martin Daunton and Rick Halpern (eds), UCL Press, London: 204–216.

O'Connor, TM 1991, *Protector Edward Stone Parker: Port Phillip Gentlemen*, UCA Historical Society, Melbourne.

Oldfield, Audrey 1999, *The Great Republic of the Southern Seas: Republicans in Nineteenth-Century Australia*, Hale & Ironmonger, Alexandria.

Peterson, Nicolas, and Will Sanders 1998, 'Introduction', in *Citizenship and Indigenous Australians: Changing Conceptions and Possibilities*, Nicolas Peterson and Will Sanders (eds), Cambridge University Press, Cambridge: 1–34.

Rae-Ellis, Vivienne 1988, *Black Robinson: Protector of the Aborigines*, Melbourne University Press, Collingwood.

Read, Peter 1988, *A Hundred Years War: the Wiradjuri People and the State*, Australian National University Press, Rushcutters Bay.

— 2000, 'Preface', in *Settlement: A History of Australian Indigenous Housing*, Peter Read (ed), Canberra, Aboriginal Studies Press: ix–xii.

— 2006, 'Shelley's mistake: the Parramatta Native Institution and the Stolen Generations', in *The Great Mistakes of Australian History*, Martin Crotty and David Andrew Roberts (eds), UNSW Press, Sydney: 32–47.

Reece, RHW 1974, *Aborigines and Colonists: Aborigines and Colonial Society in New South Wales in the 1830s and 1840s*, Sydney University Press, Sydney.

Reed, Liz 2004, 'Rethinking William Thomas, "friend of the Aborigines"', *Aboriginal History* 28: 87–99.

Reynolds, Henry 1983, 'Aborigines and European social hierarchy', *Aboriginal History* 7(2): 124–133.

— 1992[1987], *The Law of the Land*, Penguin, Ringwood.

— 1995, *Fate of a Free People*, Penguin, Ringwood.

— 1996, 'Pastoral Leases in their historical context', *Aboriginal Law Bulletin* 3(81), June: 9–11.

— 1998, *This Whispering in Our Hearts*, Allen & Unwin, St Leonards.

— and Dawn May 1995, 'Queensland', in *Contested Ground: Australian Aborigines under the British Crown*, Ann McGrath (ed), Allen & Unwin, St Leonards: 168–207.

Rhodes, David 1995, *An Historical and Archaeological Investigation of the Loddon Aboriginal Protectorate Station and Mount Franklin Aboriginal Reserve*, occasional report, no 46, Aboriginal Affairs Victoria.

Ribton-Turner, CJ 1972[1887], *A History of Vagrants and Vagrancy and Beggars and Begging*, Montclair, New Jersey.

Robert, Hannah 2002, '"Satisfying the saints" – colonial entrepreneurs in the 1830s and 1840s and the elasticity of language', in *Writing Colonial Histories: Comparative Perspectives*, Tracey Banivanua Mar and Julie Evans (eds), Melbourne University Conference and Seminar Series, Melbourne: 7–22.

Roberts, David A 2003, 'The Bells Falls massacre and oral tradition', in *Frontier Conflict: the Australian Experience*, Bain Attwood and SG Forster (eds), National Museum of Australia, Canberra: 150–158.

— 2006, '"They would specify abandon the country to the new comers": the denial of Aboriginal rights', in *The Great Mistakes of Australian History*, Martin Crotty and David Andrew Roberts (eds), University of New South Wales Press, Sydney: 14–31.

—, and Hilary Carey 2009, '"Beong! Beong! (more! more!)": John Harper and the Wesleyan Mission to the Australian Aborigines', *Journal of Colonialism and Colonial History* 10(1), (online through Project Muse).

Roberts, F David 2002, *The Social Conscience of the Early Victorians*, Stanford University Press, Stanford.

Rose, Deborah Bird 1998, 'Signs of life on a barbarous frontier: intercultural encounters in North Australia', *Humanities Research* 2: 17–36.

— 2001, 'Aboriginal life and death in Australia settler nationhood', *Aboriginal History* 25: 148–162.

Rose, Lionel 1988, *'Rogues and Vagabonds': Vagrant Underworld in Britain, 1815–1985*, Routledge, London and New York.

Rountree, Kathryn 2000, 'Re-making the Maori female body', *Journal of Pacific History* 35(1), June: 49–66.

Rowse, Tim 1993, *After Mabo: Interpreting Indigenous Traditions*, Melbourne University Press, Carlton.

— 1998a, 'Rationing's moral economy', in *Connection and Disconnection: Encounters Between Settlers and Indigenous People in the Northern Territory*, Tony Austin and Suzanne Perry (eds), Northern Territory University, Darwin: 95–124.

— 1998b, *White Flour, White Power: From Rations to Citizenship in Central Australia*, Cambridge University Press, Cambridge.

— 2000, 'The humanitarian legacy: colonialism, coexistence and reconciling stories', *Arena* 45, February-March: 33–36.

Russo, George 1980, *Lord Abbott of the Wilderness: the Life and Times of Bishop Salvado*, Polding Press, Melbourne.

Ryan, Lyndall 1980, 'Aboriginal policy in Australia – 1838 – a watershed?', *Push from the Bush* 8: 14–22.

— 1981, *The Aboriginal Tasmanians*, University of Queensland Press, St Lucia.

Samson, Jane 1998, *Imperial Benevolence: Making British Authority in the Pacific Islands*, University of Hawai'i Press, Honolulu.

Scrimgeour, Anne 2006, 'Notions of civilisation and the project to "civilise" Aborigines in South Australia in the 1840s', *History of Education Review* 35(1): 35–46.

Smandych, Russell 2004, 'Contemplating the testimony of 'Others': James Stephen, the Colonial Office, and the fate of Australian Aboriginal Evidence Acts, circa 1839–1849', *Australian Journal of Legal History* 8(2): 237–283.

Stanley, Brian 2001, 'Christianity and civilisation in English evangelical mission thought, 1792–1857', in *Christian Missions and the Enlightenment*, Brian Stanley (ed), Wm B Eerdmans, Surrey: 169–198.

State Records of South Australia 2002, *'A Little Flour and a Few Blankets': an Administrative History of Aboriginal Affairs in South Australia, 1834–2000*, SRSA, Gepps Cross.

Steele, JG 1975, *Brisbane Town in Convict Days, 1824–1842*, University of Queensland, St Lucia.

Strong, Pauline Turner 1986, 'Fathoming the primitive: Australian Aborigines in four explorers' journals, 1697–1845', *Ethnohistory* 33(2): 175–194.

Symcox, Geoffrey 1972, 'The wild man's return: the enclosed vision of Rousseau's discourses', in *The Wild Man Within: an Image in Western Thought from the Renaissance to Romanticism*, Edward Dudley and Maximillian E Novak (eds), London, University of Pittsburgh Press.

Thompson, MMH 2006, *The Seeds of Democracy: Early Elections in Colonial New South Wales*, Federation Press, Sydney.

Thorne, Susan 1999, *Congregational Missions and the Making of an Imperial Culture in Nineteenth-Century England*, Stanford University Press, California.

Toussaint, Sandy 1995, 'Western Australia', in *Contested Ground: Australian Aborigines under the British Crown*, Ann McGrath (ed), Allen & Unwin, St Leonards: 240–268.

Turner, John, and Greg Blyton 1995, *The Aboriginals of Lake Macquarie: a Brief History*, Lake Macquarie City Council, Newcastle.

Twells, Alison 1998, '"Happy English children": class, ethnicity, and the making of missionary women in the early nineteenth century', *Women's Studies International Forum* 21(3), May-June: 235–245.

Tyrell, Alex 1993, *A Sphere of Benevolence: the Life of Joseph Orton, Wesleyan Methodist Missionary (1795–1842)*, State Library of Victoria, Melbourne.

Van Gent, Jacqueline 2005, 'Changing concepts of embodiment and illness among the Western Arrente at Hermannsbug Mission', in *Indigenous Peoples and Religious Change*, Peggy Brock (ed), Brill, Leiden: 227–248.

Van Toorn, Penny 2006, *Writing Never Arrives Naked: Early Aboriginal Cultures of Writing in Australia*, Aboriginal Studies Press, Canberra.

Walker, George Washington 1898, 'Notes on the Aborigines of Tasmania', in *Notes on the Aborigines of Tasmania*, Royal Society of Tasmania (ed), Government Printer, Hobart.

Waterhouse, Richard 2005, *The Vision Splendid: a Social and Cultural History of Rural Australia*, Curtin University Press, Freemantle.

Wellings, Ben 2004, 'Crown and country: empire and nation in Australian nationalism, 1788–1999', *Journal of Australian Colonial History* 5: 148–170.

White, Richard 1981, *Inventing Australia: Images and Identity, 1688–1980*, Allen & Unwin, Sydney.

Williams, Glyndwr 1981, 'Three reactions on Cook's voyage', in *Seeing the First Australians*, Ian Donaldson (ed), Allen & Unwin, Sydney: 35–50.

Windross, John, and JP Ralston 1897, *Historical Records of Newcastle, 1797–1897*, Federal Printing, Newcastle.

Wood, Peter 1991, *Poverty and the Workhouse in Victorian Britain*, Alan Sutton, Gloustershire.

Woolmington, Jean 1983, 'Wellington Valley in 1838: a house divided against itself', *The Push from the Bush* 16, October: 24–32.

— 1985, 'Missionary attitudes to the baptism of Australian Aborigines before 1850', *The Journal of Religious History* 13(3), June: 283–293.

— 1986, 'The Civilisation / Christianisation debate and the Australian Aborigines', *Aboriginal History* 10(2): 90–98.

— 1988, '"Writing in the sand": the first missions to the Aborigines in Eastern Australia', in *Aboriginal Australians and Christian Missions: Ethnographic and Historical Studies*, Tony Swain and Deborah Bird Rose (eds), Australian Association for the Study of Religions, Adelaide: 77–92.

www.ingramcontent.com/pod-product-compliance
Lightning Source LLC
Chambersburg PA
CBHW060929170426
43192CB00031B/2883